The English Poor Law 1780–1930

GENERAL EDITOR: *E. R. R. Green, Senior Lecturer in History, University of Manchester*

THE FACTORY SYSTEM   VOLUME I: BIRTH AND GROWTH
J. T. Ward
Senior Lecturer in Economic History
University of Strathclyde

THE FACTORY SYSTEM   VOLUME II: THE FACTORY SYSTEM
AND SOCIETY
J. T. Ward
Senior Lecturer in Economic History
University of Strathclyde

FREE TRADE
Norman McCord
Reader in Modern History
University of Newcastle upon Tyne

in preparation
READINGS IN THE DEVELOPMENT OF ECONOMIC ANALYSIS
R. D. C. Black
Professor of Economics, The Queen's University of Belfast

NINETEENTH CENTURY CRIME
John J. Tobias
Senior Tutor of the Special Course,
The Police College, Basingstoke

EDUCATION 1790-1902
J. M. Goldstrom
Lecturer in Economic & Social History
The Queen's University of Belfast

SOURCES FOR SOCIAL AND ECONOMIC HISTORY

MICHAEL E. ROSE

Lecturer in Economic History
University of Manchester

The English
Poor Law 1780–1930

BARNES & NOBLE, Inc.
NEW YORK
PUBLISHERS & BOOKSELLERS SINCE 1873

First Published in the United States, 1971
by Barnes & Noble, Inc.
ISBN 389-04061-4

Printed in Great Britain

Contents

INTRODUCTION   *page* 11

PART ONE: THE REFORM OF THE OLD POOR LAW
1 Sir William Young. *The Parish Workhouse*   25
2 Thomas Gilbert. *Gilbert's Act*   26
3 *The Removal Act*   28
4 Rev David Davies. *The State of the Labourer (1795)*   30
5 Sir F. M. Eden. *The Speenhamland Scale (1795)*   33
6 Samuel Whitbread. *A Minimum Wage*   35
7 Sir F. M. Eden. *Pitt's Scheme for Poor-Law Reform*   36
8 *The Magistrates' Powers of Relief*   38
9 Select Committee on Poor Rate Returns. *The Rising Cost of Relief*   39

    CRITICS OF THE POOR LAW: 39
10A Sir F. M. Eden. *The State of the Poor*   39
10B Rev T. R. Malthus. *Essay on Population*   43
10C Patrick Colquhoun. *A Treatise on Indigence*   46
10D The Committee of 1817. *Report*   49

    THE ABUSES OF POOR RELIEF: 52
11A Select Committee on Labourers' Wages. *The Allowance System*   52
11B Samuel Makin & John Robinson. *Industrial Speenhamland* 54

5

11C Rev Phillip Hunt. *The Roundsman System*   *page* 56
11D Thomas Bowyer. *The Labour Rate*   57
11E Henry Boyce. *An Auction of Paupers*   58
11F J. D. Tweedy. *Labour on the Roads*   58
11G Select Committee on the Employment or Relief of Able
     Bodied Persons. *The Bread Scale*   60
11H Asst Commissioner Walcott. *The Overseers*   61
12 Thomas Smart. *The State of the Labourer (1824)*   62

THE REFORM OF THE POOR LAW: 64

13A W. D. Evans. *Poor Law Administration in Manchester*   64
13B *Sturges Bourne's Act*   67
13C Lister Ellis. *A Stricter Relief System*   69
13D Rev J. T. Becher. *The Anti Pauper System*   71

PART TWO: THE RECEPTION OF THE NEW POOR LAW

THE ROYAL COMMISSION ON THE POOR LAWS: 75

14 Royal Commission. *Instructions to Assistant Commissioners*   77
15 Royal Commission. *Questions for Parishes*   79
16 Edwin Chadwick. *The 1834 Report*   84
17 Nassau Senior. *The Preparation of the Poor Law Bill*   87
18 Lord Althorp, Edward Baines & William Cobbett. *The
     Poor Law Debate*   90
19 *The Times. Against the New Poor Law*   94
20 *The Poor Law Amendment Act*   95

THE FIRST YEARS OF THE POOR LAW COMMISSION: 101

21 Poor Law Commission. *The Regulation of Outdoor Relief*   102
22 W. J. Gilbert. *Rural Opposition*   103
23 Uckfield Union, Sussex. *The Effects of the New Poor Law*   105
24 R. H. Greg. *The Migration Scheme*   107

THE ANTI POOR LAW MOVEMENT: *page* 109

25 Joseph Ellison. *The Good Old System*   112
26 Richard Oastler. *The New Poor Law*   113
27 G. R. W. Baxter. *Anti Poor Law Tales*   113
28 '*Marcus on Populousness*'   116
29 G. Tinker. *The State of the Huddersfield Union*   118
30 Poor Law Commission. *Poor Relief Regulations*   120

THE FALL OF THE POOR LAW COMMISSION: 121

31 William Day. *The Difficulties of an Assistant Commissioner*   123
32 Poor Law Commission. *Indoor and Outdoor Relief*   127
33 Select Committee on the Andover Union. *Chadwick's Quarrel with the Poor Law Commissioners*   127
34 Sir George Grey. *The Poor Law Board*   132

PART THREE: THE POOR LAW IN OPERATION 1834–71

THE CENTRAL AUTHORITY AND THE BOARDS OF GUARDIANS: 135

35 Joseph Rogers. *A Corrupt Guardian*   137
36 R. A. Arnold. *A Board of Guardians at Work (1862)*   138

OUTDOOR RELIEF: 140

37A Poor Law Commission. *Outdoor Relief Prohibitory Order (December 1844)*   143
37B Poor Law Commission. *Outdoor Labour Test Order (April 1842)*   145
37C Poor Law Board. *Outdoor Relief Regulation Orders (1852)* 146
38 Blackburn Union. *A Protest Against the Relief Regulation Order* 148
39 Poplar Union. *A Labour Test*   150
40 Rev E. H. Carr. *Inadequate Relief*   152
41 Skipton Union. *Relief in Aid of Wages*   156
42 W. M. Torrens. *Poor Relief and the Cotton Famine*   156
43 Robert Rawlinson. *The Public Works Act*   158

THE WORKHOUSE: *page* 160

44A Poor Law Commission. *Workhouse Diets*   162
44B Dr Edward Smith. *Survey of Workhouse Diets*   164
45 H. Taine. *A Manchester Workhouse*   169
46 R. Tatham *A Workhouse Hospital*   171
47 *The Lancet. Report on Workhouse Infirmaries*   172
48 Poor Law Board. *Improvement of Sick Wards*   175

PAUPER CHILDREN: 178

49 Poor Law Commission. *Less Eligibility and Education*   179
50 J. P. Kay. *Pauper Schools*   181
51 *Household Words. A Pauper Palace*   185
52 Mrs N. Senior. *Pauper Schools and Boarding Out*   188

SETTLEMENT, REMOVAL AND VAGRANCY: 191

53 Bradford Union. *An Illegal Removal*   194
54 Mr Blyth. *Close and Open Parishes*   195
55 A. Power. *The Burden on Agriculture*   198
56 *The 1846 Act*   199
57 J. Beckwith & C. Heaps. *The Effects of the 1846 Act*   201
58A George Coode. *Reform of the Law of Settlement*   203
58B Joseph Ellison. *Reform of the Law of Settlement*   205
59 *The Union Chargeability Act*   206
60 Charles Buller. *The Buller Minute*   207
61 Liverpool Parish. *Rules for a Vagrant Ward*   210
62 Andrew Doyle. *The 'Terror of the Tramp'*   211

FINANCE: 213

63 R. E. Warwick. *The Inequality of the Poor Rate (Parishes)*   215
64 William Day. *Poor Law Union Finance*   217
65 William Rathbone. *The Inequality of the Poor Rate (Ratepayers)*   219

PART FOUR: THE POOR LAW UNDER ATTACK 1870–1914

THE CAMPAIGN AGAINST OUTDOOR RELIEF: *page* 222

66 G. J. Goschen. *The Goschen Minute* 225
67 Local Government Board. *Circular on Outdoor Relief (1871)* 228
68 Manchester Guardians. *Regulations on Outdoor Relief (1875)* 230
69 Dr P. F. Aschrott. *The COS at Work* 231

THE INADEQUACIES OF THE POOR LAW: 234
70 Robert Blatchford. *A Socialist View of the Poor Law* 239
71 B. S. Rowntree. *The Investigation of Poverty* 241
72 Alfred Marshall. *Outdated Ideas* 247
73 Samuel Barnett. *Lack of Uniformity* 248
74 George Lansbury. *A Working-class Guardian* 250

BETTER TREATMENT: 252
75A Local Government Board. *Advice on Treatment of Old People* 252
75B G. Cuttle. *Old People in Essex Workhouses* 254
76 T. J. Macnamara. *Better Treatment for Children* 256
77A Joseph Chamberlain. *The Chamberlain Circular (1886)* 258
77B *The Unemployed Workmen Act (1905)* 260

THE ROYAL COMMISSION ON THE POOR LAWS: 262
78 Local Government Board. *The Statistics of Pauperism* 268
79 Beatrice Webb. *The Aims of the Royal Commission* 268
80 Royal Commission. *The Majority Report* 271
81 Royal Commission. *The Minority Report* 274
82 National Committee for the Prevention of Destitution. *The Crusade* 278
83 J. Austen Chamberlain. *The Conservatives and the Minority Report* 280

PART FIVE: THE BREAK-UP OF THE POOR LAW 1914–30

THE EFFECTS OF WORLD WAR I: *page* 283

84 Local Government Board. *War Victims and the Poor Law*   285
85 Ministry of Health. *The Reduction of Pauperism*   286
86 *The Maclean Report*   288

POST-WAR DEPRESSION AND POPLARISM: 290

87 Ministry of Health. *Restrictions on Outdoor Relief*   294
88 *Pall Mall Gazette. Poplarism*   296
89 Poplar Board of Guardians. *Poplar's Answer*   299

THE END OF THE BOARDS OF GUARDIANS: 302

90 Joseph Jackson. *No Relief for Blacklegs*   304
91 Gateshead Union. *The Guardians in the Red*   305
92 John Wheatley. *Opposition to the Default Bill*   306
93 *The Boards of Guardians (Default) Act*   309
94 *Chester-le-Street*   311
95 Sidney Webb. *Speech on the Local Government Bill*   314
96 *The Local Government Act (1929)*   317

EPILOGUE   321
SUGGESTIONS FOR FURTHER READING   325
ACKNOWLEDGEMENTS   330
INDEX   331

Introduction

The English Poor Law has its origins in the social and economic upheavals of the sixteenth century. Tudor Governments proved sensitive to social unrest caused by enclosures, industrial unemployment and rising prices, since they feared that such discontents might be used by their political opponents. Working through their representatives in the counties, the justices of the peace, they experimented with methods of allaying distress, preventing vagrancy and maintaining a degree of social stability. These were codified at the turn of the century in the Acts of 1597 (39 Eliz, c 3) and 1601 (43 Eliz, c 2). This latter Act, the '43rd of Elizabeth', was seen by later generations as the basis of the English poor law system. Sir George Nicholls in the first volume of his *History of the English Poor Law* described it as 'the foundation and groundwork of our English Poor Law', and the Webbs held that 'the celebrated legislation of 1597–1601 . . . gave to the whole system of poor relief the moulding which it has ever since preserved'.[1] The Act of 1601 made it compulsory for each parish to provide for the poor by levying a rate on all occupiers of property within its bounds. An unpaid parish officer, the overseer of the poor, was to be appointed. His duties were to levy and collect the rate and to see that it was expended in the relief of the aged and infirm poor, the apprenticing to a trade of the children of

[1] Sir George Nicholls. *History of the English Poor Law*, Vol 1 (1904), 181. S. & B. Webb. *English Local Government. English Poor Law History, Part 1 The Old Poor Law* (Reprint 1963), 61.

paupers, and the 'setting on work' of the able-bodied poor. This principle of compulsory provision made the English poor law system unique, marking it off even from Scotland and Ireland where no such provision existed until the nineteenth century.

In the early seventeenth century, the Government attempted, often at the cost of much unpopularity, to supervise the poor law administration of the parishes. This attempt at central control broke down during the Civil War, leaving the justices of the peace and the overseers in each locality to interpret the provisions of the 1601 Act as they thought best. This high degree of local discretion in the administration of poor relief was to prove a vital factor in the future development of the poor law.

The Restoration of 1660 was followed by an Act which deserves to be ranked with that of 1601 as providing the foundation of the English poor law system. This was the Act of Settlement of 1662 (14 Ch II, c 12) which gave powers to parish overseers, on complaint to justices, to return to their parish of settlement any newcomers to the parish who had no legal settlement within it. Like the Act of 1601, the Act of Settlement was merely a codification of existing practice. It was never rigidly enforced since it proved impossible to create such a high degree of labour immobility in an economically expanding society. Numerous loopholes, both statutory and informal, had to be made in it. Nevertheless it served to strengthen the local, parochial basis of the poor law, and the increasingly complex problems of settlement and removal created difficulties for future generations of poor law administrators and fat fees for their legal advisers (see Part Three).

The Acts of 1601 and 1662 form the basis of what came to be known as the Old Poor Law. Although many other Acts dealing with aspects of poor law administration reached the statute book in the seventeenth and eighteenth centuries, they were mainly a gloss on these two. Within the elastic bounds of these laws, the Old Poor Law came to be shaped according to the ideas and experience of the men on the spot—the overseers, the wealthier ratepayers and the justices. Legislation reflected these ideas. An

Act of 1722, Knatchbull's Act, revealed a growing tendency to deal stringently with the able-bodied poor and grant them relief only within an institution in which they would be set to work. Sixty years later, Gilbert's Act of 1782 (2) betrayed a growing feeling that such methods had failed, and that the able-bodied poor must be found work outside the confines of the poorhouse. Both these measures, however, were permissive. It was left to local administrators to adopt such facets of them as were thought to be suited to the prevailing conditions of their parish, town or county. As J. D. Marshall has remarked, the Old Poor Law was profoundly adaptable.[1]

It is not intended to illustrate the working of the Old Poor Law in this book. It begins in the last two decades of the eighteenth century when the system was beginning to feel the impact of the massive social and economic changes set in motion by the first Industrial Revolution. Part One deals with the problems of the poor law in the new type of society which was emerging under the impact of industrialisation, urbanisation and war. Part Two examines the preparation of, and reaction to, the Poor Law Amendment Act of 1834—the most important piece of poor law legislation since 1601, as contemporaries realised when they christened it the New Poor Law despite its claim to be only an amendment of the 43rd of Elizabeth. Part Three looks in detail at the working of the nineteenth-century poor relief system once the storm over the 1834 Act had to some extent subsided; and Part Four at the rising tide of criticism of the system in that period of acute social conscience and consciousness which stretches from the late 1870s to the outbreak of World War I— criticism which culminated in a second massive Royal Commission of enquiry into the poor law, between 1905 and 1909. Part Five covers the final, less familiar, episode, the fortunes of the English poor law during World War I and its collapse under the weight of the mass unemployment of the 1920s. The collection of documents ends with the Local Government Act of 1929, a statute which followed the recommendations of the

[1] J. D. Marshall. *The Old Poor Law 1795–1834* (1968), 11.

Majority Report of the Royal Commission of 1909 by winding up the boards of poor law guardians and handing over their responsibilities to the county and borough councils.

The Act of 1929 did not of course mean the end of the poor law. The statutes of 1601, 1662 and 1834 were not finally repealed until 1948; their spirit still walks abroad in our 'Welfare State'. But for a book of this type, 1930 is a convenient stopping place, since it was the year which saw the dismantling of the local administrative structure of the nineteenth-century poor law. To go beyond this date would involve us with the origins of the Welfare State, and would stretch this collection of documents well beyond the limits of a single volume.

It is the aim of this book to trace through documentary material the development of the English poor law in the nineteenth and twentieth centuries, and I have tried not to wander into closely related fields such as public health, old age pensions, national insurance or other aspects of social welfare. The documents have been selected mainly from sources which might prove difficult of access to the average student. Particular weight has been placed on official sources, especially the reports and correspondence of the central authorities for poor relief, the Poor Law Commission, the Poor Law Board, the Local Government Board and the Ministry of Health, together with Parliamentary enquiries into, and speeches on, poor law matters. Inevitably with a locally based institution like the poor law much of the material deals with problems in particular localities, but I have not drawn extensively on the great mass of poor law material in local libraries and record offices because of the difficulties of making anything like a representative sample. Even in my attempt to illustrate national trends, I may be accused of paying overmuch attention to my favourite county, the West Riding of Yorkshire. I hope, however, that students will be encouraged to move from this sample of poor law documents to the wealth of archive material in their own locality. Local research has done much in recent years to modify our conceptions of the poor law system but much more remains to be done. It is, as I have frequently been told, 'a grim subject', yet H. L. Beales, writing some forty years ago, underlined its importance. 'If there is little pomp in this pageant, there yet may be discovered the ebb and flow of the tide of national prosperity, the waxing and waning of social and economic systems, the rise and decline of habits of social thought and methods of social control.'[1]

[1] H. L. Beales. 'The New Poor Law', *History* (1931).

PART ONE

The Reform of the Old Poor Law

The political, social and economic upheavals which marked the second half of the eighteenth century brought with them increasing scrutiny and criticism of existing institutions. Radicals from Wilkes onwards clamoured for a reform of Parliament, the revolt of the American colonies shattered the old colonial system, and the writings of Adam Smith heralded the downfall of mercantilist economics. From this process of critical enquiry the poor law system could not escape. In the early decades of the century, indeed, considerable dissatisfaction had been expressed at the way in which the original Poor Law Act of 1601 was being administered. This was particularly directed at the treatment of the able bodied unemployed poor, whom the Act of 1601 had required to be 'set on work'. The critics argued that the Act ought to be more strictly interpreted with regard to this class, and increasing favour was shown to the idea of institutional relief for them. Some parishes pooled their resources in order to provide workhouses or 'houses of industry', in which paupers could be maintained and employed in spinning, weaving or other simple manufacturing processes. Not only was it hoped that the produce of their labour could be sold in order to offset a part of the cost of their relief, but also that the prospect of being set to regular work in a disciplined institution would deter the idle and feckless from seeking relief, thus further reducing the burden of the poor rate. In 1722 Parliament accordingly passed an Act (9 Geo I, c 7) giving parishes the power to buy or hire workhouse premises and to refuse all relief to paupers who would not enter them.

By the end of the eighteenth century, however, this institutional method of relief was in its turn attracting considerable criticism. Many of the houses of industry proved too expensive for parishes to support. Workhouse masters who had contracted with parishes to take in their paupers at so much per head were accused of embezzling ratepayers' money and of making the lives of their charges a misery. Workhouses were portrayed as abodes of corruption for the young and of wretchedness for the sick and aged. Opinion was swinging round towards a policy of giving outdoor relief, particularly to those thrown out of work in periods of depression or to those whose earnings were inadequate for their support at a time of rising food prices.

Gilbert's Act of 1782 (2) gave expression to this trend of opinion. In a parish or union of parishes under this Act, the workhouse became a poorhouse to which only the aged and infirm were to be admitted. The able-bodied unemployed were to be found work and subsidised out of the poor rates if their earnings proved to be insufficient for their maintenance. The Act, however, was a permissive one and by 1830 less than 1,000 of the 15,000 parishes in England and Wales had placed themselves under it. Nevertheless, it has been described by Sidney and Beatrice Webb as 'perhaps the most influential, for both good and evil, of all the scores of Poor Law statutes between 1601 and 1834'. It decisively reversed the relief policy laid down by the Act of 1722, and legitimised the practice of those parishes that were already granting outdoor relief to underpaid workers.

Another feature of the English poor law system which began to attract a good deal of hostile criticism at this time was the laws of settlement. Economic writers, led by Adam Smith, maintained that these laws hindered the mobility of labour, and thus prevented the unemployed man from finding work. Thomas Malthus condemned their use to oppress the poor (10B). By the time that Malthus's *Essay on Population* appeared, however, some of the earlier criticism had caused the settlement laws to be modified. An Act of 1795 (35 Geo III, c 101) ordered that no paupers were to be returned to their parish of settlement until they actually became chargeable to the poor rates of the parish in which they were living, and that the removal of sick persons was to be suspended until they had recovered from their illness (3).

By the time this Act was passed, the poor law system found itself faced with one of the severest crises in its history. The outbreak of war with France brought economic disturbance and there were commercial crises in 1793 and 1797. The harvests of 1794, 1795, 1799 and 1800 were poor, and this, together with the demands of the armed forces for grain and the difficulties of importing corn while the war lasted, led to a steep rise in the price of bread, the staple food of the labourer. For agricultural labourers, many of whom were already barely managing to exist (4), the steep rise in food prices brought with it the grim prospect of utter destitution and starvation. The ruling classes were faced with the possibility of mounting discontent and bread riots in the countryside at a time when they were haunted by the spectre of Jacobinism. Thus magistrates urged local poor law authorities to take some action to alleviate the sufferings of the poor. One course of action was to extend the system of granting allowances of poor relief to labourers whose wages were insufficient to maintain them and their families. In some areas, the local justices produced scales of relief according to an applicant's earnings, the size of his family, and the current price of bread. The most famous of these scales was that drawn up by the justices of Berkshire, meeting at the Pelican Inn, Speenhamland, near Newbury, at Easter 1795 (5), though this was by no means the first or the only example of such a scale. Nor was the cash allowance to supplement wages the only way in which local authorities met the crisis of the 1790s: in some areas, corn was bought by parishes or by private charities and sold to the poor at reduced prices.

Action to meet the crisis was not just local. In 1795, and again in 1800, Samuel Whitbread, one of the ablest of the younger Foxite Whigs, moved in Parliament for legislation which would have allowed magistrates to fix minimum wages, as they were already empowered to fix maximum wages under an Act of 1563 (6); but the attempt failed in face of strong opposition. William Pitt, the Prime Minister, was one of the leading speakers against it, yet he was responsible for drafting a Bill in 1796 which, among other things, would have empowered overseers and justices to grant allowances of poor relief to supplement wages (7). Like Whitbread's proposal, however, this scheme aroused considerable opposition, and the Bill was shelved. One measure that did reach the statute book was an Act (36 Geo III, c 23) which permitted the payment of outdoor relief to applicants even if they refused to enter the workhouse, and also gave local justices power to order such relief over the heads of the parochial authorities (8).

This Act, which severely weakened the Act of 1722 and increased the powers of justices over the parishes, was the nearest Parliament got to giving legislative sanction to the allowance system. Nevertheless the system spread quite widely over the country during the next twenty years. In years of economic distress and high food prices—1799, 1800, 1811 and 1812—magistrates and overseers found it useful to resort to the allowance system in order to alleviate distress and counter discontent. Resort to such a policy in a period when wages were lagging behind prices, together with the granting of relief to families of militiamen and to those made destitute by the agrarian and industrial changes of the period, brought a steep rise in the national poor relief bill (9). Landowners and farmers, who bore the chief burden of the poor rate, could stand the increase during the war when prices, rents and profits rocketed. With the ending of the war, however, depression hit agriculture, particularly the corn-growing sector of southern and eastern England. Yet, despite the fall in prices, the cost of poor relief continued to rise, reaching a peak of over £8 million in 1818. Thus the poor law system found itself being subjected once more to searching criticism. Increasingly, people listened to those critics who had disapproved of the more generous out-relief system, and had argued that, for the good of his character, the poor man ought to be forced to look after himself, making provision through friendly societies for periods of emergency, adopting a more frugal standard of living, and limiting the size of his family by abstaining from early marriage. Both Sir Frederick Morton Eden and the Rev Thomas Malthus, the most famous of these critics, were willing to contemplate the complete abolition of compulsory poor relief (10A & B). Patrick Colquhoun wished to retain the system, but to amend it radically so that it distinguished closely between poverty and indigence, relieved the deserving and tried to restore the undeserving to a useful position in society (10C). Many people, influenced by the writings of a Glasgow minister, the Rev Thomas Chalmers, advocated the adoption of the Scottish system of relief, which relied mainly on private charity.

Economic distress in both manufacturing and agricultural districts in 1816 forced the Government to act on the poor laws. In 1817, a Select Committee of the House of Commons met to consider the problem. Its report clearly revealed the change in public opinion: it strongly criticised the system of compulsory relief for the poor, approved the Scottish system of private charity and the deterrent effect of the workhouse system, and recommended a limit on poor law expenditure, together with the encouragement of parish schools and benefit clubs and an improved system of relief administration (10D).

Although the Committee's report brought little immediate legislation, it stimulated further examination and analysis of the poor law system. More select committees met to enquire into the poor law and various aspects of relief, and the pamphleteers were once again busy propounding solutions to the problem of poverty. Such enquiries highlighted the abuses of poor relief to which overseers, particularly in the depressed rural areas, had resorted when faced with surplus population, inadequate wages, and severe unemployment or underemployment, particularly in the winter. One of the most common abuses was the so called 'roundsman' system by which unemployed labourers were sent round the parish from one farm to another until they found someone willing to set them to work at a wage subsidised by the parish (11C). A variant on this method, which was favoured by some would-be reformers as being less likely to interfere with the independent working of the labour market, was the 'labour rate' system. Each ratepayer in the parish agreed to employ a certain number of labourers according to his assessment to the poor rate, or, if he had no need of that number of workers, to pay to the parish the equivalent value of their wages (11D). In some parishes, unemployed labourers were put up for auction, or sent to work on the roads, with varying degrees of success (11E & F).

None of these methods found any favour with the growing body of reformers who followed the teaching of the political economists and held that labour must be left free to find its own level. The allowance system of relief to supplement wages was specially condemned, and select committees were appointed in 1824 and again in 1828 to enquire into its extent and results. The first of these reported that the system was most prevalent in the southern and eastern counties of England, much less so in the more prosperous manufacturing districts of the north (11A). No one knows how widespread the allowance system was, even in rural areas. Probably its use was spasmodic. Overseers might resort to it during bad winters when there were high prices and heavy underemployment, only to stop it when conditions improved. The slow improvement in arable farming after the slump of the early 1820s, and the increasing dissatisfaction with the system, probably reduced its use. In 1832, few parishes would admit to using it, though a considerable number, both agricultural and industrial, admitted to paying allowances to labourers with large families.

The allowance system and its variants did little to improve the condition of the agricultural labourer (12). Bread scales were often cut below the levels of the 1790s (11G). Discontent was rife in the countryside, and there were outbreaks of rioting in

East Anglia in 1816 and throughout the southern counties in 1830. Such disturbances seemed to the reformers to be further proof of the widespread demoralisation which the poor law system was causing amongst the labouring classes.

If it was the rural areas and the plight of the agricultural labourer that attracted most attention from poor law reformers, the urban poor law administrator was not without his problems. Periodic commercial crises threw large numbers out of work, poor relief costs rose astronomically, and private charity had to be called on to help relieve the prevailing distress. Handicraft workers in some trades found their economic position undermined by sweated labour or factory competition, and were forced to ask for help from the parish. The allowance system was not confined to the rural areas (11B). Problems of settlement increased as immigrants flocked to the towns. In some cases, those who applied for relief in a period of depression were moved back to their parishes of settlement. In many more, applicants were given relief on the spot, and their parish of settlement charged with its cost. The growing number of vagrants, particularly Irish, entering the towns were given short shrift, however, and were quickly passed on to the next parish. All this served to increase and complicate the tasks of administration; the old system of using a part-time, unpaid, unenthusiastic and sometimes corrupt, overseer, supervised haphazardly by an annual or bi-annual vestry meeting, attracted increasing criticism (11H), and by the turn of the century it had become unworkable in the rapidly expanding industrial towns. Full-time salaried officials were increasingly employed to carry out the routine administrative duties, under the control of small committees that met regularly and exercised a close supervision. In towns like Manchester the administration of poor relief was highly organised by 1815 (13A). The Select Committee of 1817 approved such reforms, and urged the more widespread adoption of the system of select vestries to control poor relief and of salaried assistant overseers to administer it; and an Act of 1819 (59 Geo III, c 12) gave powers to parishes to adopt such measures if they so desired.

By 1828, nearly 3,000 parishes in England and Wales had taken advantage of these clauses of the Act (13B).

In some places the adoption of a select vestry brought with it the reform not only of relief administration but also of relief policy. Grants of outdoor relief, particularly to able-bodied men and women, were more closely scrutinised. Offering relief in a disciplined workhouse was accepted as one way of scaring away malingerers (13C). Perhaps the most famous of these experiments in relief policy was that carried out at Southwell in Nottinghamshire in the 1820s under the leadership of George Nicholls, later to be a member of the Poor Law Commission, and the Rev J. T. Becher, who did much to publicise the experiment, which he christened 'The Anti Pauper System' (13D). By prohibiting relief in aid of wages, making more use of indoor relief, improving their accounting procedure, and stimulating agencies of working-class thrift and education, the Nottinghamshire reformers claimed to have reduced the burden of the poor rates and to have greatly improved the character of the local labourers. Their claims have been shown to be greatly exaggerated, but they were well received by poor-law reformers and considerably influenced the decisions of the Royal Commission on the Poor Laws of 1832-4.

Between 1780 and 1830 there were numerous attempts to reform the poor-law system. In administration, the reformers tried to base relief on a wider area than the parish, and to improve efficiency by using salaried officers and smaller, more specialised, committees. In relief policy, there was first the attempt to find employment for the poor and to maintain their living standards by subsidies from the rates; then, increasingly from 1800, the policy changed to one of educating the poor in self-reliance and deterring them from seeking poor relief. Yet despite all this reforming activity, there remained in 1830 many parishes where the rates were still rising, the overseer illiterate, and the vestry corrupt and incompetent. Agricultural labourers remained ill paid and discontented, and this smouldering discontent burst into riotous flame in 1830. The Whig Government severely suppressed the revolt, but many of its members and supporters realised that this was not enough. Once Parliament had been reformed, the poor-law system must be subjected to a similar, once for all process.

1 Sir William Young   The Parish Workhouse

Sir William Young (1749–1815) was MP for St Mawes, Cornwall, from 1784 to 1806 and for Buckingham from 1806 to 1807. From 1807 until his death he was Governor of Tobago. He was elected a Fellow of the Royal Society in 1786, and of the Society of Antiquaries in 1791. A keen poor-law reformer, he unsuccessfully promoted a Bill in 1788 which would have given parish vestries the power to fix a rate of wages during the winter.

––––––

The contract being signed, the parish officers think themselves exonerated from every duty of office, and when a poor man, casually out of employ, applies for relief or work, they send him to the contractor or master of the workhouse, who hath neither means to employ him, nor influence, nor leisure to procure him employ. The contractor cannot afford, or will rarely give, a small intermediate stipend whilst the labourer himself is in search of employ. The contractor, as a condition of relief by food, ejects the man and family from his cottage and brings them to the workhouse, where the helpless and hopeless increase misery to desperation. Indolence, a carelessness of life and character, and progressively a loss of feeling for the little wretches who no longer look to him for support, oppress and vitiate this poor man's heart. Finally, he leaves his wife and children a lasting burden on the parish, to go—he knows not whither; to do—he knows not what.

The 9th of George I[1] chap. 7th is the very pandar to vagrancy and its succession of idleness, vice and crime.

The overseer having made his contract for the year, cares not

[1] Knatchbull's Act of 1723 which gave parish officers the power to establish a workhouse and to refuse relief to those who would not enter it.

how many he sends to the poor house; thence the contractor, overburdened, too often connives at the petty larcenies of his poor for supplemental support. In the woods and turnip fields are the forsaken children educated! Sir William Young. *Considerations on the Subject of Poor Houses and Work Houses* (1796), 9–10

2 Thomas Gilbert Gilbert's Act

Thomas Gilbert (1720–98), the sponsor of the Act, was land agent to Lord Gower and MP for Newcastle-under-Lyme and later for Lichfield. In 1765 he obtained the sinecure post of Comptroller of the Great Wardrobe and in 1784 became chairman of the Committee of Ways and Means. His brother, John, was agent to the Duke of Bridgewater, and it was Thomas who persuaded the Duke to employ James Brindley as engineer for the Duke's canal schemes.

As well as changing policy with regard to the relief of the poor, the Act was also aimed at improving the administrative system. It provided for a union of parishes to set up a common workhouse. This was to be controlled by a board of guardians appointed by the local magistrates, and their work was to be supervised by a visitor, also appointed by the magistracy. Outdoor relief in each constituent parish was to be administered by the guardian for that parish. In 1786, Gilbert drafted a Bill for the appointment of commissioners to supervise the administration of poor relief in each county, but this failed to gain acceptance.

22 Geo. III CAP. 83

An Act for the better Relief and Employment of the Poor.

"Whereas, not withstanding the many laws now in being for the relief and employment of the poor, and the great sums of money raised for those purposes, their sufferings and distresses are nevertheless very grievous; and, by the incapacity, negligence or misconduct of the overseers, the money raised for the relief of the poor is frequently misapplied, and sometimes expended in defraying the charges of litigations about settlements indiscreetly and unadvisedly carried on; and whereas by a clause in an Act passed in the ninth year of the reign of King George the First, intituled, 'An Act for the Amendment of the Laws relating to the Settlement, Employment and Relief of the Poor', power is given to the churchwardens and overseers in the manner therein mentioned to purchase or hire houses, and contract with any person for the lodging, keeping, maintaining and employing the poor, and taking the benefit of their work, labour, and service for their maintenance; and where any parish, town or township, should be found too small to unite two or more for those purposes, with the consent of the major part of the parishioners or inhabitants and the approbation of a justice of the peace; which provisions from want of proper regulations and management in the poor houses or workhouses that have been purchased or hired under the authority of the said Act, and for want of due inspection and control over the persons who have engaged in those contracts, have not had the desired effect, but the poor in many places, instead of finding protection and relief, have been much oppressed thereby:"

XXIX . . . Be it further enacted, that no person shall be sent to such poor house or houses, except such as are become indigent by old age, sickness or infirmities, and are unable to acquire a maintenance by their labour; and except such orphan children as shall be sent thither by order of the guardian, or guardians of the poor, with the approbation of the visitor; and except such children as shall necessarily go with their mothers thither for sustenance.

XXXII   And be it further enacted, that where there shall be, in any parish, township or place, any poor person or persons who shall be able and willing to work, but who cannot get employment, it shall and may be lawful for the guardian of the poor of such parish, township or place, and he is hereby required on application made to him by or on behalf of such poor person, to agree for the labour of such poor person or persons, at any work or employment suited to his or her strength or capacity, in any parish, township or place, near the place of his or her residence, and to maintain, or cause such person or persons to be properly maintained, lodged and provided for, until such employment shall be procured, and during the time of such work, and to receive the money to be earned by such work or labour, and apply it in such maintenance, as far as the same will go, and make up the deficiency if any; . . . W. C. Glen. *The Statutes in Force Relating to the Poor* (1857), 103, 117–18

3 The Removal Act

The original settlement Act of 1662 (13 & 14 Ch II, c 12) had granted temporary immunity from removal to harvest labourers and others seeking work providing they could produce a certificate from their parish of settlement acknowledging that parish's responsibility for them. This provision was further widened by an Act of 1697 (8 & 9 Wm III, c 30). An Act of 1793 (33 Geo III, c 54) allowed members of friendly societies to remain undisturbed outside their parishes of settlement provided they did not apply for relief. The 1795 Act extended this provision to all persons, and also ordered justices to suspend orders of removal against the sick.

Thus the laws of settlement were made more humane, though the constant addition of statute to statute on the subject of settlement served to confuse the legal issues. The extent to which the laws of settlement hindered the mobility of labour is questionable. Adam Smith emphatically believed that they did, but Sir Frederick Eden believed such a notion to be exaggerated. Certainly the Act of 1795, together with the increasing reluctance of parochial authorities to enter the legal tangle which pauper removal involved, made the laws of settlement one of the least significant barriers to labour mobility in the early nineteenth century.

35 Geo. III CAP. 101

An Act to prevent the Removal of Poor Persons until they shall become actually chargeable. (22nd June, 1795)

". . . And whereas many industrious poor persons, chargeable to the parish, township or place where they live, merely from want of work there, would in any other place, where sufficient employment is to be had, maintain themselves and families without being burthensome to any parish, township or place; and such poor persons are for the most part compelled to live in their own parishes, townships, or places, and are not permitted to inhabit elsewhere, under pretence that they are likely to become chargeable to the parish, township or place into which they go for the purpose of getting employment, although the labour of such poor persons might, in many instances, be very beneficial to such parish, township or place: And whereas the remedy intended to be applied thereto, by the granting of certificates in pursuance of the Act passed in the eighth and ninth years of the reign of King William the Third, intituled, 'An Act for supplying some Defects in the Laws for the Relief of the Poor of this Kingdom,' hath been found very ineffectual, and it is necessary that other provisions should be made relating thereto."

Be it therefore enacted, by the King's most excellent Majesty, by and with the advice and consent of the Lords spiritual and temporal, and Commons, in this present parliament assembled, and by the authority of the same, that, from and after the passing of this Act, so much of the said in part recited Act of the thirteenth and fourteenth years of King Charles the Second, as enables the justices to remove any person or persons that are likely to be chargeable to the parish, township or place into which they shall come to inhabit, shall be and the same is hereby repealed; and that from thenceforth no poor person shall be removed, by virtue of any order of removal, from the parish or place where such poor person shall be inhabiting to the place of his or her last legal settlement until such person shall have become actually chargeable to the parish, township or place in which such person

shall then inhabit, in which case two justices of the peace are
hereby empowered to remove the person or persons in the same
manner, and subject to the same appeal, and with the same
powers, as might have been done before the passing of this Act
with respect to persons likely to become chargeable. W. C. Glen.
The Statutes in Force Relating to the Poor (1857), 154–5

4 Rev David Davies   The State of the Labourer in 1787

The Rev David Davies (d 1819?) was a graduate of Jesus
College, Oxford, and rector of the parish of Barkham in Berkshire. In his book Davies portrayed the very poor living standards of the agricultural labourers in his parish, defended the
poor from some of the allegations of improvidence made
against them, and urged that their condition be improved by
finding employment for labourers in winter, creating work for
their wives and children, fixing minimum wage standards and
making allowances out of the poor rate for those with large
families. Although published in 1795, the material contained
in the book was collected in 1787. With the rapid rise in prices
in the 1790s, the position of Barkham's labourers presumably
deteriorated in the eight years between collection and publication.

Weekly expenses of a Family, consisting of a Man and his
Wife, and five Children, the eldest eight years of age, the youngest
an Infant. (Easter 1787).

	s.	d.
Flour: 7½ gallons, at 10d per gallon	6	3
Yeast, to make it into bread, 2½d; and salt 1½d ..	0	4
Bacon, 1 lb. boiled at two or three times with greens: the pot liquor, with bread and potatoes, makes a mess for the children	0	8
Tea, 1 ounce, 2d: ¾ lb. sugar 6d; ½ lb. butter or lard 4d	1	0
Soap, ¼ lb. at 9d per lb.	0	2¼
Candles, ⅓ lb. one week with another at a medium,		

at 9d	0	3
Thread, thrum, and worsted, for mending apparel, etc.	0	3
Total	8	11¼

Weekly earnings of the Man and his Wife, viz.

The man receives the common weekly wages 8 months in the year	7	0
By task work the remaining 4 months he earns something more: his extra earnings, if equally divided among the 52 weeks in the year, would increase the weekly wages about	1	0
The wife's common work is to bake bread for the family, to wash and mend ragged clothes, and to look after the children; but at bean-setting, haymaking and harvest, she earns as much as comes one week with another to about	0	6
Total	8	6
Weekly expenses of this family	8	11¼
Weekly earnings	8	6
Deficiency of earnings	0	5¼

The expenses already set down are only the weekly outgoings, exclusive of house-rent, fuel, clothing, lying in, sickness, and burials: these being best allowed for by the year, may be called annual outgoings, and are as under:

	£	s.	d.

Rent of a cottage, or part of an old farm-house, with a small piece of garden ground, for a family, is from two pounds to two guineas: say   2   0   0

Fuel: this is turf from the common, and when bought costs 12s. per family; but as a man can cut in a week nearly enough to serve his family all the year, and the farmers (if the distance be not great) will give the carriage for the ashes, let this be charged at little more than one week's wages 0 10 0

Clothing: 1. The man's: wear of a suit per annum 5s.; wear of a working jacket and breeches 4s.; two shirts 8s.; one pair of stout shoes nailed 7s.; two pairs of stockings 4s.; hat, handkerchief, etc. 2s.; Sum £1–10–0d.

2. The wife's: wear of gown and petticoats 4s.; one shift 3s.6d.; one pair of strong shoes 4s.; one pair of stockings 1s.6d.; two aprons 3s.; handkerchiefs, caps, etc. 4s. Sum £1.

3. The children's: their clothing is (usually) partly made up of the parents' old clothes, partly bought at second hand: what is bought (supposing three children to a family) cannot well be reckoned at less than £1: where there are more than three children 7s. may be added; and where there are fewer 7s. may be deducted for each—Let the whole be estimated at £3–10–0d.

[Note: Very few poor people can afford to lay out this sum in clothes; but they should be enabled to do it; some cottagers breed a few fowls, with which they buy what sheets and blankets they want; but those who live in the old farmhouses are seldom allowed (to use their own words) 'to keep a pig or a chick']

Lying-in: the child's linen 3s. or 4s.; the midwife's fee 5s.; a bottle of gin or brandy always had upon this occasion, 2s.; attendance of a nurse for a few days, and her diet, at least 5s.; half a bushel of malt brewed, and hops, 3s.; to the minister for churching 1s.;—call the sum £1 and suppose this to happen once in two years; this is per annum 10s.

Casualties: 1. In sickness there is the physick to be paid for, and the loss of time to be allowed for:

2. Burials: poor people having many children, sometimes lose one: for both these together it seems
moderate to allow per annum 10s.

Sum of these annual outgoings   .. £7   0   0

This sum (£7) being divided by 52, the number of weeks in
a year, gives 2s. 8¼d per week. If therefore anyone desires to know
the whole weekly expense of a family, (consisting of a man and
his wife with three children) in order to compare it with the
whole of their weekly earnings, he must add 2s. 8¼d to the
current weekly expense of the family, as before set down, at the
foot of its account. Rev David Davies. *The Case of Labourers in
Husbandry Stated and Considered* (1795), 8, 15–16

5 Sir F. M. Eden   The Speenhamland Scale (1795)

Faced with the rapidly deteriorating condition of the agricultural labourers in the county in the spring of 1795, the
magistrates of Berkshire met at the Pelican Inn, Speenhamland, near Newbury, and, having rejected a proposal to fix a
minimum wage, drew up a table by which overseers could see
the minimum income required for the maintenance of a
labourer and his family at a given price of bread, and thus
could make up his weekly earnings out of the poor rates if they
fell below that amount. This Speenhamland scale, possibly
because of the publicity given to it by Eden, became the best
known example of the allowance system, which came to be
referred to by later poor law historians as the 'Speenhamland
System'. It was, however, by no means the only scale of its kind
in existence, nor was it the first to be drawn up, since a bread
scale of this kind had been introduced in Dorset in 1792.
It was, in fact, a method of regularising existing practice
rather than of introducing a new system of poor relief.
It was regarded at the time as a useful expedient for allaying the discontent of the labouring classes without unduly
increasing their wages, though by the time the Royal Commission on the Poor Laws had made their Report in 1834, it
c

had come to be regarded as the master evil of the old poor-law system.

The very great price of the necessaries of life, but more particularly of bread-corn, during the whole of last year, produced numberless extraordinary demands for parochial assistance. In many parishes in the county of Berks, relief from the Poor's Rates was granted, not only to the infirm and impotent, but to the able-bodied and industrious, who had, very few of them, ever applied to the parish for relief; and then only during temporary illness or disability. There was no doubt, but that the circumstances of the times required an increase in the income of the labourers in husbandry, who, in this county at least, compose the most numerous body of those liable to want assistance from the parish. But there existed a difference of opinion, respecting the mode of making such increase. In order to apply some adequate remedy to the evil, a meeting of the magistrates for the county was held about Easter 1795, when the following plans were submitted to their consideration:—1st, that the magistrates should fix the lowest price to be given for labour, as they were

This shews, at one view, what should be the weekly Income of the Industrious Poor, as settled by the Magistrates for the county of Berks, at a meeting held at Speenhamland, May the 6th, 1795.	Income should be for a Man.	For a single Woman.	For a Man and his Wife.	With one Child.	With two Children.	With three Children.	With four Children.	With five Children.	With six Children.	With seven Children.
	s. d.	s. d.	s. d.	s. d.	s. d.	s. d.	s. d.	s. d.	s. d.	s. d.
When the gallon loaf is¹ 1 0	3 0	2 0	4 6	6 0	7 6	9 0	10 6	12 0	13 6	15 0
when — 1 1	3 3	2 1	4 10	6 5	8 0	9 7	11 2	12 9	14 4	15 11
when — 1 2	3 6	2 2	5 2	6 10	8 6	10 2	11 10	13 6	15 2	16 10
when — 1 3	3 9	2 3	5 6	7 3	9 0	10 9	12 6	14 3	16 0	17 9
when — 1 4	4 0	2 4	5 10	7 8	9 6	11 4	13 2	15 0	16 10	18 8
when — 1 5	4 0	2 5	5 11	7 10	9 9	11 8	13 7	15 6	17 5	19 4
when — 1 6	4 3	2 6	6 3	8 3	10 3	12 3	14 3	16 3	18 3	20 3
when — 1 7	4 3	2 7	6 4	8 5	11 6	12 7	14 8	16 9	18 10	20 11
when — 1 8	4 6	2 8	6 8	8 10	11 0	13 2	15 4	17 6	19 8	21 10
when — 1 9	4 6	2 9	6 9	9 0	11 3	13 6	15 9	18 0	20 3	22 6
when — 1 10	4 9	2 10	7 1	9 5	11 9	14 1	16 5	18 9	21 1	23 5
when — 1 11	4 9	2 11	7 2	9 7	12 0	14 5	16 10	19 3	21 8	24 1
when — 2 0	5 0	3 0	7 6	10 0	12 6	15 0	17 6	20 0	22 6	25 0

¹ Gallon Loaf—a loaf weighing 8lb 11oz.

empowered to do by the 5th Eliz. c. 4.:[1] and, 2dly, that they should act with uniformity, in the relief of the *impotent* and *infirm* Poor, by a Table of universal practice, corresponding with the supposed necessities of each family. The first plan was rejected, by a considerable majority; but the second was adopted, and the Table (*on page 34*) was published as the rule for the information of magistrates and overseers. Sir F. M. Eden. *The State of the Poor*, Vol I (1797), 576–7

6 Samuel Whitbread   A Minimum Wage

Samuel Whitbread (1758–1815), the son of a wealthy London brewer, entered Parliament in 1790 as member for Bedford. He became a close friend and supporter of Charles James Fox and later emerged as one of the leading figures in the radical wing of the Whig Party. He led the attack on Henry Dundas in 1805 and after 1807 was prominent in pressing the Government to negotiate a peace with France. In July 1815, believing his political career to be at an end, he committed suicide.

In 1795 and 1800, both lean years, Whitbread attempted to get legislation to alter the Act of 1563 so that magistrates could fix minimum as well as maximum wages. In doing so, he was swimming against the tide of economic opinion, which was coming to regard all legislation regulating economic affairs as mischievous. On both occasions his efforts were opposed by William Pitt in speeches worthy of a disciple of Adam Smith.

In 1807, Whitbread drafted a full-scale Bill for poor law amendment which included such measures as reform of the settlement laws, equalisation of poor rates, provision of cottages for the poor, and parochial schools financed out of the rates. This attempt also failed, though the educational clauses of the Bill were commended by Malthus.

'The right hon. gentleman[2] had contended, that nothing effectual could be done by regulations, that all must be the

---

[1] *Statute of Artificers* (1563).   [2] William Pitt.

result of principle: and that, in amending the Poor Laws, no regulation could be made respecting the amount of wages, but that labour should be left to find its own level. It was impossible, however, that labour should find its own level, as the laws on that head now stood. What first gave rise, in his mind, to the idea of the bill he wished to introduce, was, the situation to which the poor were reduced in 1795. Their distresses then were nearly the same as they are now; and very exemplary attention was likewise then shown by the richer classes to alleviate their distresses, but, before they received that relief, the pressure under which they laboured was extreme. The farmers would not raise the price of labour; he consulted the Statute-book, but could discover nothing in it that would compel the farmers to do their duty. The justices, he found, had no power to grant relief; but they were armed with power to oppress the poor. In virtue of the fifth Elizabeth c.4,[1] the justices had the power of regulating the maximum of labour. This was highly oppressive to the labouring poor. A law therefore appeared necessary for enabling the justices to regulate also the minimum of labour. . . . The more he examined the Poor Laws, the more convinced he was, that the fault lay not in the laws themselves, but in the execution of them. Where they were well executed, the poor enjoyed as much comfort as it was possible for them to enjoy. But where they were not duly enforced, the poor endured the most intolerable miseries. *Parliamentary History*, Vol XXXIV, cols 1427–8

---

7 Sir F. M. Eden   Pitt's Scheme for Poor-Law Reform
In December 1796 William Pitt laid before Parliament a Bill for the reform of the poor laws containing 130 clauses, an elaborate and complicated measure which embodied many of the ideas put forward by earlier writers. Its first 47 clauses were given over to regulations for the establishment of schools

---

[1] Statute of Artificers (1563). Section 11 of this Act gave power to magistrates to fix wage rates, although under Section 13, penalties only seem to have been imposed on those who paid or received wages *higher* than the prescribed rate.

of industry. In its proposals for the reform of administration, it followed closely the ideas of Thomas Gilbert, for example its recommendation of salaried county guardians to supervise parochial administration. The Bill also attempted to give legislative expression to the practice of making up inadequate wages out of the poor rates, which had spread rapidly during the crisis of 1795. Such a comprehensive scheme could not fail to attract the opposition of local poor-law authorities; over forty petitions against it were submitted to the House of Commons in the six months after its presentation and this opposition was sufficient to kill it.

Heads of a Bill for the Better Support and Maintenance of the Poor.

Prepared according to the Plan opened by Mr. Pitt, to the House of Commons, in the Present Session of Parliament, 1796.

. . . LIV. And be it further enacted, that if any poor person residing in any parish under the authority of this Act, and not being able to earn the full rate of wages usually given in such parish, or the parish or parishes united therewith, shall, with the previous consent of the person or persons appointed to the management of the poor of any such parish or united parishes, contract and agree to work at any inferior rate or wages, which wages shall not be sufficient for the maintenance and support of such poor person singly, or in conjunction with his or her family, it shall and may be lawful for such officers of the Poor, with the approbation of one or more Justice or Justices of the Peace in the district, to make up such deficiency as may be necessary for the support of such poor person, and his or her family, (regard being had to the earnings of such family), out of the Rates made for the relief of the Poor, without compelling such poor person to be employed in any school of industry, or in any other manner, under the authority of this Act. Sir F. M. Eden. *The State of the Poor*, Vol III, Appendix XI (1797), cccxxiv

8 The Magistrates' Powers of Relief

This statute clearly reflects the change in attitudes to outdoor relief that had occurred in the late eighteenth century, particularly with the necessity of granting emergency relief to hard-pressed labourers during the price rise of the 1790s. In its first section, the Act severely criticised the Act of 1722 (9 Geo I, c 7), which it claimed had been found to be 'inconvenient and oppressive' since it prevented an industrious poor person receiving the type of relief best suited to his case. Thus the Act empowered local magistrates to order outdoor relief for pauper applicants even in parishes where the overseer had a contract to send all paupers to the workhouse. This considerably increased the powers of justices over the parochial authorities, and may well have encouraged some parishes to adopt the provisions of Gilbert's Act, since parishes under that Act were exempted from such interference. The Royal Commission of 1834 was strongly critical of this extension of the magistrates' power of granting relief, arguing that it had too often been used carelessly and outdoor relief had been granted indiscriminately under it.

---

36 Geo III CAP. 23

An Act to amend so much of an Act, made in the ninth year of the reign of King George the First, intituled, "An Act for amending the Laws relating to the Settlement, Employment and Relief of the Poor" as prevents the distributing occasional relief to poor persons in their own houses, under certain circumstances and in certain cases. (24th December, 1795).

... II. And be it further enacted by the authority aforesaid, that it shall and may be lawful for any His Majesty's justices of the peace for any county, city, town or place, usually acting in and for the district wherein the same shall be situated, at his or their just and proper discretion, to direct and order collection and relief to any industrious poor person or persons, and he, she or they shall be entitled to ask and to receive such relief at his, her or their homes, house, or houses, in any parish, town, township or place, notwithstanding any contract shall have been or shall be made with any person or persons for lodging, keeping, maintaining and employing any and all poor persons in a house or houses for such purpose hired or purchased, and the churchwarden or churchwardens, overseer or overseers, for such parish, town, township or place, are required and directed to obey and perform such order for relief given by any justice or justices as aforesaid. *The Statutes at Large*, Vol X (1795–1800), 19

9 Select Committee on Poor Rate Returns   The Rising Cost of Relief

In 1803 and again in 1813, Parliament demanded a return from each parish of the amount it had spent in poor relief over the past year. From 1813 onwards these returns were required annually in order to keep some check on the rise in relief costs. The continued increase after the war to a peak of £8 millions in 1818 caused considerable alarm amongst ratepayers in both agricultural and manufacturing areas since the pinch of post-war depression was making the poor rate a far more difficult burden to bear. (Cont pp 40–41).

CRITICS OF THE POOR LAW
10A Sir F. M. Eden   The State of the Poor

Sir Frederick Morton Eden was the son of Sir Robert Eden, at one time Governor of Maryland. He was the founder and chairman of the Globe Insurance Company, but his chief claim to fame was the investigation into the state of the labouring classes which he carried out in order to discover the effects of the high food prices of 1794 and 1795. He visited some parishes personally, corresponded with clergymen and leading inhabitants of others, and also employed an investigator to carry out some of the research. The completed work was published in three volumes in 1797. The first volume contained a history of the poor law and a critique of the present system, and the other two contained the reports from

AN ACCOUNT SHOWING THE AMOUNT OF MONIES ASSESSED AND LEVIED IN ENGLAND AND WALES,

At the several Periods for which Returns have been required by Parliament; distinguishing the Payments made thereout, for Other Purposes than the Relief of the Poor; the Sums expended in Law, Removals, &c. and the Sums expended for the Relief of the Poor:—Also, the Average Price of Wheat in each Year for which it can be ascertained.

YEARS.	TOTAL SUM Assessed and Levied.	PAYMENTS thereout for other Purposes than the Relief of the Poor.	SUMS Expended in Law, Removals, &c.	SUMS Expended for the Relief of the Poor.	TOTAL SUMS EXPENDED.	Average Price of WHEAT.
	£.	£.	£.	£.	£.	£. s.
Average of } 1748–49–50 -	730,135	40,164	* - -	689,971	† —	—
1776 - - -	1,720,316	137,655	35,071	1,521,732	1,694,458	—
Average }						

1803	5,346,204	1,034,105	190,672	4,677,691	5,302,076	03	2
1812–13 – –	8,640,842	1,861,073	325,107	6,656,105	8,865,838	128	8
1813–14 – –	8,388,974	1,881,565	332,966	6,294,584	8,511,863	98	–
1814–15 – –	7,457,676	1,763,020	324,664	5,418,845	7,508,853	70	6
1815–16 – –	6,937,425	1,212,918	*	5,724,506	†	61	10
1816–17 – –	8,128,418	1,210,200	*	6,918,217	†	87	4
1817–18 – –	9,320,440	1,430,292	*	7,890,148	†	90	7
1818–19 – –	8,932,185	1,300,534	*	7,531,650	†	82	9
1819–20 – –	8,719,655	1,342,658	*	7,329,594	8,672,252	69	5
1820–21‡ –	8,411,893	1,375,868	*	6,958,445	8,334,313	62	5

* For these periods there is no particular account of the sums expended in Law, or in Removals.

† For these periods there is no account of the sums *expended*, as distinguished from those *assessed and levied*.

‡ For this year, (1820–21) the Order required a Return, not of the sum *assessed and levied*, but of the sum *levied*.

Select Committee on Poor Rate Returns. *Report*, V, Appendix A (1822).

parishes investigated by Eden and an appendix of statistical and other material on poor relief.

Upon the whole, therefore, there seem to be just grounds for concluding, that the sum of good to be expected from the establishment of a compulsory maintenance for the Poor, will be far outbalanced by the sum of evil which it will inevitably create; that the certainty of a legal provision weakens the principles of natural affection, and destroys one of the strongest ties of society, by rendering the exercise of domestic and social duties less necessary; that a Poor's Tax will unavoidably be burthensome and unequal; and that the distribution of a large public fund, confided, as it must be, to officers, who cannot but be invested with discretionary powers, will ever be the pregnant source of partiality and peculation.

The preceding observations chiefly regard a national provision, which is designed for the relief of those, who, either from infancy, old age, or sickness, are incapacitated from acquiring the necessaries of life. It is seldom, however, that public charity is confined to this object. It generally professes to act upon the wide-extended view of supplying the able with employment, as well as of furnishing the impotent with subsistence. The two leading principles of the 43d of Elizabeth were, that those who were incapable of working should be supported by their parish, and that those who were capable of working should be employed. With respect to the practicability or utility of the last-mentioned provision of the Statute, I shall content myself with referring the Reader to a subsequent part of this Work; and with remarking, that it is impossible to provide a national fund for setting the Poor to work in any species of employment, without in some degree injuring those who are engaged in similar undertakings. If, for instance, a parish work-house undertakes the manufacture of mops, ropes, and sacking; those who before subsisted by means of these trades are sure to be the sufferers. Whether the mops are made by the private manufacturer, or by the parish children, no more will be sold than the Public have occasion for. The managers of the work-house, however, without being able to increase the demand, can generally obtain a preference and a certain sale for their goods, by selling them rather below the market price. The concern, though a losing one, is carried on by the contributions of the parishioners; and a poor industrious manufacturer will, perhaps, often have the mortification to reflect, that, in contributing his portion of Poor's Rate, he is helping the parish to undo him. To invest a public body with a part of that stock, which, for the sake of profit, sets the greater part of useful labour in motion, seems indeed repugnant to the sound principles of political economy. The capital stock of every society, if left to its free course, will be divided among different employments, in the proportion that is most agreeable to the public interest, by the private views of individuals. When it is thus employed, it will accumulate: and it is its accumulation only, which can afford regular and progressive employment to industry. Projects, which, without increasing the demand for any article of consumption, interfere with established manufactures, and oblige the fair trader, (whose capital is limited,) to enter into competition with the parish, (whose capital can, upon any emergency, be recruited by an order of Justices,) are, it may well be supposed, as injurious to the general interests of the community, as the monopolizing speculations of Governments in foreign commerce. They operate in the same manner, "by "repelling from a particular trade that stock which would other- "wise go to it, or by attracting towards a particular trade that "which would not otherwise come to it." Sir F. M. Eden. *The State of the Poor*, Vol I (1797), 467–8

10B Rev T. R. Malthus   Essay on Population

Thomas Robert Malthus (1766–1834) was the son of Daniel Malthus, a country gentleman of Dorking in Surrey. Educated by a tutor, Gilbert Wakefield, a founder of the famous War- rington Academy, and at Jesus College, Cambridge, Malthus became a Fellow of his college in 1793 and three years later obtained a living in Surrey. In 1805, he became Professor of

History and Political Economy at the East India College at Haileybury, a post which he held until his death.

Malthus is best known for his work on population theory, particularly for his thesis that the rate of population growth tends always to outstrip the means of subsistence unless sufficient checks are imposed. His first *Essay on Population*, published in 1798, was a slender treatise, intended mainly as a refutation of the idealism expressed by William Godwin in his *Political Justice*. The second edition of 1802 was a much expanded version of the original, and four more editions were published before Malthus' death.

Like Eden, Malthus believed that the poor law did nothing to better the condition of the poor. On the contrary, it made them spendthrift and careless of the future. It encouraged early and improvident marriages and thus promoted the rapid growth of population. Undoubtedly Malthus's theory of population and his critique of the poor law greatly strengthened the arguments of those who desired a more closely regulated and less attractive system of poor relief. The word 'Malthusian' became a term of abuse frequently hurled at the reformers of 1834, who were credited with all manner of devilish schemes for checking population growth (28). Despite this, Malthus, as his attack on the settlement laws in this passage shows, was genuinely concerned to promote the happiness and improve the condition of the poor.

I feel no doubt whatever that the parish laws of England have contributed to raise the price of provisions and to lower the real price of labour. They have therefore contributed to impoverish that class of people whose only possession is their labour. It is also difficult to suppose that they have not powerfully contributed to generate that carelessness and want of frugality observable among the poor, so contrary to the disposition frequently to be remarked among petty tradesmen and small farmers. The labouring poor to use a vulgar expression seem always to live from hand to mouth. Their present wants employ their whole attention, and they seldom think of the future. Even when they have an opportunity of saving they seldom exercise it, but all that is beyond their present necessities goes, generally speaking, to the ale-house. The poor-laws of England may therefore be said to diminish both the power and the will to save among the common people, and thus to weaken one of the strongest incentives to sobriety and industry, and consequently to happiness.

The poor-laws of England were undoubtedly instituted for the most benevolent purpose, but there is great reason to think that they have not succeeded in their intention. They certainly mitigate some cases of very severe distress which might otherwise occur, yet the state of the poor who are supported by parishes, considered in all its circumstances, is very far from being free from misery. But one of the principal objections to them is that for this assistance which some of the poor receive, in itself almost a doubtful blessing, the common people of England is subjected to a set of grating, inconvenient and tyrannical laws, totally inconsistent with the genuine spirit of the constitution. The whole business of settlements, even in its present amended form, is utterly contradictory to all ideas of freedom. The parish persecution of men whose families are likely to become chargeable, and of poor women who are near lying-in, is a most disgraceful and disgusting tyranny. And the obstructions continually occasioned in the market of labour by these laws, have a constant tendency to add to the difficulties of those who are struggling to support themselves without assistance.

The evils attendant on the poor-laws are in some degree irremediable. If assistance be distributed to a certain class of people, a power must be given somewhere of discriminating the proper objects and of managing the concerns of the institutions that are necessary, but any great interference with the affairs of other people, is a species of tyranny, and in the common course of things the exercise of this power may be expected to become grating to those who are driven to ask for support. The tyranny of Justices, Churchwardens and Overseers, is a common complaint among the poor, but the fault does not lie so much in these persons, who probably before they were in power, were not worse than other people, but in the nature of all such institutions.

The evil is perhaps gone too far to be remedied, but I feel little doubt in my own mind that if the poor-laws had never existed, though there might have been a few more instances of very severe distress, yet that the aggregate mass of happiness among the common people would have been much greater than it is at present. T. R. Malthus. *Essay on Population* (1798), 86-7, 91-4

10C Patrick Colquhoun   A Treatise on Indigence

Patrick Colquhoun (1745-1820) was born in Dumbarton, the son of a county registrar. As a young man he went to Virginia where he made his fortune. He returned to Glasgow in 1766 and took a prominent role in commercial affairs, leading delegations to London to make representations to the Government on behalf of local industries. He was founder and chairman of the Glasgow Chamber of Commerce and was made Lord Provost of Glasgow in 1782 and 1783. In 1789 he moved to London, becoming a magistrate in 1792 through the influence of Henry Dundas. He took a strong interest in local government and suggested methods of improvement in such works as *Treatise on the Police of the Metropolis* (1795) and *The Commerce and Police of the River Thames* (1800).

Unlike Eden and Malthus, Colquhoun did not desire the abolition of the poor-law system but rather its centralisation, so that it could be used to distinguish carefully between poverty and indigence, prevent the deserving poor from falling into the latter condition and restore the idle to a useful position in society, thus reducing the waste which indigence entailed.

Many of Colquhoun's schemes closely resemble those of his contemporary friend and admirer, Jeremy Bentham. The idea of a centralised poor law authority was of course taken up by the Royal Commission of 1832–4, but Colquhoun's notion of a restorative function for the poor law is more in tune with some of the ideas of the early twentieth-century poor law reformers (see Chapter 4).

In contemplating the affairs of the poor, it is necessary in the first instance to have a clear conception of the distinction between Indigence and Poverty.

Poverty is that state and condition in society where the individual has no surplus labour in store, and, consequently, no property but what is derived from the constant exercise of industry in the various occupations of life; or in other words, it is the state of every one who must labour for subsistence.

Poverty is therefore a most necessary and indispensable ingredient in society, without which nations and communities could not exist in a state of civilisation. It is the lot of man—it is the source of wealth, since without poverty there would be no labour, and without labour there could be no riches, no refinement, no comfort, and no benefit to those who may be possessed of wealth —inasmuch as without a large proportion of poverty surplus labour could never be rendered productive in procuring either the conveniences or luxuries of life.

Indigence therefore, and not poverty, is the evil. It is that condition in society which implies want, misery and distress. It is the state of any one who is destitute of the means of subsistence, and is unable to labour to procure it to the extent nature requires. The natural source of subsistence is the labour of the individual; while that remains with him he is denominated poor: when it fails in whole or in part he becomes indigent.

The condition of man is susceptible of four material distinctions:

Indigence $\begin{cases} \text{1. Utter inability to procure subsistence} \\ \text{2. Inadequate ability} \end{cases}$

              3. Adequate ability and no more—Poverty

              4. Extra ability, which is the ordinary state of man, and is the source of wealth.

But it may happen, and does sometimes happen in civil life, that a man may have ability to labour and cannot obtain it. He may have labour in his possession, without being able to dispose of it.

The great desideratum, therefore, is to prop up poverty by judicious arrangements at those critical periods when it is in danger of descending into indigence. The barrier between these two conditions in society is often slender, and the public interest requires that it should be narrowly guarded, since every individual who retrogrades into indigence becomes a loss to the body politic, not only in the diminution of a certain portion of productive labour, but also in an additional pressure on the community by the necessary support of the person and his family who have thus descended into indigence.

It is the province of all governments by wise regulations of internal police to call forth the greatest possible proportion of industry, as the best and surest means of producing national happiness and prosperity.

The great object is first to establish a foundation, a rallying point, a centre of action, a fixed responsible agency, a resource of talents, knowledge, application and industry, equal, if possible, to the difficult task of improving the condition of society in all those ramifications, where a gangrene either exists or is threatened.

1. By diminishing the number of the innocent indigent by judicious and timely props.

2. By restoring the culpable indigent to at least a useful condition in society, by a variety of combined regulations, applicable to persons discharged from prisons and unable to obtain work for want of character:—to others, under similar circumstances, in point of character, who have not been imprisoned:—to unfortunate females, abandoned by the world and degraded by prostitution:—to the race of gypsies and others imitating their manners:—to vagrants of all descriptions:—and finally, to the means of diminishing the temptations and resources which are

rendered so prolific for the commission of moral and criminal offences.

And thus, by an all pervading system of well regulated police, having its chief seat or central point in the metropolis, and from thence maintaining a close and connected chain of correspondence, by receiving information and communicating the same with regularity and promptitude to all parts of the Kingdom, by a permanent authority, competent (in consequence of the continually accumulating fund of information and experience so collected and preserved) to report to his Majesty in Parliament such measures as shall in any degree be conducive to the great objects of the institution—The improvement of the condition of the labouring people—the increase of the productive labour of the country—the more effectual prevention of moral and criminal offences—to the lessening the demand for punishment—the diminution of the public burdens attached to pauper and criminal police, by turning the hearts and arresting the hands of evil-doers—by forewarning the unwary, and preserving in innocence the untainted. P. Colquhoun. *A Treatise on Indigence* (1806), 7–9, 108–9

10D The Committee of 1817   Report

The economic depression at the end of the Napoleonic wars brought an increase in poor rates and in working-class discontent, to the alarm of ratepayers, overseers and magistrates. In February 1817 a motion in the House of Commons for an enquiry into the poor-law system was accepted by the Government and a committee was set up under the chairmanship of William Sturges Bourne. Parish officers and other witnesses from rural and urban areas were questioned, and, in July 1817, the committee produced its report, which clearly revealed to what extent the criticisms of writers like Eden and Malthus had been accepted, and pointed the way forward to the reforms of 1834.

D

The Committee are well aware, that however important and desirable it undoubtedly is to equalize this heavy burthen [of poor rates], yet if new funds are provided, it should at the same time be remembered, that a facility of expenditure will be also created. But whether the assessment be confined to land and houses, or other denominations of property be made practically liable to the same charge, Your Committee feel it their imperious duty to state to the House their opinion, that unless some efficacious check be interposed, there is every reason to think, that the amount of the assessment will continue as it has done, to increase, till at a period more or less remote, according to the progress the evil has already made in different places it shall have absorbed the profits of the property on which the rate may have been assessed, producing thereby the neglect and ruin of the land, and the waste or removal of other property, to the utter subversion of that happy order of society so long upheld in these kingdoms.

What number of years, under the existing laws and management, would probably elapse, and to what amount the assessments might possibly be augmented, before the utmost limitation would be reached, cannot be accurately ascertained; but with regard to the first, Your Committee think it their duty to point out, that many circumstances which, in the early periods of the system, rendered its progress slow, are now unfortunately changed. The independent spirit of mind which induced individuals in the labouring classes to exert themselves to the utmost, before they submitted to become paupers, is much impaired; this order of persons therefore are every day becoming less and less unwilling to add themselves to the list of paupers. The workhouse system, though enacted with other views, yet for a long time acted very powerfully in deterring persons from throwing themselves on their parishes for relief; there were many who would struggle through their difficulties, rather than undergo the discipline of a workhouse; this effect however is no longer produced in the same degree, as by two modern statutes the justices have power under certain conditions to order relief to be given out of the workhouses, and the number of persons to whom relief is actually given, being now far more than any workhouses would contain, the system itself is from necessity, as well as by law, materially relaxed.

These impressions, upon subjects of such great importance, could not fail to induce Your Committee to take into their consideration whatever plans could be referred to or suggested, the object of which might be to check and modify the system itself, a duty to which they were the more strongly urged, by the view which had presented itself to their consideration of the state of society, created by an extensive system of pauperism, and which led them, for the sake of the paupers themselves, to seek for the means of setting again into action those motives which impel persons, by the hope of bettering their condition on the one hand, and the fear of want on the other, so to exert and conduct themselves, as by frugality, temperance and industry, and by the practice of those other virtues on which human happiness has been made to depend, to ensure to themselves that condition of existence in which life can alone be otherwise than a miserable burthen; the temptations to idleness, to improvidence, and want of forethought, are under any circumstances so numerous and enticing, that nothing less than the dread of the evils, which are their natural consequence, appears to be sufficiently strong in any degree to control them; as long indeed as fresh funds can be found for their relief, those evils may in some degree be mitigated; but when such resources can no longer be found, then will these evils be felt in their full force; and as the gradual addition of fresh funds can only create an increased number of paupers, it is obvious that the amount of the misery which must be endured, when these funds can no longer be augmented, will be the greater (though the longer delayed) the greater the supplies are, which may be applied to the relief of pauperism, inasmuch as the sufferings to be endured must be increased with the number of sufferers.

Select Committee on the Poor Laws. *Report*, VI (1817), 8, 9, 10

THE ABUSES OF POOR RELIEF
11A Select Committee on Labourers' Wages The Allowance System

This committee was set up to discover the extent to which agricultural labourers were being subsidised out of the poor rates. The committee examined witnesses and circulated a questionnaire to magistrates throughout England and Wales. Its report condemned the allowance system, also reporting it to be far less prevalent in the north of England than in the southern counties, where wages were lower.

From the evidence and other information collected by Your Committee, it appears that, in some districts of the country, all able-bodied labourers are sent round to the farmers, and receive a part, and in some instances the whole of their subsistence from the parish, while working upon the land of individuals. This practice was, doubtless, introduced at first as a means of employing the surplus labourers of a parish; but by an abuse, which is almost inevitable, it has been converted into a means of obliging the parish to pay for labour, which ought to have been hired and paid for by private persons. This abuse frequently follows immediately the practice of sending the unemployed labourers upon the farms in the parish. The farmer, finding himself charged for a greater quantity of labour than he requires, naturally endeavours to economize, by discharging those labourers of whom he has the least need, and relying upon the supply furnished by the parish for work, hitherto performed entirely at his own cost. An instance has been quoted, of a farmer's team standing still, because the farmer had not received the number of roundsmen he expected. Thus the evil of this practice augments itself: and the steady hard working labourer, employed by agreement with his master, is converted into the degraded and inefficient pensioner of the parish.

In other parts of the country this practice has been carried to
a very great extent, for the sake of diminishing the income of
the clergyman of the parish, and for paying the expenses of one
class of men out of the revenue of another. In the parish of
Hurstmonceaux, in Sussex, it appears, that the wages of labour
were reduced in this manner to sixpence a day: and a clergyman
of a neighbouring parish has been threatened with the adoption
of a similar practice.

This practice is the natural result of another, which is far
more common, namely, that of paying an allowance to labourers
for the maintenance of their children. In some counties, as in
Bedfordshire, this payment usually begins when the labourer has
a single child, wages being kept so low, that it is utterly impossible for him to support a wife and child without parish
assistance.

. . . We are happy to be able to say, that the evil of which we
complain is partial, and that many counties in England are
nearly, if not totally, exempt from the grievance. In Northum-
berland, wages are twelve shillings a week; and labourers, having
families, do not usually receive assistance from the poor rate. In
Cumberland, wages vary from twelve shillings to fifteen shillings
a week, and the report is equally satisfactory. In Lincolnshire,
the wages are generally twelve shillings per week, and the
labourers live in comfort and independence. At Wigan, in Lancashire, wages are seven or eight shillings a week, and relief is
afforded to a man with three children; in the division of Oldham,
in the same county, a great manufacturing district, wages are
from twelve shillings to eighteen shillings a week, and no such
practice is known. In Yorkshire, wages are generally twelve
shillings a week; but in some parts of that extensive county, the
practice of giving married labourers assistance from the parish
appears very prevalent. In Staffordshire, wages are about ten
shillings; and labourers, having families, only occasionally receive relief from the poor rate. In the divisions of Oswaldslow,
in the county of Worcester, the practice of paying part of the
wages of labour out of the poor-rate, has been entirely put a

stop to by the vigilance of the Magistrates. If we turn to the midland, southern and western parts of the country, we find a great variety in the rate of wages. In the Wingham division, in Kent alone, it appears, that the lowest wages paid were, in one parish, sixpence; in four, eight-pence; in eleven, one shilling and sixpence; in four, two shillings, and, in the greater number, one shilling a day. In Suffolk, Sussex, Bedfordshire, Buckingham-shire, Dorsetshire and Wiltshire, the plan of paying wages out of the poor rate, has been carried to the greatest extent. Norfolk, Huntingdonshire and Devonshire, are likewise afflicted by it. In some of these counties wages are eight shillings or nine shillings; in others, five shillings; and in some parts they have been and are so low as three shillings a week for a single man; four shillings and sixpence for a man and his wife. Select Committee on Labourers' Wages. *Report*, VI (1824), 3, 5

___

11B Samuel Makin & John Robinson Industrial Speenhamland

The two witnesses were Coventry ribbon manufacturers, both of whom employed over 100 workers. They alleged that some master manufacturers were employing young workers as ap-prentices without going through the proper legal forms of indenture. As a condition of their employment, half the wages of these 'illegal' apprentices was retained by their employer, hence the phrase 'half pay' apprentices. The complaint that underpaid workers were having their earnings made up out of the poor rate, thus enabling master manufacturers to flood the market with cheap goods, was common in many handi-craft industries after 1815. Allegations about similar practices in the Sheffield cutlery trades led to a public enquiry in 1820 and the adoption of a stricter system of relief admin-istration.

___

If a skilful person cannot obtain more than 5s. 6d. a week, and that not being a maintenance, where does he get the rest from?—Why sometimes of the parish; it is astonishing to see how very bare some of them live, some instances of which have come under my own eye.

Then those half-pay apprentices who may only get 2*s.*, 1*s.* 9*d.* or 1*s.* 6*d.*, to what do they resort to get sufficient to sustain life?— They have generally friends who can assist them, who put them out apprentice, and they live upon them; and if their friends are in distress themselves, they apply to the parish.

Then the Committee are to conclude, that in both these cases, the system has operated very much to increase the poor rates?— I have not a doubt of it.

What is now the rate of the poor's rates at Coventry, or what has it been within the last twelve months?—I think they must amount to somewhere about 19*s.* in the pound.

Have you served the office of director of the poor?—No; I have not.

If you can, the Committee will thank you to inform them, generally, concerning the great number that resort to poor rates for relief, under this state of things; the Committee suppose this effect is to be attributed to two causes, the one the under-selling of each other, and the other the system of half-pay apprentices? —It certainly is; for I know, that if I wish to purchase goods ready made, I could purchase them a vast deal lower than I could make them, and which I have done in many instances.
Evidence of Samuel Makin

How is it possible that goods can be manufactured at so low a rate, you only paying 5*s.* 6*d.* a week journeyman's wages, that you can purchase goods so much cheaper than you can manufacture them, as you state?—The masters that encourage the half-pay system, get their goods made at half-pay; some get them manufactured at full thirty per cent. lower than I do.

Then you conceive the poor's rates pay the difference of wages?—Yes; they have even to support, in part, those who work for me.

Do you conceive those goods were sold, under circumstances of distress, to the person of whom you bought them; and, therefore, sold at a cheaper rate than they otherwise would have been, or that it arises from the way in which they are manufactured?—I believe it arises from the way in which they are manufactured, generally; there may be something of distress in it, for aught I know.

Could you purchase any quantity at that price?—Any quantity, this day.

Do you know where they are manufactured?—Yes.

Are they manufactured at Coventry?—In Coventry, and its neighbourhood; and many of them are paying full thirty per cent. less than I am paying, shamefully low as my price is.

And the difference is made up by poor rates?—Of course, for they have no other means of subsistence. *Evidence of John Robinson.* Select Committee on Silk Ribbon Weavers. *Report*, IX (1818), 36, 126

11C Rev Phillip Hunt   The Roundsman System

The witness, a Bedford JP, here explains the system by which unemployed labourers were sent round the parish looking for work at wages subsidised by the parish. The origins of the system are obscure, but it had doubtless been in existence since the eighteenth century, and had been encouraged by statutes such as Gilbert's Act, which enjoined on the parish guardian the duty of finding work for the able-bodied unemployed. It was particularly common in winter, when there was little to do on the farms. The increased use of threshing machines and the decline of cottage industries such as spinning had further reduced employment.

Will you state exactly what the system that is called the system of roundsmen, is?—It is sending in rotation to each of the occupiers in the parish those unemployed labourers (who have a parochial settlement in the Parish) to work for such farmers, and to have their wages paid, in whole or in part, out of the poor rates.

When a part is to be paid by the farmer, is that sum fixed by the parish?—Yes.

Are those men, called roundsmen, considered as good labourers?—Quite otherwise; they became roundsmen, perhaps, in consequence of their not being so well liked as the other labourers; and by being employed as roundsmen, they become still worse, by the indolent habits they thus acquire. Select Committee on Labourers' Wages. *Report*, VI, *Evidence of Rev Phillip Hunt* (1824), 36

11D Thomas Bowyer The Labour Rate

The witness, a maltster and corn factor from Buckden in Huntingdonshire, handed in a pamphlet containing the details of this plan for a labour rate to the committee. The labour rate was seen by some people as a more equitable method of adjusting the burden of rural unemployment. It was, however, sharply condemned by the Royal Commission of 1832–4 for weighing unfairly on the small farmer and tradesman who employed little or no labour, for confining labourers to their parish of settlement, and for destroying the distinction between pauperism and independence.

A Plan to regulate the Employment of the Labouring Poor, as acted upon in the Parish of Oundle.

(Since the first edition of this little pamphlet was published in February last, experience has fully proved the utility of the plan proposed; and it is now adopting in most of the neighbouring villages, sanctioned with the approbation of the Magistrates of the county.)

The Plan is as follows:

A separate rate for the above purpose, distinct from all other rates, is made upon the parish, which rate being regularly allowed and published as "A Rate for the Relief of the Poor," the payment of it, of course, may be legally enforced, in cases where any of the occupiers have neglected to employ a sufficient number of men and boys, at the wages fixed upon to exonerate them from the rate.

The principle of the plan is this, that every occupier who is liable to be assessed, shall pay labourers' wages according to his assessment; leaving him the choice to whom to pay it,—either to the labourer himself, if he chooses to employ one, or otherwise to the overseer, to whom ultimately the labourer must apply for support. It also gives the employer a proper control over his labourers, and it occasions a competition for the best hands, while, at the same time, it insures the best pay to those who best merit it, and stimulates others to try for the like advantages. Select Committee on Labourers' Wages. *Report, VI, Evidence of Thomas Bowyer* (1824), 23

11E Henry Boyce   An Auction of Paupers

This piece of evidence, from a witness who had been an overseer in the parish of Waldershare in Kent for twenty-five years, shows the desperate straits to which parish officers were sometimes reduced in order to find employment for the able-bodied poor.

... In the parish of Ash, there is a regular meeting every Thursday, and the paupers are put up to auction.

What do they fetch?—That will depend on the character of the man; the best will fetch the full pay of twelve shillings per week.

Every Saturday?—Every Thursday, they are put up.

Are they all put up to auction, all the labourers?—Only those out of employ.

Does that include the whole number, or is there a considerable portion that do not come to the auction?—There are a great portion; those who go to the auction, the extent of their wages is twelve shillings a week; if a person bids eight or ten, it is made up by the poor rates. Select Committee on the Employment or Relief of Able Bodied Persons. *Report, IV, Evidence of Henry Boyce* (1828), 21

11F J. D. Tweedy   Labour on the Roads

These passages are taken from the report of one of the assistants to the Royal Commission of 1832–4 who was investigating the state of poor-law administration in the West Riding of Yorkshire. Since parishes were responsible for the upkeep of their roads as well as of their poor, the employment of able-bodied paupers in repairing the parish roads seemed an obvious solution, especially as the overseer often combined his office with that of surveyor of the highways. In some cases, road labour was carefully supervised and used to deter those thought to be workshy from seeking relief, but, frequently, as the second extract shows, the system was merely another despairing and ill-contrived effort to find something for the able-bodied poor to do.

In Tickhill the assistant overseer is also assistant surveyor of the highways, and the overseers are surveyors. There are 28 miles of highways, exclusive of six miles of turnpike-road which is under the direction of the turnpike road surveyor; the men who are out of employ are therefore set to work, either in the quarries to get stone, or in breaking stones or in cleaning the road; and for this work they are paid out of the composition, and if that be not sufficient, it is eked out of the poor rate; for the last year the composition has been sufficient. . . . The work is let to the men generally, say 10d a yard for getting and breaking limestone, and 4d a yard for walling stones that are thrown out: if done by regular labourers, the rate of pay would be 1s.3d or 1s.4d per yard; those who do not work by the piece are paid at from 1s. to 1s.4d per day; a regular day labourer would earn 2s.3d; this plan, the overseers find, causes the able-bodied to seek for other work as soon as they can.

In Pollington, they send many of them upon the highways, but they only work four hours per day; this is because there is not sufficient employment in that way; they sleep more than they work, and if any but the surveyor found them sleeping, they would laugh at them. In Rawcliffe, they employed a man in the winter of 1830–1 to look over them, but they threatened to drown him, and he was obliged to withdraw. Royal Com-

mission on the Poor Laws. *Report of J. D. Tweedy*, Appendix A,
Part 1 (1834), 842, 848

11G Select Committee on the Employment or Relief of Able Bodied Persons   The Bread Scale

In some counties, tables drawn up by the magistrates to guide
parish overseers in giving relief to labourers with insufficient
earnings continued in existence after the war, though their
use became much less frequent as the allowance system came
under criticism. With the drastic fall in corn prices after 1813,
relief scales were severely reduced, specially in areas feeling
the effects of agricultural depression. This scale is the one in
use in the Hindon Division of Wiltshire in 1828. It had been
drawn up by the magistrates in March 1817, and calculated
the exact amount required to sustain each member of a family
with the price of bread at 1s 3d (6p) the gallon loaf. If the
labourer and his family earned less than this amount, their
earnings were subsidised out of the poor rates. In calculating
family earnings, only half the wife's wage was taken into
account if she had two children under four; with three children
or more under four, her earnings were ignored completely.
Nevertheless, the scale was considerably less generous than the
Speenhamland scale of 1795 (5) where the minimum weekly
needs of a man and wife with six children were estimated at
16s (80p) when the gallon loaf stood at 1s 3d.

EXAMPLE of the Operation of the Hindon Scale

Minimum of Weekly Support for a family taking the price of bread at 1s.3d the Gallon Loaf; being the actual price of bread of the best description, at Salisbury, the 24th June 1828.	Weekly Earnings of the same family, according to the price of labour, in the neighbourhood of Hindon and Salisbury 24th June, 1828.
⌣——— Per Week	⌣——— Per Week

	s.	d.		s.	d.
The man in employment, not found by the parish.	2	2½	– –	7	0
Wife 1		7	Half earnings 1		0
Son .. (10 years old) ..1		4		1	0
Daughter (9 years old) ..1		4	–		
Child.. (7 years old) ..1		1½	–		
Do. .. (6 years old) ..1		1½	–		
Do. .. (3 years old) ..1		0½	–		
Do. .. (2 years old) ..1		0½	–		
			Earnings 9		0
			Relief 1		9½
	10	9½		10	9½

(Copied exactly from a statement furnished by a Wiltshire Magistrate.) Select Committee on the Employment or Relief of Able Bodied Persons. *Report*, IV, Appendix (1828), 62

11H Asst Commissioner Walcott   The Overseers

A good deal of the blame for the alleged inefficiency of poor-law administration in the early nineteenth century fell on the overseer, the officer responsible for the collection of poor rates and the distribution of parish relief. Often a small farmer or tradesman, chosen from amongst his fellow parishioners at a vestry meeting, the overseer had a difficult job. If he was too lavish with relief, the rates would increase and his fellow ratepayers would complain bitterly; if he attempted to reduce the relief, he might be threatened with physical violence by paupers or be reprimanded by a local magistrate for failing in his duties. Also there might be legal complications over cases of settlement or illegitimacy which would sorely tax his small degree of literacy. Thus the best policy might be to do as little as possible during the six or twelve months of unpaid office.

The Royal Commission of 1832–4 highlighted examples of incompetence in its Report. In judging the overseers, however, account should be taken of the difficulties under which they laboured, and also of the fact that there were parishes in which poor-law administration was both honest and reasonably efficient.

As a body, I found annual overseers wholly incompetent to discharge the duties of their office, either from the interference of private occupations, or from a want of experience and skill; but most frequently from both these courses. Their object is to get through the year with as little unpopularity and trouble as possible, their successors therefore have frequently to complain of demands left unsettled, and rates uncollected, either from carelessness or a desire to gain the trifling popularity of having called for fewer assessments than usual. In rural districts the overseers are farmers; in towns generally shopkeepers; and in villages usually one of each of those classes. *Asst Commissioner S. Walcott—North Wales*. Royal Commission on the Poor Laws. *Report*, Appendix A, Part 2 (1834), 184.

---

12 Thomas Smart   The State of the Labourer (1824)
Despite the large amounts spent in poor relief during and after the Napoleonic wars, the condition of the agricultural labourer, particularly in the arable counties of the south-east, had improved little since the late eighteenth century (4). He still clung to the margin of subsistence, and in bad times only kept his head above it by grasping the lifebelt of poor relief or private charity. Thomas Smart, a labourer from Eversholt in Bedfordshire, was no doubt brought before the Select Committee as an example of the frugal labourer scorning poor relief, whom the poor law reformers wished to encourage. Nevertheless at 46, with 13 children, only seven of whom were still alive, his standard of life had little to commend it. With or without poor relief, the rural labourer in southern England was in a wretched condition.

What have been your wages for the last five years?—Ten shillings and eight shillings.

What is the food on which you have supported yourself and your family?—Bread and cheese and what we could get; sometimes we were short and sometimes we got enough for them.

Did you get meat on Sundays?—I have not had a bit of meat for a month together sometimes.

What do you drink?—Water.

Have you no bacon?—We get a little bacon; that is the chief meat we get when we get any.

You do not keep a pig?—No.

Have you a garden?—Yes.

Is that of much use to you?—A great deal of use to me.

Do you get potatoes?—Yes, I get plenty of potatoes.

Do you ever get any milk?—Now and then we get a halfpenny worth of milk, but the farmers are very shy of letting us have it

What is the extent of your garden?—I do not know; it is a good bit of ground, it is a good bit under a rood.

Do you use tea in your family?—Yes.

And sugar?—No, sometimes we do not.

Do you have tea for breakfast?—The children do, and sometimes water gruel, and what we can get; we cannot always get tea.

Have you any idea what your clothes for yourself and your family have cost you in a year?—My shoes cost about 15s. a year, for a pair of strong shoes to go to work in, and the rest of my family makes it another pound. I dare say it stands me in £2 for shoe bills.

Did you ever know of a practice in your parish of paying a part of the wages of labour out of the poor rate?—They do at this time.

Do they do it as much as they used to, or did they do it more a few years back?—They did not use to do it as they do now. They do it now more than ever?—Yes.

The men to whom they pay this money have families of children?—Yes; they take it out of the parish; they have an allowance from the parish.

Have you ever applied to them for any addition to your wages?—No, I never did; I always try to do without. Select Committee on Labourers' Wages. *Report*, VI, *Evidence of Thomas Smart* (1824), 54-5

THE REFORM OF THE POOR LAW

13A W. D. Evans   Poor Law Administration in Manchester

The rapid growth of the industrial towns during the late eighteenth and early nineteenth centuries quickly revealed the deficiencies of the amateur system of parochial administration. The population of Manchester and Salford grew from 90,000 in 1801 to 155,000 by 1821. Thus it soon became quite beyond the powers of the part-time churchwardens and overseers to collect the poor rates and manage the affairs of the poor. For towns like Manchester it became imperative to employ full-time salaried poor-law officers controlled by small specialised committees, and to organise the giving of poor relief so as to prevent abuses. By 1808, Manchester was employing ten permanent overseers, sixty-one district overseers, seven assessors of factories and seven rate collectors. Even with such a staff, the tasks of investigating and granting relief applications remained an arduous one, as the witness, one of Manchester's stipendiary magistrates, told the Parliamentary Select Committee.

Can you give the Committee any information as to the effect of the Poor Laws and the general management of the poor, in the manufacturing district of Manchester and neighbourhood? —I believe I can give pretty extended information as to the

nature and system of management in Manchester and the neighbourhood; having had from the time of my appointment the
exclusive magisterial direction of the poor in the townships of
Manchester and Salford, and having concurred with other
gentlemen in the direction of the different surrounding townships. The parish of Manchester comprises a great number of
townships, not less than thirty; but what is, properly speaking,
considered as the town of Manchester, consists of the two townships of Manchester and Salford. I believe Manchester, by the
Returns of Population in the year 1811, contained, of inhabitants, between seventy-eight and seventy-nine thousand, and
Salford between nine-teen and twenty thousand. There are three
churchwardens annually appointed for the parish of Manchester
at large, who, with thirteen sidesmen undertake the general
direction of the poor of the township of Manchester; the churchwardens and sidesmen being generally gentlemen of the first
respectability and opulence in the place, and whose duties are
of the most laborious kind, to such an extent, that a Tyburn
ticket[1] for the exemption from parish offices within the parish
of Manchester, I apprehend, will fetch a price five times more
than in any other parish in England, selling for from two to
three hundred pounds. Those gentlemen hold a board once a
week or oftener; it used to be weekly on the Friday; but, in
consequence of the increase of poor lately, that has not been
sufficient, and they have been obliged to hold them on other
days. An annual printed account is made of the expenditure and
receipts of the township of Manchester, and a similar one for
the township of Salford. . . . The churchwardens hold a regular
board, as I have already mentioned, once or oftener in the week,
as may be requisite, always on the Friday; and, in consequence
of the late increase of poor, more frequently. I omitted to state
that there are an indefinite number of overseers of the poor, in
consequence of a local Act of Parliament for the building of a

---

[1] A certificate granted to a person who helped to secure the conviction of
a felon. The certificate gave the holder an exemption from parochial offices
in the parish in which the felony was committed.

E

workhouse, enabling the churchwardens and sidesmen to appoint an indefinite number of overseers with salaries; and a great number of persons are so employed, very laboriously, in various departments: amongst those there are four, who are peculiarly called the visiting overseers; the township being divided into four districts, in respect of each of which the officer has the looking after the families, and seeing whether they are proper objects of relief, and making such other inquiries as may enable the churchwardens, if necessary, and the magistrate, to decide upon the applications that are made. Upon the application to the board, the sheets, of which I now hold the specimens, are in the hands of the clerk or other officer, who fills up the blanks with the particulars of the applications, stating the circumstances of the parties, the situation of their family, and what they apply for; in a subsequent column, the relief they apply for is entered; and on the Wednesday the churchwardens and the visiting overseers attend me at the New Bailey court house, where the complaints of such as are dissatisfied are heard one by one; and from those schedules I have an opportunity of seeing, from a single point of view, the state of the family, what are their earnings, what are their employments, their sources of income, and the relief which has been given; and can decide, subject to any enquiries requisite, on the additional relief which may be ordered, or such directions which, as a magistrate, it may be necessary I should give; and, in consequence of the number of the Irish poor, the schedules are distinctly distributed; one applicable to those who belong to Manchester; another, those of the Irish, kept in separate blocks. A book has been latterly kept, in which the persons, who apply to me as a magistrate, are entered previously to their coming into the room; with the regularity of a list of causes, they are called in their order, and that is ready to be produced if it is desired.—Upon their coming to me, I either confirm the order the churchwardens have made, or make such order as may appear requisite; that the party shall be admitted into the poor house, or additional relief given for a certain time; that a certain sum shall be given for casual relief, or give such directions as may be necessary according to the circumstances of the case. Almost the whole of the business of the township is conducted by means of printed documents of various kinds; a printed order from the visiting overseer to the treasurer to pay a certain weekly relief, an order to admit into the workhouse, or any other given orders. If there is an apprehension that the party is not giving a true account of the earnings, there is a printed blank calling upon the master to fill up the weekly earnings of the party, and also requesting him to state what an industrious person in that line can make; and various other printed documents, applicable to the different occasions which may arise. Select Committee (House of Lords) on the Poor Laws. *Evidence of W. D. Evans Esq* (1817), 103–5

13B Sturges Bourne's Act

Improved administration was seen by some reformers as a possible answer to rising poor-relief costs. This Act of 1819 gave powers to such parishes as desired them to appoint small committees, or select vestries, of leading inhabitants to scrutinise the granting of poor relief, and also salaried assistant overseers to help the unpaid part-time overseer with his mounting burden of work. The Act saved parishes which wished to improve their administration from the lengthy and expensive process of obtaining a private Act of Parliament giving them such powers. The Select Committee of 1817 had recommended this reform and its chairman, William Sturges Bourne, was responsible for piloting the measure through Parliament.

59 Geo. III CAP. 12

An Act to amend the Laws for the relief of the Poor. (31st March, 1819).

"For the better and more effectual execution of the laws for the relief of the poor, and for the amendment thereof"; May it please your Majesty that it may be enacted, and be it enacted, by the King's most excellent Majesty, by and with the advice of the Lords spiritual and temporal, and Commons, in this present parliament assembled, and by the authority of the same, that it shall be lawful for the inhabitants of any parish in vestry assembled, and they are hereby empowered to establish a select vestry for the concerns of the poor of such parish; and to that end to nominate and elect, in the same or subsequent vestry, or any adjournment thereof respectively, such and so many substantial householders or occupiers within such parish, not exceeding the number of twenty or less than five, as shall in any such vestry be thought fit to be members of the select vestry; . . . and every such select vestry is hereby empowered and required to examine into the state and condition of the poor of the parish, and to enquire into and determine upon the proper objects of relief, and the nature and amount of the relief to be given; and in each case shall take into consideration the character and conduct of the poor person to be relieved, and shall be at liberty to distinguish in the relief to be granted, between the deserving, and the idle, extravagant, or profligate poor; and such select vestry shall make orders in writing for such relief as they shall think requisite, and shall inquire into and superintend the collection and administration of all money to be raised by the poor's-rates, and of all other funds and money raised or applied by the parish to the relief of the poor; and where any such select vestry shall be established, the overseers of the poor are required in the execution of their office, to conform to the directions of the select vestry.

VII And be it further enacted, that it shall be lawful for the inhabitants of any parish in vestry assembled, to nominate and elect any discreet person or persons to be assistant overseer or overseers of the poor of such parish, and to determine and specify the duties to be by (him) or them executed and performed, and to fix such yearly salary for the execution of the said office as shall by such inhabitants in vestry be thought fit; . . . . and every person to be so appointed assistant overseer shall be, and he is hereby authorised and empowered to execute all such of the duties of the office of overseer of the poor as shall in the warrant for his appointment be expressed, in like manner and as fully, to all intents and purposes, as the same may be executed by any ordinary overseer of the poor; . . . W. C. Glen. *The Statutes in Force Relating to the Poor* (1857), 238–41

13C Lister Ellis   A Stricter Relief System

In some parishes, the appointment of a select vestry led to the adoption of a stricter system with regard to outdoor relief. Such was the case in Liverpool, as Lister Ellis, a former overseer of the town and a member of the select vestry for two years, told the Select Committee of 1828.

When was the select vestry established?—In 1821. . . . . When was the change of system of refusing relief, as the general rule to all applicants out of the workhouse, adopted by the select vestry? —Within six months of the first appointment of the select vestry.

What was the precise resolution adopted, by the select vestry operating in this change at the end of 1821, as regarded the relief not to be given out of the walls of the workhouse?—No person was relieved with money who was able to labour, not one fraction, whatever the number of his family consisted of; but labour was offered to those who were able to work.

But money relief was absolutely and peremptorily refused?— Yes; and no sum was given nor is now given beyond five shillings per week, let their family be ever so numerous; with a family of five or six children, for instance.

Is that given out of the walls in any case?—There are cases where it is given out of the walls; where there is no husband able to work.

At the same time this alteration of the rule with respect to relief took place did any new regulations of the workhouse also take place of a more strict kind?—They did.

What was the nature of those regulations?—There was several new branches of manufacture introduced; calicoes to a very considerable extent, that is, in the house; there was an establishment for the manufactory of pins, straw bonnets, shoes, for sale; exclusive of what the parish required for their own use; and in fact, ever since the establishment of the select vestry, no person has been in that house but who has been employed, and beneficially employed, up to the present period.

Was the discipline of the workhouse rendered more severe, when the intercourse with persons without the walls was cut off? —It was cut off altogether, with the exception of two days per week, when they are permitted to go out of the workhouse boundaries.

Is the dietary of the workhouse of the humblest description consistent with the health of the persons within the walls?—I have the bill of fare for every day in the year.

Is it as humble as is consistent with the health of the parties?— In some cases more is given than is necessary, such as tea, sugar and butter, to persons above a certain age, whether they have been in the habit of using it or not; this is given by order of a general vestry, and extends to all persons above sixty years of age.

Then they are liberally treated?—Yes.

Generally speaking, is the dietary to able bodied men within the walls as spare and humble as that of the labouring classes out of the workhouse?—I think it better, they get it much more comfortably from the way of cooking adopted.

On the whole, is there a salutary fear of going into the workhouse among the labouring classes in Liverpool?—Not sufficiently so; there is generally a reluctance for it, but the moment they get acquainted with the sort of treatment they experience and the sort of labour imposed on them, there is no apparent dissatisfaction, although every person and child after a certain age is compelled to labour to a certain extent.

What is the description of persons who receive relief out of the workhouse?—They are principally the aged, the infirm and the blind.

Any able bodied persons?—No able-bodied person whatever.

Did you not say that some able-bodied men were employed by the parish in breaking stones?—Yes, they are casual poor; they are paid for the labour they do by the cubic yard; they are paid the price of 2s.4d.; no stone to be less than five ounces weight, nor that will not pass through a ring of a certain size.

Are they able, to a certain extent, to provide for their family by task work?—Yes, but it is a task work they dislike exceedingly; there is not one instance in fifty that a man remains at it for a month, he exerts himself, and contrives to procure employment.

. . . . The result of this change of system at Liverpool has been, that whereas in the year 1821, 4,715 individuals were relieved at a cost of £36,013; in the year 1827, 2,607 persons have been relieved at a cost of £19,395?—Yes, that is right, that is the result.

And since that period a vast increase of population has taken place?—Very great indeed. Select Committee on the Employment or Relief of Able Bodied Persons. IV, *Evidence of Lister Ellis* (1828), 52–6

13D Rev J. T. Becher   The Anti Pauper System

John Thomas Becher (1770–1848) was vicar of Rumpton in Nottinghamshire, a prebendary of Southwell, and, after 1816, chairman of the Newark Quarter Sessions. Disturbed by the increase of the poor rates, he called a meeting of local landowners and farmers in October 1823. The meeting decided to set up an incorporated workhouse under Gilbert's Act and forty-nine parishes joined together in the Thurgarton Hundred Incorporation. The relief policy of the Incorporation did not, however, follow that of Gilbert's Act, which reserved the workhouse for the aged and infirm; at Southwell, relief to supplement wages was stopped, parish employment discontinued and relief in the workhouse offered as a test of whether an applicant was in real need or not. By this new policy, Becher claimed to have reduced relief expenditure at Southwell from over £2,000 in 1821 to £551 in 1828.

Another publicist of the Southwell system was George Nicholls, a retired sea captain, who became overseer at Southwell after 1821, and in 1834 was appointed a member of the Poor Law Commission. In his *History of the English Poor Law*, published in 1853, Nicholls claimed the credit for having reformed poor relief in Southwell and makes no mention of Becher. Nor does he mention the Rev Robert Lowe, squire and parson of nearby Bingham, who introduced a similar system of relief into his parish in the early 1820s.

In the Antipauper System, all our arrangements should be strictly comfortable to the laws of the realm. We do not profess to amend the provisions of the legislature, but to enforce them. The rights of the poor are few, therefore they should be scrupulously respected; for the retrenchment of their imaginary claims will naturally inspire them with a disposition to resist any such innovation. But, when they become convinced that their privileges are preserved without violation, and that our measures are founded upon legal and equitable principles, any opposition created by the impulse of the moment, will gradually subside into patient and good tempered acquiescence.

The fundamental and operative law upon this important subject is the statute passed in the 43rd year of Queen Elizabeth, by which all the preceding enactments for the maintenance of the impotent poor were modified, matured and consolidated. This should constitute the basis of our superstructure: and, to obtain an authentic exposition of its principles, we must constantly consult the elaborate Report of the Select Committee of the House of Commons on the Poor Laws in 1817; for which we are principally indebted to the Right Honourable William Sturges Bourne, the Chairman of the Committee.

However, before we can enforce discipline, so as to control the vicious and refractory, we must provide a place of refuge as

well as of restraint. For this purpose, commence your measures
for the reformation of the poor by the establishment of a parochial workhouse, affording the means of distributing males,
females and children, both by day and by night, into separate
classes; and of subdividing these classes into distinct wards,
according to the conduct and character of the paupers.

If the population of the parish will not suffice for this, unite
with the surrounding parishes, and provide an incorporated
workhouse, under the statute 22 Geo. 3 c. 83. Let the system of
management insure every tenderness towards the infirm, the
aged, and the guiltless, while it imposes wholesome restraint
upon the idle, the profligate, and the refractory.

. . . . The provisions for the workhouse should be purchased
under the immediate superintendence of the parish officers, or
the governor, or the secretary. The dietary of the paupers should
be plain, but wholesome and sufficient. Any privations injurious
to health should be peremptorily prohibited.

Do not contract with any person for the lodging, keeping or
maintaining of your paupers. Such engagements frequently con-
sign the poor to the dominion of a merciless and rapacious
master, who sacrifices duty and discipline to self interest; while
he endeavours to acquire an unjust profit by sustaining them
with food defective in quality, or deficient in quantity. Besides
which, it cannot be imagined that the moral improvement of
the individuals placed under the care of such contractors, will
occupy any considerable portion of their time or attention.

Let the churchwardens, the overseers of the poor, and the
guardians, if such officers have been appointed, assemble
monthly, or weekly, if necessary, and execute all the functions
of a select vestry. Let them investigate carefully the legal settlement, the character, the conduct, and the means of subsistence
attainable by every pauper claiming parochial relief;

Let it, however, be remembered that the advantages resulting
from a workhouse must arise, not from keeping the poor in the
house, but from keeping them out of it; by constraining the

inferior classes to know and feel how demoralizing and degrading is the compulsory relief drawn from the parish to silence the clamour, and to satisfy the cravings, of wilful and woful indigence; but how sweet and wholesome is that food and how honourable is that independence, which is earned by persevering and honest industry.

. . . . The labourer is worthy of his hire. Never pauperize him by reducing his wages below their just amount, or by making up the deficiency out of the poor rate. This extinguishes the incitement to industry and economy. The superficial observer may deem it a saving: but such a system debases the feelings, the principles and the habits of the working classes. It is a fraudulent, illegal and ruinous misapplication of the parochial funds, which never ought to be practised by the rate payers, nor tolerated, much less recommended, by the magistracy.

. . . . If a poor person applies for relief on account of his numerous family, let it be recollected, that a labourer's ordinary wages should support himself, his wife, and four children under ten years of age: but some of the children under this age, if exceeding four in number, may be sent during the day time into the workhouse, there to be fed and schooled, as at Southwell. If the poorhouse be situated at a distance, a working school may be established upon the same principle within the parish, at which such children may be schooled and victualled. J. T. Becher. *The Anti Pauper System* (1828), 17–19, 20–1, 23

PART TWO

The Reception of the New Poor Law

The agrarian riots of 1830 together with the continuing rise in the cost of poor relief brought increased pressure on the government for some final solution to the poor-law problem. The Whig Government, embroiled in the struggle over the passage of the First Reform Bill, delegated the problem to a Royal Commission for investigation.

THE ROYAL COMMISSION ON THE POOR LAWS

Seven Commissioners were appointed in 1832 under the chairmanship of the Bishop of London, and two more were added in the following year. To help them in their investigation, the Commissioners were empowered to appoint Assistant Commissioners who were to visit parishes in the districts assigned to them and ask questions about the state of poor relief administration (14). In the meantime the Commission sent out detailed questionnaires to a number of urban and rural parishes—parish overseers, rectors or prominent local inhabitants being asked to furnish information about the state of their parishes, with particular reference to the question of parochial relief given to the able-bodied poor (15). Replies were received from about 10 per cent of the 15,000 parishes in England and Wales, containing about 20 per cent of the country's population.

Armed with a mass of information which, when published,

filled fifteen folio volumes, the Royal Commission proceeded to draw up its report. This was largely the work of two of the Commission's members—Nassau Senior, first holder of the Drummond Chair of Political Economy at Oxford, and Edwin Chadwick, a Manchester-born lawyer and private secretary to Jeremy Bentham until the philosopher's death in 1832. There is little doubt that these two had already made up their able minds as to the remedies they would propose, and that they used the evidence collected by the Royal Commission selectively rather than analytically in order to stampede public opinion into backing the measures they put forward (16).

A Poor Law Amendment Bill was drawn up on the lines recommended by the Royal Commission, and laid before the cabinet for discussion. Although most members of the government were persuaded of the need for poor-law reform, some of them felt the proposed remedies to be too extreme, particularly the idea of a powerful central authority to interfere in local affairs. Thus the powers reserved for the central authority in the Bill were considerably whittled down despite the protests of Senior, who acted as chief adviser to the government on the Bill (17).

On 17 April 1834 the Bill, in its revised form, was introduced into the House of Commons by Lord Althorp, the Chancellor of the Exchequer (18a). Its reception in both Houses was generally favourable, though some members were anxious about the powers to be granted to the central authority, and wished to keep them to a minimum (18b). The most virulent attack came from the ageing Radical, William Cobbett, who castigated the measure as a 'Poor Man's Robbery Bill', designed to reduce yet further the living standards of the labouring poor (18c).

Despite opposition from *The Times* and from Cobbett, the Poor Law Amendment Bill passed comfortably through all its Parliamentary stages and received the royal assent on 14 August 1834. The New Poor Law was launched. Under its terms, a central authority of three members, the Poor Law Commission, was established with powers to group parishes into unions for the purposes of poor-law administration, and to supervise the actions of the new local poor-law authorities, the boards of guardians, particularly with regard to the granting of relief to the able-bodied poor. The Act made no stipulation on the method of giving relief. Decisions on the withdrawal of outdoor relief and the introduction of a workhouse test were left to the Commission, though it was given very feeble powers to enforce such decisions (20). It could not order boards of guardians to spend more than one-tenth of their annual rate on the provision of an adequate workhouse; and it could not dissolve existing unions of parishes under Gilbert's Act or local Acts without the consent of their guardians. Until 1844, boards of guardians were responsible for appointing their own auditor to examine their accounts for illegal expenditure. For the task of cleansing the Augean stables of the English poor-law system, the Poor Law Commission was given a broom with remarkably few bristles.

14 Royal Commission   Instructions to Assistant Commissioners

The Royal Commission appointed twenty-six assistant commissioners to carry out on-the-spot investigations of poor law administration. Before beginning their travels in the autumn of 1832, the assistant commissioners were issued with a booklet, probably written by Nassau Senior, instructing them how to perform their duties.

INSTRUCTIONS.

The Central Commissioners are directed by His Majesty's Commission to make a diligent and full inquiry into the practical operation of the Laws for the relief of the Poor in England and Wales, and into the manner in which those laws are administered, and to report whether any, and what, alterations, amendments, or improvements may be beneficially made in the said laws, or in the manner of administering them; and how the same may be best carried into effect.

This extensive inquiry may be conveniently divided into four heads:—

I. The form in which parochial relief is given.

II. The persons to whom it is given.

III. The persons by whom it is awarded.

IV. The persons at whose expence it is given.

It is probable that this inquiry will suggest considerable alterations in the existing law; and it is also probable that those alterations may be facilitated by some further measures, such as—

V. Affording facilities for emigration.

VI. Facilitating the occupation and even the acquisition of land by labourers.

VII. Removing the tax on servants, so far as it is found to interfere with their residence under their employers' roof.

VIII. Improving the rural police.

On these points there is already much information before the public, and much more may be expected from the replies to the queries circulated by the Commissioners. Those replies must, however, in general, be imperfect, from the absence of details and vouchers as to matters of fact, and of reasons where opinions are stated. There is no comparison between the information afforded by them to the central Commissioners, and that which could be obtained if it were in their power to sift the facts and the opinions contained in the different replies by the inspection of documents and cross-examination of witnesses; if they could ascertain the state of the poor by personal inquiry among them, and the administration of the poor laws, by being present at vestries and at the sessions of magistrates.

As the constitution of the Central Board renders it impossible that these offices can be adequately performed by them in person, it is proposed that they should be executed by Assistant Commissioners.

The duty of an Assistant Commissioner will be, to proceed to the district, which will be indicated to him by the Board, taking with him whatever replies may have been returned from that district, and sets of blank queries for distribution. He will also be furnished with letters from the Home Department, which he can direct and deliver as he may find it expedient, requesting assistance in his inquiries.

He will communicate with the clergy, magistrates, and parish officers, deliver the printed queries to those who have not received them, and arrange the times and places of meeting at which the replies already given, or to be given, are to be explained, and the parish books and other vouchers produced.

The inspection of these documents will enable him to judge of the correctness of the replies, and probably offer him subjects of further inquiry. An investigation into all the circumstances connected with a single entry, may give him a better insight into the actual management of a parish, than could have been derived from any voluntary statements. He will endeavour, as far as possible, to be present at vestry meetings, and at the petty sessions of magistrates.

He will keep a full daily journal of his proceedings, and give to the Central Board, at least once a week, a sketch of his proceedings. The Commissioners wish to leave it in the discretion of each Assistant Commissioner, either to make one final report at the termination of his labours, or distinct reports, from time to time, as soon as he has sufficient materials, but they would much prefer the latter course where it is practicable. Instructions from the Central Board of Poor Law Commissioners to Assistant Commissioners (ND), 2-6

15 Royal Commission   Questions for Parishes

In 1832, the Royal Commission sent out a questionnaire on poor-law administration to a number of rural parishes in England and Wales. Later another questionnaire containing rather differently phrased questions was sent to a number of urban parishes. The questionnaires were usually answered by the overseer or by some prominent local inhabitant such as the rector or a JP. The completed questionnaires were published by the Commission in Appendices to their Report. The following is a sample of the rural questions and of the replies to them from two parishes in Berkshire.

_____

14.—Could the Family subsist on these earnings? and if so, on what food?—

15.—Could it lay by any thing? and how much?—

16.—What class of Persons are the usual Proprietors of Cottages?—

17.—Are there many cases in your Parish where the Labourer owns his Cottage?—

18.—The Rent of Cottages?—

19.—Whether Gardens to the Cottages?—

20.—Whether any Land let to Labourers; if so, the quantity to each, and at what Rent?—

21.—Are Cottages frequently exempted from Rates, and is their Rent often paid by the Parish?—

22.—Have you a Workhouse? State the Number, Age, and Sex of its inmates?—

23.—What Number of Individuals received Relief last week, not being in the Workhouse?—

24.—Whether any Allowance is made from the Poor's Rate on account of large Families; and if so, at what number of Children does it begin?—
Whether any Wages paid out of the Poor's Rate?—

Have you many able-bodied Labourers receiving Allowance or regular Relief from your Parish?—

25.—Is Relief or Allowance given according to any and what Scale?—

26.—Is any and what attention paid to the character of the Applicant, or the causes of his distress?—

27.—Whether the system of Roundsmen is practised, or has been practised?—

COUNTY OF BERKS—*continued.*

ANSWERS.

BINFIELD.

James Randall,
Rector.

14.—It could, feeding on good bread; but that must be with better management than they usually exercise, and supposing also that they have no sickness or other casualty.

15.—They could not.

16.—Farmers, Builders, small Tradesmen and Labourers.

17.—Yes; many Labourers built cottages on the waste before the inclosure of the Parish in 1817, and their encroachments were then confirmed.

18.—Average about £.3. 10.

F

19.—All have gardens, from ¼ to ½ an acre.

20.—Mr. Elliott, one of the principal land-owners, has let land to 12 Labourers, and would let more if it was desired. It is let in lots of half an acre, except two, which are of one acre each. Rent £.1 per acre per annum.

21.—Not often exempted; nor is their rent often paid by the parish.

22.—Not a regular *Workhouse*. We have a Poor-house, under the care of a Master and Matron. The inmates are 6 Men, all past 70, and 8 Women, of whom 4 past 70, 2 of them being Wives of 2 of the old Men, 2 more past 50, and the 2 others past 40. Three Boys, aged 16, 10 & 9. One young Child.

23.—Thirteen.

24.—The practice of the parish paying partly for work done for individuals once obtained here, but has been quite abolished for four or five years past. There are about six Labourers with large families, and of indifferent character for industry, who receive relief so often as to be almost constant; but there is no stated allowance on account of large families.

25.—Old and impotent persons have a regular allowance of 2s. 6d. per week, if in the house, and 3s. if out. Others are relieved according to the exigency of the case.

26.—The character of the applicant, and causes of distress, are always inquired into.

27.—It has never been practised here.

County of BERKS—*continued.*

ANSWERS.

BOXFORD.

John Wells,
Rector.

14.—A man, with such a family, could earn enough to subsist on; their food being, animal food in small quantity, bread and potatoes.

15.—Nothing could be laid by.

16.—Persons of large property, or persons who, having very small property, have built cottages on speculation.

17.—Hardly one.

18.—The greater part under 50s.; but some as high as 70s.

19.—Yes; most of the cottages have gardens.

20.—Some land has been let to cottagers whose gardens are small, but not more than 40 poles to each, at the rent of 3d. per pole.

21.—All cottages are rated, but the rate seldom levied. The rent is never paid by the parish.

22.—No.

23.—Ninety-nine; in which number are included the old men

who work on the roads, and all the children exceeding three in each family, on whose account relief is granted to their parents.

24.—All able-bodied Labourers, having more than three children, receive regular relief. Relief now begins after three children, but previously to this week it began after two. Wages not paid out of the Poor Rates.

25.—

26.—Some attention, but not enough.

27.—No.

Royal Commission on the Poor Laws. *Report*, Appendix B1, Part 2 (1834)

---

16 Edwin Chadwick   The 1834 Report

In the first part of the report of the Royal Commission of 1832–4 Nassau Senior exposed what he regarded as the shortcomings of the old system and illustrated them with examples drawn from the reports of the assistant commissioners. Chadwick followed this with a section headed *Remedial Measures*, from which the following is an extract. This set forward proposals for the reform of the poor law, the most important being the suggestions that relief to able-bodied paupers be given only in a 'well regulated' workhouse, and that a central board be established to control the local poor law authorities.

It may be assumed that, in the administration of relief, the public is warranted in imposing such conditions on the individual relief, as are conducive to the benefit either of the individual himself, or of the country at large, at whose expense he is to be relieved.

The first and most essential of all conditions, a principle which we find universally admitted, even by those whose practice is at variance with it, is, that his situation on the whole shall not be made really or apparently so eligible as the situation of the independent labourer of the lowest class. Throughout the evidence it is shown, that in proportion as the condition of any pauper class is elevated above the condition of independent labourers, the condition of the independent class is depressed; their industry is impaired, their employment becomes unsteady, and its remuneration in wages is diminished. Such persons, therefore, are under the strongest inducements to quit the less eligible class of labourers and enter the more eligible class of paupers. The converse is the effect when the pauper class is placed in its proper position below the condition of the independent labourer. Every penny bestowed, that tends to render the condition of the pauper more eligible than that of the independent labourer, is a bounty on indolence and vice. We have found, that as the poor rates are at present administered, they operate as bounties of this description, to the amount of several millions annually.

We therefore submit, as the general principle of legislation on this subject, in the present condition of the country:

That those modes of administering relief which have been tried wholly or partially, and have produced beneficial effects in some districts be introduced, with modifications according to local circumstances, and carried into complete execution in all.

The chief specific measures which we recommend for effecting these purposes are—

FIRST, THAT EXCEPT AS TO MEDICAL ATTENDANCE, AND SUBJECT TO THE EXCEPTION RESPECTING APPRENTICESHIP HEREINAFTER STATED, ALL RELIEF WHATEVER TO ABLE BODIED PERSONS OR TO THEIR FAMILIES, OTHERWISE THAN IN WELL-REGULATED WORK-HOUSES (i.e. PLACES WHERE THEY MAY BE SET TO WORK ACCORDING TO THE SPIRIT AND INTENTION OF THE 43rd. OF ELIZABETH) SHALL BE DECLARED UNLAWFUL, AND SHALL CEASE, IN MANNER AND AT

PERIODS HEREAFTER SPECIFIED: AND THAT ALL RELIEF AFFORDED
IN RESPECT OF CHILDREN UNDER THE AGE OF 16, SHALL BE CON-
SIDERED AS AFFORDED TO THEIR PARENTS.

It must be remembered that the pauperized labourers were
not the authors of the abusive system, and ought not to be made
responsible for its consequences. We cannot, therefore, recommend that they should be otherwise than gradually subjected to
regulations which, though undoubtedly beneficial to themselves,
may, by any sudden application, inflict unnecessary severity.
The abuses have grown up in detail, and it appears from our
evidence that the most safe course will be to remove them in
detail. We deem uniformity essential: but, in the first instance,
it is only an approximation to uniformity that can be expected,
and it appears that it must be obtained by gradations in detail,
according to local circumstances. And although uniformity in
the amount of relief may be requisite, it may not be requisite
that the relief should be invariably the same in kind. In Cumberland, and some others of the northern counties, milk is generally
used where beer is used in the southern counties. The requisite
equality in diet would probably be obtainable without forcing
any class of the inmates of the workhouses in the northern
counties to take beer, or those of the southern counties to take
milk.

By many it is considered that the only means by which the
system can be effectually amended, is the management of the
whole poor law administration as a branch of the general
government. The advocates of a national rate, and those who
are willing and desirous that the Government should take upon
itself the whole distribution of the funds for the relief of the
poor, do not appear to have considered the expense and difficulties in the way of obtaining such an agency throughout the
country.

We have received no definite plan for the purpose, and have
prepared none. We trust that immediate measures for the cor-

rection of the evils in question may be carried into effect by a comparatively small and cheap agency, which may assist the parochial or district officers, wherever their management is in conformity to the intention of the legislative; and control them wherever their management is at variance with it. Subject also to this control, we propose that the management, the collection of the rates, and the entire supervision of the expenditure, under increased securities against profusion and malversation, shall continue in the officers appointed immediately by the rate-payers. This course, we believe, will be the most easily practicable, and will best accord with the recommendations of the majority of the witnesses, and with the prevalent expectation of the country.

WE RECOMMEND, THEREFORE, THE APPOINTMENT OF A CENTRAL BOARD TO CONTROL THE ADMINISTRATION OF THE POOR LAWS, WITH SUCH ASSISTANT COMMISSIONERS AS MAY BE FOUND REQUISITE; AND THAT THE COMMISSIONERS BE EMPOWERED AND DIRECTED TO FRAME AND ENFORCE REGULATIONS FOR THE GOVERNMENT OF WORK-HOUSES, AND AS TO THE NATURE AND AMOUNT OF THE RELIEF TO BE GIVEN AND THE LABOUR TO BE EXACTED IN THEM, AND THAT SUCH REGULATIONS SHALL, AS FAR AS MAY BE PRACTICABLE, BE UNIFORM THROUGHOUT THE COUNTRY. Royal Commission on the Poor Laws. *1834 Report* (1905 Edition), 228, 261–2, 295–7

17 Nassau Senior   The Preparation of the Poor Law Bill

Nassau Senior, and William Sturges Bourne (1769–1845), who had chaired the 1817 Select Committee on the Poor Laws, were chosen as the two members of the Royal Commission who should advise the government on the drafting of the Poor Law Amendment Bill. In his diary Senior described the lengthy discussion of the Bill by the Cabinet, some of whose members had severe misgivings as to the Royal Commission's recommendations, particularly the question of central control.

Lord Althorp (1782–1845), the Chancellor of the Exchequer, was the member of the Government responsible for piloting the Bill through the House of Commons (18a). Other ministers were the Duke of Richmond, Charles Gordon-Lennox (1791–1860), who had joined the Whig Ministry as Postmaster-General after quarrelling with the Tory party over the question of Catholic Emancipation; Lord Lansdowne, Henry Petty-Fitzmaurice (1780–1863), President of the Council; and Lord Ripon, Frederick John Robinson (1782–1859), a former Chancellor of the Exchequer and for a brief period in 1827 Prime Minister, who was Lord Privy Seal. Both Ripon and Richmond resigned from the Government over the question of the Irish Church Commission in May 1834.

The 11th Clause enabling the Commissioners to unite parishes for workhouse purposes and to issue rules for the maintenance, classification and employment of paupers in united workhouses was approved.

But the 12th Clause which enabled the Commissioners to rate parishes in order to raise the funds necessary for that purpose was opposed and became the subject of a discussion which lasted during the remainder of the meeting. Lord Althorp said that he objected on constitutional grounds, to giving the Commissioners power to levy a tax on parishes against their will. He was supported in this objection by the Duke of Richmond and opposed by Lord Lansdowne and Lord Ripon. The rest of the Cabinet appeared undecided. Mr. Sturges Bourne and I stated that the greater part of the opposition to improvement arose from persons interested in the perpetuation of abuses. That every alteration however economical in its ultimate results must require some immediate outlay, that if the Commissioners required the workhouse door to be locked, the answer might be "there is no lock: it would cost half a crown to get one and we will not raise the half crown." It was proposed to obviate this by allowing a majority to bind the minority. To which we replied that a minority interested in abuses is always more active and successful than a majority desirous of improvement. And we called on Lord Althorp and the Duke to state what plan of poor law reform they could substitute for the workhouse system, assuming as we did that if this power were refused the workhouse system must fail.

[*No decision on this clause was taken after further discussion, and Senior was asked to make such alterations in the Bill's clauses as he thought likely to suit the views of a majority of the Cabinet. A Committee of the Cabinet was set up to discuss the Bill, and it was decided to limit the expenditure on a workhouse which the Commissioners could demand to the amount of one year's rates. On Sunday, 13 April, however, Senior was called in after a Cabinet meeting and told that the members had resolved that the Commissioners should have no power to order expenditure on workhouses without the consent of a majority of property owners or ratepayers in the locality.*]

It was agreed that we should meet the Cabinet again on Tuesday to consider the clauses they altered and the remainder of the Bill.

The proposal that no expenditure for fitting the Workhouse for its purposes should be incurred without the consent of the parishes seemed to me to be so fundamental an injury to the Bill that I called on Lord Lansdowne on Tuesday to ask whether he thought I might continue to beg the Cabinet, not indeed to reopen a question which they had disposed of after hours of debate, but to add a new clause enabling the Commissioners to oblige parishes to expend a sum not exceeding 1/10th of their rates in altering or enlarging their Workhouse without which power the bill ought to be instituted "an act to amend the laws for the relief of the poor in such parishes as shall consent thereto." Lord Lansdowne said that he quite agreed with me as to the mischief of the alteration and recommended me to propose such a clause.

The Cabinet was held at Lord Althorp's. Before the members were assembled Lord Althorp came to me in an adjoining room and I went over with him the same ground. He said that the clause as originally drawn enabling the Commissioners to compel the erection of Workhouses, or even as altered by the Committee, enabling them to compel a year's rates to be so employed would undoubtedly have shipwrecked the whole measure. That the landed interest were looking for nothing but immediate relief and that relief to be purchased through expenditure would be rejected at once. But he thought the proposal of compelling not more than 1/10th of the rates to be employed in altering or enlarging workhouses ought to be adopted.

The Cabinet had by this time assembled and we went through the rest of the Bill making only verbal alterations. Lord Althorp then stated the substance of our conversation and the suggestion was approved. Nassau Senior. *MS Diary* (March–April 1834), 28–30, 68–71

18 Lord Althorp, Edward Baines & William Cobbett The Poor Law Debate

The Poor Law Amendment Bill was introduced in the House of Commons in April 1834 and received the royal assent in August. Three extracts are given here from the many lengthy Parliamentary speeches on the Bill. The first is taken from the speech of Lord Althorp, Chancellor of the Exchequer, introducing the first reading in the House of Commons. The second is from a brief intervention by Edward Baines (1774–1848), MP for Leeds and proprietor of the *Leeds Mercury*, during the report stage of the Bill. The third is from a speech on the third reading by the Bill's strongest Parliamentary opponent, William Cobbett (1762–1835), MP for Oldham.

(*a*) *Lord Althorp:*

He felt justified, therefore, under the circumstances, in submitting the present measure to the House. It was a measure he conceived, at all events, grounded upon prudence and caution. It was absolutely necessary that there should be a discretionary power vested in some quarter to carry into effect recommendations calculated he hoped, to introduce sound principles and the fruits of salutary experience into the administration of the Poor-laws. The principal subject then for them to consider was, where that discretionary power should be placed. If they vested it in the local authorities, or in the local magistracy, however well intentioned they might be, deprived as they would be of those sources of general information and comparison open to a board of Commissioners, and however excellent their motives, biassed as they must be by local prejudices and local feelings, it was plain that such a quarter would not be the fittest one to invest with a discretionary power for carrying the measure into effect. It was therefore his intention to propose, that his Majesty should be authorized to appoint a central board of Commissioners, vested with such power for that purpose. It would be necessary to invest the Board with extraordinary power, to enable it to accomplish the object proposed, but that power would be subject to the constant control of the Parliament and the Executive Government. There was one part of the administration of the Poor-laws which, however difficult it might be to effect, yet was essentially necessary, and without which no discretionary power ought to be extended, and that was, to fix a day (and that day he should propose, in the measure he sought to introduce, to be in one of the summer months of the next year, when the agricultural labourers would, of course, be in full employment), when the allowance system, as it was called, should entirely and altogether cease. He was aware of the great difficulties which might be suggested to this proposition, but having for many years acted as a magistrate in a county in which the allowance system had been adopted, from his own experience of its operation, he was perfectly satisfied that so long as that system was permitted to exist, it would be impossible to carry into effect any suggested improvement, or to bring the Poor-laws into a better condition... He repeated, therefore, that before it was possible successfully to proceed with the amendment of the present system of Poor-laws, whatever difficulty might appear, it was absolutely necessary to get rid of this most leading error—the allowance system—an error which was the foundation of almost all the evils arising from the existing system. Having stated thus much, he again came to the consideration of the discretionary powers with which it would be necessary to vest the Central Commissioners. He need not say, that an immense advantage would be obtained by the establishment of an uniformity of system throughout the country, and therefore he proposed, that the Commissioners should have power to make general rules and orders as to the mode of relief and for the regulation of work-houses, and the mode of relief afforded therein. He admitted, that these were great discretionary powers to be given to any body of men, but he should propose, as a check against any abuse, that before any such rule, order, or regulation so proposed by the Commissioners should be valid, it should be submitted to the Secretary of State, and remain forty days, and it could only be brought into action if during that period an Order in Council, issued for that purpose, did not prohibit it from being carried into effect.

(b) Edward Baines:

Mr. *Baines* proposed a clause to restrain the Commissioners from the exercise of their powers in any parish or township maintaining its own poor, where the rates, on an average of the three last years, shall not have exceeded 2s. 6d. in the pound, unless at the requisition of the rate-payers in special vestry. The hon. Member observed, that the majority of the petitions pre-sented to the House against this Bill were opposed to the power given to the Commissioners, and its extension to all parts of the country, where, such as at Manchester, and other places, there was no necessity for the exercise of that power, the parishes being well administered. Instead of 5s. and 15s. in the pound, in most of the manufacturing parishes, the rates were scarcely one-eighth of the annual rental. The measure here recommended would withdraw one quarter of the population of the country from the operation of the Bill, and the remaining three-fourths were quite sufficient for the Administration of the Commissioners. If these three-fourths were well administered, then it would be an induce-ment to parishes to require their superintendence. The exception he proposed would not vitiate the Bill, or prevent the experiment being tried; on the contrary, it would facilitate the experiment.

(c) William Cobbett:

In the instructions to the Commissioners there were two things to which he wished to call the attention of the House. The one was an express desire upon the part of Government—to do what? Why, to so manage the thing that the people of England might be gradually used to coarser food than at present. That would, indeed, be bringing the north to the south! Another thing was, that there were to be 200 workhouses. These workhouses, he foresaw, would be so many military stations. No doubt there would be a police station attached to each of them. To be sure there would. The effect of one of the instructions would possibly be an attempt to reconcile the people to potatoes and sea-weed as a diet. The Poor-law Commissioners in their report said, that in one parish, which they mentioned, every man who had been a farmer for thirty-years preceding was at the time the report was drawn up subsisting upon the poor-rates. Were these men to be treated in the manner, in the harsh and cruel manner, prescribed by this Bill? How many tradesmen, at present residing in Fleet-street, might within a short time be obliged to look to the poor-rates for support, and were these men to be driven to a workhouse in a workhouse dress? Were their families to be dragged from them, or they from their families, and were one and all of them to be treated worse than negro slaves or even than favourite hounds? Would not this be the effect of the Bill? Was it not the object contemplated by the Commissioners, who might be said to be the mentor under whose auspices this Bill was brought forward, while the noble Lord was but the Ministerial Telemachus? The object of the Bill was to raise the character of the English labourer. Raise the character of the English labourer, forsooth! The English labourer, no doubt had reason to be grateful for it. His own opinion was that the object of the Bill was, to rob the poor man to enrich the landowner . . . If the poor man when in distress were thus deprived of his lawful means of relief, what principle in nature or justice was there to prevent his taking whatever he could lay his hands on to prevent himself from starving? Robbery and violence would then become a matter of dire necessity, the sacredness of property would no longer be protected, and how would the House like the idea of that? They were now about to dissolve the bonds of society; they were going to break faith with the poor man; and then what claim could they pretend to have upon him in return? But he was sure the Parliament could not pass this Bill, and if any future Parliaments should dare to do so, it would be a cry of war upon the cottage, which the hand of Providence would answer with a cry of war upon the princely mansion. It was said in Scripture, "Cursed be he who oppresseth the poor;" and how was he to be cursed? Why, "God shall smite him with the plagues of Egypt, the scab and the itch." Let the House read the Bible and this Bill at the same time, and then see if they could find it in their consciences to pass it. He was very sure, that if they did pass it, the curses he had announced to them would fall upon them, and that something more terrible would take place in the country than had been seen or heard of for the last two centuries. Hansard. *Parlt Debates*, 3rd Series, Vol XXII, Cols 880-81, 883, XXIV, Cols 929, 1050-52

19 The Times   Against the New Poor Law

Press comment on the new Bill was, in general, initially favourable, but *The Times* proved to be an important exception. Its hostility was probably the result of the opposition of its proprietor John Walter, a Berkshire squire, to the new centralised system of control. Since the newspaper was influential and widely read, particularly by country gentlemen, its attitude caused the Government considerable embarrassment, and it remained a thorn in the flesh of the Poor Law Commission and the Poor Law Board for many years.

This poor law system is an invention merely: it leaps forth *de novo* like Pallas out of the head of Jupiter, complete and perfect, from the plotting pericrania of Mr. Senior and other political economists. No seed or sprig of it is to be found in the records of our ancient history, and which being buried at first and laid in obscurity, time and chance might bring into light and develop. To say the truth, in one word, it is AGAINST the deep-rooted and long-formed habits of this nation, the principle of all which is that the people should be made to govern themselves as much as possible, at least in their domestic concerns and relations.

Whether this bill will pass into a law we cannot tell; we know that, should it be carried, it will disgrace the statute-book which contains Magna Charta and the Bill of Rights; and that no Englishman, who is not dead to shame, will again hear the words British liberty pronounced without a blush or a sigh. Let us, however, confidently hope that we shall not be saddled with this hastily adopted measure. We give Ministers the fullest credit for the best intentions and believing as we do that they ardently wish for the good and happiness of the country, we are convinced that they will feel the strongest sentiments of gratitude towards those who keep them from the infliction of so dreadful a scourge on the land. *The Times* (30 April 1834)

___

20 The Poor Law Amendment Act

The most important clauses of the Poor Law Amendment Act of 1834 were those setting up the new central authority, the Poor Law Commission, and establishing its powers. In deference to the considerable unease shown in Parliament and the country at the prospect of a powerful central authority, the Act left local justices, guardians and overseers with powers of independent judgement in certain cases.

___

4 & 5 WILL IV. CAP. 76.

AN ACT for the Amendment and better Administration of the Laws relating to the Poor in England and Wales.
[14th August, 1834.]
"WHEREAS it is expedient to alter and amend the laws relating

to the relief of poor persons in England and Wales;" Be it therefore enacted, by the King's most excellent Majesty, by and with
the advice and consent of the Lords spiritual and temporal, and
Commons, in this present parliament assembled, and by the
authority of the same, that it shall be lawful for His Majesty,
his heirs and successors, by warrant under the royal sign manual,
to appoint three fit persons to be commissioners to carry this Act
into execution, and also from time to time, at pleasure, to remove
any of the commissioners for the time being, and upon every or
any vacancy in the said number of commissioners, either by
removal or by death, or otherwise, to appoint some other fit
person to the said office; and until such appointment it shall be
lawful for the surviving or continuing commissioners or commissioner to act as if no such vacancy had occurred.

II. And be it further enacted, that the said commissioners
shall be styled "The Poor Law Commissioners for England and
Wales;" and the said commissioners or any two of them, may
sit, from time to time as they deem expedient, as a board of
commissioners for carrying this Act into execution;

XV. And be it further enacted, that from and after the
passing of this Act the administration of relief to the poor
throughout England and Wales, according to the existing laws,
or such laws as shall be in force at the time being, shall be subject to the direction and control of the said commissioners, and
for executing the powers given to them by this Act the said
commissioners shall and are hereby authorized and required,
from time to time as they shall see occasion, to make and issue
all such rules, orders, and regulations for the management of
the poor, for the government of workhouses and the education
of the children therein, and for the management of parish poor
children under the provisions of an Act made and passed in the
seventh year of the reign of His late Majesty King George the
Third, intituled "An Act for the better Regulation of Parish
Poor Children of the several Parishes therein mentioned within
the Bills of Mortality, and the superintending, inspecting, and

regulating of the houses wherein such poor children are kept and maintained, and for the apprenticing the children of poor persons, and for the guidance and control of all guardians, vestries, and parish officers, so far as relates to the management or relief of the poor, and the keeping, examining, auditing, and allowing of accounts, and making and entering into contracts in all matters relating to such management or relief, or to any expenditure for the relief of the poor," and for carrying this Act into execution in all other respects, as they shall think proper; and the said commissioners may, at their discretion, from time to time, suspend, alter, or rescind such rules, orders, and regulations, or any of them: Provided always, that nothing in this Act contained shall be construed as enabling the said commissioners or any of them to interfere in any individual case for the purpose of ordering relief.

XVI. And be it further enacted, that no general rule of the said commissioners shall operate or take effect until the expiration of forty days after the same, or a copy thereof, shall have been sent, signed and sealed by the said commissioners, to one of His Majesty's principal secretaries of state;

XXIII. And be it further enacted, that it shall be lawful for the said commissioners, by and with the consent in writing of a majority of the guardians of any union, or with the consent of a majority of the rate-payers and owners of property entitled to vote in manner hereinafter prescribed, in any parish, such last-mentioned majority to be ascertained in manner provided in and by this Act, to order and direct the overseers or guardians of any parish or union not having a workhouse or workhouses to build a workhouse or workhouses, and to purchase or hire land for the purpose of building the same thereon, or to purchase or hire a workhouse or workhouses, or any building or buildings for the purpose of being used as or converted into a workhouse or workhouses;

XXIV. And be it further enacted, that for the better and

G

more effectually securing the repayment of any sum or sums of
money which may be borrowed for the purposes aforesaid, with
interest, it shall be lawful for the said overseers or guardians to
charge the future poor rates of such parish or union with the
amount of such sum or sums of money: Provided always, that
the principal sum or sums to be raised for such purposes, whether raised within the year or borrowed, shall in no case exceed
the average annual amount of the rates raised for the relief of
the poor in such parish or union for three years ending at the
Easter next preceding the raising of such money, and that any
loan or money borrowed for any of the purposes aforesaid shall
be repaid by annual instalments of not less than one-tenth of
the sum borrowed, with interest on the same, in any one
year.

XXV. And be it further enacted, that it shall be lawful for
the said commissioners, and they are hereby empowered, without requiring any such consent as aforesaid, by any writing
under the hands and seal of the said commissioners, to order
and direct the overseers or guardians of any parish or union
having a workhouse or workhouses, or any building capable of
being converted into a workhouse or workhouses, to enlarge or
alter the same, according to such plan and in such manner as
the said commissioners shall deem most proper for carrying the
provisions of this Act into execution; and the overseers or
guardians to whom any such order shall be directed are hereby
authorized and required to assess, raise, and levy such sum or
sums of money as may be necessary for the purposes specified
in such order, by such powers, ways, and means as are now
by law given to or vested in churchwardens and overseers or
guardians of the poor for altering, enlarging, and maintaining
workhouses for the use of the poor in their respective parishes
or unions: Provided always, that the principal sum or sums to
be raised for such purposes, and charged upon any parish, shall
not exceed in the whole the sum of fifty pounds, nor in any
such case exceed one-tenth of the average annual amount of the
rates raised for the relief of the poor in such parish for the three

years ending at the Easter next preceding the raising of such money.

XXVI. And be it further enacted, that it shall be lawful for the said commissioners, by order under their hands and seal, to declare so many parishes as they may think fit to be united for the administration of the laws for the relief of the poor, and such parishes shall thereupon be deemed a union for such purpose, and thereupon the workhouse or workhouses of such parishes shall be for their common use; and the said commissioners may issue such rules, orders, and regulations as they shall deem expedient for the classification of such of the poor of such united parishes in such workhouse or workhouses as may be relieved in any such workhouse, and such poor may be received, maintained, and employed in any such workhouse or workhouses as if the same belonged exclusively to the parish to which such poor shall be chargeable; but, notwithstanding such union and classification, each of the said parishes shall be separately chargeable with and liable to defray the expence of its own poor, whether relieved in or out of any such workhouse.

LII. And whereas a practice has obtained of giving relief to persons or their families who, at the time of applying for or receiving such relief, were wholly or partially in the employment of individuals, and the relief of the able bodied and their families is in many places administered in modes productive of evil in other respects: And whereas difficulty may arise in case any immediate and universal remedy is attempted to be applied in the matters aforesaid; Be it further enacted, that from and after the passing of this Act, it shall be lawful for the said commissioners, by such rules, orders, or regulations as they may think fit, to declare to what extent and for what period the relief to be given to able-bodied persons or to their families in any particular parish or union may be administered out of the workhouse of such parish or union, by payments in money, or with food or clothing in kind, or partly in kind and partly in money, and in what proportions, to what persons or class of persons, at what times and places, on what conditions, and in what manner such out-door relief may be afforded; and all relief which shall be given by any overseer, guardian, or other person having the control or distribution of the funds of such parish or union, contrary to such orders or regulations, shall be and the same is hereby declared to be unlawful, and shall be disallowed in the accounts of the person giving the same, subject to the exceptions hereinafter mentioned: Provided always, that in case the overseers or guardians of any parish or union to which such orders or regulations shall be addressed or directed shall, upon consideration of the special circumstances of such parish or union, or of any person or class of persons therein, be of opinion that the application and enforcing of such orders or regulations, or of any part thereof, at the time or in the manner prescribed by the said commissioners, would be inexpedient, it shall be lawful for such overseers or guardians to delay the operation of such orders or regulations, or of any part thereof, for any period not exceeding the space of thirty days, to be reckoned from the day of the receipt of such orders or regulations; and such overseers or guardians shall, twenty days at the least before the expiration of such thirty days, make a statement and report of such special circumstances to the said commissioners; Provided also, that in case the overseers or guardians of any parish or union in which such orders or regulations shall be in force shall depart from them or any of them in any particular instance or instances of emergency, and shall within fifteen days after every such departure report the same and the grounds thereof to the said commissioners, and the said commissioners shall approve of such departure, or if the relief so given shall have been given in food, temporary lodging, or medicine, and shall have been so reported as aforesaid, then and in either of such cases the relief granted by such overseers or guardians, if otherwise lawful, shall not be unlawful or subject to be disallowed. W. C. Glen. *The Statutes in Force Relating to the Poor* (1857), 372, 376-7, 380-83, 399-400

THE FIRST YEARS OF THE POOR LAW COMMISSION

In an attempt to keep the difficult problem of poor-law reform free from the tangled world of politics, the Poor Law Amendment Act had laid down that the three members of the Poor Law Commission should not have seats in Parliament, and should be responsible to the legislature only indirectly through the Home Secretary. Once the Act had received the royal assent, the Government was faced with the task of finding three extra-Parliamentary figures to launch the New Poor Law. Their choice fell on Thomas Frankland Lewis, a country gentleman and a member of the important Select Committee on the Poor Laws of 1817; George Nicholls, the retired East India captain whose poor-law reforms in the parish of Southwell had greatly influenced the 1834 reformers; and John Shaw-Lefevre, a protegé of Lord Althorp. Edwin Chadwick, to his bitter disappointment, was only made secretary to the Poor Law Commission.

Once installed in its headquarters at Somerset House, the Commission lost no time in appointing assistant commissioners who were to have the task of grouping parishes into unions, and of supervising the administration of the boards of guardians under the direction of the central authority. Work began in the most heavily pauperised areas of southern England. Unions of between fifteen and twenty parishes were formed, each parish electing a representative to the board of guardians, which met weekly at the nearest market town. Justices of the peace resident within the Union also attended the board as *ex officio* members. Once a board of guardians was established, it took over the duty of relieving the poor from the parish overseers, and received from the Poor Law Commissioners a detailed set of regulations on how to conduct its business (21).

For the first two years of its existence, the Poor Law Commission's task proved relatively easy, despite some isolated outbreaks of resistance to the new system (22). In general the new regime was welcomed by farmers and landowners in the southern counties (23). The work was greatly aided by two years of good harvests and general prosperity. Manufacturers in the northern industrial areas found themselves working their mills at full capacity, and often experiencing labour shortages, which compelled them to raise wages. Some of them, therefore, wrote to Somerset House suggesting that the Poor Law Commissioners help to transfer redundant agricultural labourers and their families from the south to the industrial towns of Lancashire and Yorkshire, where there was plenty of work in the mills, particularly for women and children (24). The Poor Law Commission accordingly appointed two agents, R. H. Muggeridge in Manchester and Robert Baker in Leeds, who were to put manufacturers in search of workers in touch with parish authorities in the south of England. About 4,000 labourers and their families were sent northwards between 1835 and 1837, but the scheme came to grief when economic depression hit the industrial areas in 1837. Some of the migrants had to turn once again to the poor-law system for relief and were moved back to the parishes they had left. Anti Poor Law and Chartist agitators made valuable propaganda out of a scheme which they claimed, not entirely without justice, had been designed to reduce wages and prevent strikes in northern factories. The hitherto smooth progress of the New Poor Law was about to be rudely interrupted.

21 Poor Law Commission   The Regulation of Outdoor Relief

Once a board of guardians had been established, the Poor Law Commission issued it with a set of detailed instructions. On the vital question of relief to the able-bodied poor, the Commission ordered the adoption of a very stringent mode of distributing outdoor relief, as a preliminary to the total abolition of outdoor relief to this class and the establishment of a workhouse test.

Relief.

21. Immediately from and after the first meeting of the board of guardians above directed, the guardians of the Union, and

the churchwardens and overseers of the several parishes and places comprised therein, and the relieving officers for the said Union, immediately from and after the time of their appointment shall, to such extent as in the convenient and proper discharge of their several duties they may be enabled, observe and conform to, and carry into effect the following Rules and Regulations, relating to the relief of the poor in the said Union; and from and after the *third day of October* 1835, the said rules and regulations shall become peremptory and binding upon the parties above mentioned, and shall not be departed from in any case, nor shall any relief be thereafter given from the poor-rates of any parish or place in the said Union contrary thereto:—

Firstly. No relief shall be given in money (except in cases of sickness or accident) to any able-bodied male pauper who is in employment (the same not being parish work), and in the receipt of earnings; nor to any part of his family who shall be dependent on him, or for whose relief and maintenance he shall be liable.

Secondly. If any able-bodied male pauper shall apply to be set to work by the parish, one-half at least of the relief which may be afforded to him or to his family shall be in kind.

Thirdly. One-half at least of the relief which may be afforded to widows or single women, not being aged or infirm, shall be in kind.

Fourthly. No relief shall be given to any able-bodied male pauper by payment or payments of, for or on account of the rent for his house or lodging, or for the house or lodging of any part of his family who shall be dependent upon him, and for whose relief and maintenance he shall be liable, or by allowance towards such rent. Poor Law Commission. *First Annual Report*, Appendix A, No 6 (1835)

22 W. J. Gilbert   Rural Opposition

Although the new system was generally welcomed by rate-payers in the southern counties, the Assistant Commissioners encountered some resistance to their proceedings. An account of such an incident, from W. J. Gilbert in Devon, is given here. The Poor Law Commission was anxious to play down such occurrences and portray them as the work of self-interested parties or persons of bad character. In fact, opposition may have been more serious than the printed accounts reveal.

Your orders and rules being calculated to lessen the resort to the beer-shop, and curtail the improper exercise of parish influence and parish funds, have here, as elsewhere, excited opposition amongst those parties who benefited by former abuses. The leaders of the opposition are to be found amongst the constant overseers (gentlemen accustomed to accept the office for 5*l.* a year, and quit it with a well-furnished purse); the little shopkeeper, at whose house the poor were paid, and who received the amount for old debts and encouraged new, from which the pauper never got free; the beer-shop keeper, at whose house great part of the relief was expended; and the little farmer or the lime-kiln owner, whose influence at the vestry enabled him to pay one half his labour from the parish funds, under the name of relief in aid of wages, or to speak correctly, relief in aid of vestrymen.

Wherever disturbances have taken place, they have been traced to the instigation of some or one of these parties. In the north of the county, where there were some disturbances, we found that the poor people were acting under the grossest deception.

There was not anything too horrible or absurd to be circulated, and nothing too incredible for their belief. Few really understood the intended proceedings of the guardians, and the opposition was not against the execution of the law, but the falsehoods in circulation. As soon as the intentions of the law were understood, the most riotous submitted and received the alterations gladly. Amongst other ridiculous statements circulated, the peasantry fully believed that all the bread was poisoned, and that the only cause for giving it instead of money was the facility it afforded of destroying the paupers; that all the children beyond three in a family were to be killed; that all young children and women under 18 were to be spared; that if they touched the bread they would instantly drop down dead; and I saw one poor person at North Molton look at a loaf with a strong expression of hunger, and when it was offered to her, put her hands behind her and shrink back in fear lest it should touch her. She acknowledged she had heard of a man who had dropped down dead the moment he touched the bread.

It was also believed that to touch the bread was like "taking bounty," and the guardians would immediately seize them, kill their children, and imprison the parents.

Other stories to excite the small rate-payers were,—that the chairman was to have 1,200*l.* a year, and all the guardians in proportion, and that 20,000*l.* were to be immediately levied on the rate-payers for a workhouse. Poor Law Commission. *Second Annual Report*, Appendix B, No 9 (1836)

23 Uckfield Union, Sussex   The Effects of the New Poor Law

This published report of the auditor of the Uckfield Union in Sussex for the quarter ending December 1835 was doubly gratifying to the Poor Law Commissioners, since it purported to show that not only was relief expenditure falling in what had been a heavily pauperised area but also that the character of the labouring poor was improving.

The annual average expenditure in the parishes forming this Union, for the years ending 1831—32, and 33, from whence our mediums have been taken, produces £16,643 as the sum annually disbursed in parochial relief; this will show an average monthly expenditure of £1386, while a similar average on the Union expenditure, including the repairs and alterations to the workhouses, will be found not to exceed £550 being a difference of £836 per month, by which it will be seen *a saving of £10,000 per annum will be effected;* and I will venture to assert, after having considered the question in all its bearings, that that sum may be looked on with reference to the ensuing year as a permanent reduction.

But the mere saving of this sum is not the only nor yet the most important point of view in which the changes of the law should be regarded; the moral reformation effected, by checks given to vice, improvidence, and indolence,—the stimulus offered to industry, and *the means it has left in the hands of the rate-payers to reward that industry*—have solved the question of surplus labour, by proving (in this Union at least) that where there exists a wish for employment, employment is to be found.

In the month of December, 1834, in the corresponding quarter of last year, upwards of two hundred and fifty labourers were out of employment, and receiving relief in consequence for their families, although the state of the weather was not of such severity as at all to impede the usual routine of a labourer's occupations.

In the quarter just past, at the end of a week's frost and when the snow had stopped most of the operations in agriculture, the greatest number of able bodied men in the work-houses was twenty-eight; which asylum was sought by many, rather as a temporary refuge from the effects of circumstances, over which they had no control,—from a suspension of labour, not from want of employment.

Yet among this number there were, as there always will be, more or less, some, who, from a long continued course of idleness and misconduct, could find no one to employ them, who had hitherto subsisted on parish pay, then derived from a fund which is now devoted to the remuneration of labour. The well-regulated system of employment, the irksome confinement, the discipline of our workhouses, and I trust a sincere desire to reform, has induced some who were unmarried to enlist as soldiers, and by thus entering the ranks in His Majesty's Service, they now form part of that body of men whose duty it is to support and maintain those laws and that peace which but a few months since they were among the foremost to outrage and disturb.

It is not from these circumstances alone that we have proofs of the beneficial operations of the bill; it may be sought for from other sources,—not in the encomiums of its friends, but in the complaints of its enemies, none of whom feel it more severely or complain more bitterly than the keepers of beer shops, and in short all that class of persons who were thriving on the improvidence and demoralization of the labourer, but who now suffer from his reform.

The great mass of those individuals who were so clamorous against the new enactments, on the ground of cruelty to the poor, are now silenced by the fact, that nearly two-thirds of the sum that they contributed, is left in their own hands, for their *own* distribution, *according to their own discretion;* to such as were sincerely actuated by the feelings they expressed, and who concealed no sinister motives under the mask of charity, it must be gratifying to reflect that the sum formerly abstracted from the funds of private benevolence is thus restored to its natural channel; those humane persons will now have the satisfaction of dispensing that relief as charity, to be received with gratitude, which was formerly claimed as a right, and exacted by intimidation. *Operations of the Poor Law Amendment Act in the County of Sussex* (1836), 8–11

24 R. H. Greg   The Migration Scheme
This letter written by Robert Hyde Greg (1795–1875), the son of Samuel Greg, the famous cotton millowner of Styal in Cheshire, to Edwin Chadwick, the secretary of the Poor Law Commission, inspired the migration scheme from the south to Lancashire and the West Riding (see p 102). Henry Ashworth was a cotton manufacturer with a large mill at Turton, near Bolton.

Manchester, 17 September 1834.

I HAVE for some time thought of addressing you on the same matter as my friend Ashworth did some time ago; namely, the propriety of opening a communication between our (strange to say) underpeopled districts and the southern overpeopled ones.

It is at this moment a most important suggestion, and deserves to be put into immediate operation.

It must be looked upon as a happy coincidence that at the period of depriving or curtailing perhaps the facilities of gaining a livelihood to the people of one half of England, and causing a fall in their present low wages, and a scramble amongst them for employment, there should exist a difficulty in obtaining labourers at extravagant wages in these northern counties. This fortunate occurrence should be taken advantage of.

But for the operation of the poor laws in binding down the labourers to their respective parishes, in the mode and to the degree I need not attempt to explain to you, of all men, there would have existed a free circulation of labour throughout the country, to the benefit alike of the northern and southern parts. Nothing but the poor laws has prevented this circulation, or could prevent it, short of the labourers being reduced again to the state of *adscripti glebæ*. * * * *

At this moment our machinery in one mill has been standing for 12 months for hands. In another mill we cannot start our new machinery for the same want. My parlours are without doors, having been sent some time since to be altered, and their progress having been stopped by a meeting of the joiners. The carpenter in the village in which I reside (12 miles from here), cannot get on with my work, having, as he says, been short of men all the year. * * * *

The suggestion I would make is this, that some official channel of communication should be opened in two or three of our large towns with your office, or any office, to which the most over-charged parishes might transmit lists of their families. Manu-facturers short of labourers, or starting new concerns, might look over the lists and select, as they might require (for the variety of our wants is great), large families or small ones, young children or grown up, men, or widows, or orphans, &c.

If this could be done, I doubt not in a short time, as the thing became known and tried, we should gradually absorb a considerable number of the surplus labourers of the south, and be supplied from there instead of from Ireland.

It must be understood at once, that we cannot do with refuse population and insubordinate sturdy paupers. We should require fair play. Hard working men, or widows with families, who preferred gaining an honest living to a workhouse, would, I am confident, be in demand.

I may add, that I think something on a small scale might be attempted soon. We are now in want of labour. Next year will, unless some unforeseen accident occurs, be naturally a year of increase in our manufactures, buildings, &c., and should this prove the case, any farther demand for labour would still further increase the unions, drunkenness and high wages.

Whilst food is cheap and wages high, the want of education (I do not merely mean the ability to read and write, which few here are without), but education which may affect manners, morals, and the proper use of their advantages, is extremely felt and to be deeply deplored. I do hope Government will not allow another session to pass without making some struggle to effect this most desirable object. Poor Law Commission. *First Annual Report*, Appendix C, No 5 (1835)

THE ANTI POOR LAW MOVEMENT

When the Poor Law Commission sent their Assistant Commissioners into northern England to organise the New Poor Law system, they found themselves faced with a resistance whose organisation and ferocity was unlike anything they had met before. In 1837, economic depression was spreading fears of unemployment and short-time working amongst industrial workers in counties like Lancashire and the West Riding, particularly amongst those employed in declining handicraft industries such as woolcombing or calico-weaving. The proposal to introduce the New Poor Law into these areas heightened the workers' fears, since resort to the parish in periods of distress might now be met, not with the grant of a small dole, but with the offer of the workhouse, the dreaded *Bastile*. Nor were working men the only ones to fear and distrust the new system. Many local officials, overseers, members of select vestries, magistrates and ratepayers felt that they had already reformed their administration. This was efficient, as the low rates proved, and it was adapted to the circumstances of the area. A strict workhouse system, they felt, was quite useless in the face of the massive distress caused by industrial depression. They resented the intrusion of London men and London methods into their affairs (25).

Not only did the northern counties distrust the New Poor Law, they were well organised to resist it. The Ten Hours Movement after 1830 had led to the establishment of a network of Short Time Committees throughout the textile-manufacturing districts of Lancashire and the West Riding, and these committees now opposed the New Poor Law. Local Anti Poor Law committees were established and their work co-ordinated by a West Riding Anti Poor Law Committee and a South Lancashire Anti Poor Law Association. Meetings were organised and petitions calling for the repeal of the New Poor Law sent to Westminster. The erstwhile leaders of the Ten Hours Movement, Richard Oastler of Fixby, near Huddersfield; William Busfeild Ferrand, squire of Bingley; George Stringer Bull, curate of Bierley, near Bradford; Joseph Rayner Stephens, a Nonconformist preacher of Ashton under Lyne; and John Fielden, cotton manufacturer of Todmorden, now emerged as leaders of the Anti Poor Law Movement.

Oastler and his fellow leaders addressed Anti Poor Law meetings, and wrote pamphlets and letters to sympathetic newspapers like the *Leeds Intelligencer* or the *Sheffield Iris* in which they denounced the New Poor Law as being cruel, unchristian, and dictatorial (26). Most of these speeches and writings consisted of highly charged emotional outbursts full of prophetic violence and often of lurid tales of cruelties inflicted on wretched paupers in the workhouses of southern England (27). Most of these alleged cruelties were investigated by the Poor Law Commission, who found though some were true, many were at best half truths, and others, like the *Marcus* affair (28) of 1839, were complete fabrications. The Anti Poor Law agitators were determined to portray the Poor Law Commissioners as inhuman tyrants.

Emotional speeches and wild tales of cruelty roused northern workers to fury. In some areas, attempts to put the new system into operation were answered by riots. The task of the Assistant Commissioners was made more difficult by the fact that many overseers, magistrates and members of the new boards of guardians were determined to obstruct the operation of the new system (29). In face of this hostility, the Poor Law Commission was forced to tread warily; and they were urged to proceed with caution by the Home Secretary, who was alarmed by the violence in the north. Thus boards of guardians were at first established merely to carry out the provisions of the Registration Act of 1836. Even when they were asked to take over poor relief duties from the parishes, the regulations issued to them by the Poor Law Commission allowed them to continue to give relief as under the old poor law system (30).

Popular resistance to the New Poor Law in the north was not long lived. When the workhouse system and its alleged cruelties failed to appear in northern towns, many working men left the paternalist Anti Poor Law movement for Chartism, which seemed to have more to offer them. Suspicion of the Poor Law Commission remained strong, however, among many members of boards of guardians. Having been granted considerable powers of discretion in the performance of their duties, they were resolved to defend this freedom against central interference. 'The rabble are easily quieted', wrote one Assistant Commissioner in 1838, 'but where a majority of a board of guardians is opposed to the Commissioners, the whole proceedings are attended with extreme difficulty.'

25 Joseph Ellison   The Good Old System

A witness before the Parliamentary Select Committee on the
Poor Law Amendment Act of 1837, Joseph Ellison was a
member of the Dewsbury board of guardians and had served
on the select vestry of the township of Gomersal before the
Poor Law Amendment Act had been extended to the West
Riding.

Notwithstanding that scarcity of work, your poor rates have
been so low as 1/– upon the rack rent, for buildings, and 2/–
for lands?—Yes, in the last year.

That being the case, you think you would have good reason
to believe that you could not have the law more satisfactorily
conducted, both for the rate payers and the rate receivers, than
it has been during the last year under the operation of the old
law?—We do think so: and at a late meeting of our select vestry
every one concurred in the answer I have just now given to
you, that under no system of management could things be
carried on more satisfactorily, both to the rate payers and to the
paupers; and this is the opinion of nineteen-twentieths of the
ratepayers of that township where I reside. The general feeling
is this, "What a pity that a system that has worked so well, and
has produced so much good, should be now broken up!" That
is the universal exclamation. I am not speaking of the working
classes, for they do not understand these things; but amongst
the most respectable portion of the ratepayers, the clergymen
and such gentry as we have, and the principal ratepayers, that
is the universal feeling. Indeed, you need not be surprised at
that, when the rates have been reduced, within the last twenty
years, to the amount that I have stated. The clergy are, I believe,
to a man, opposed to the new law; they have seen the good
effects of the old system, and are satisfied that it cannot be
improved upon; but I am speaking always of the Select Vestry
Act;[1] that was the greatest improvement that ever took place in
the Poor Law, so far as regards manufacturing districts. Select

[1] Sturges Bourne's Act, 59 Geo III, c 12 (1819). See 13B.

Committee on the Poor Law Amendment Act. XVIII, *Evidence of Joseph Ellison*, Q 5292–3 (1837–8)

_____

26 Richard Oastler   The New Poor Law

Richard Oastler (1789–1861), son of a Leeds clothier, was agent for an estate at Fixby in the West Riding. A prominent leader of the Ten Hours Movement, he won the adulation of many northern workers, despite his paternalistic Evangelical and Tory beliefs. In 1838 he was dismissed by his employer, Mr Thornhill, and later imprisoned for debt.

_____

CHRISTIAN READER.

Be not alarmed at the sound of the Title. I can not *bless* that, which GOD and NATURE CURSE. The Bible being true, the Poor Law Amendment Act is false! The Bible containing the will of God,—this accursed Act of Parliament embodies the will of Lucifer. It is the Sceptre of Belial, establishing its sway in the Land of Bibles!! DAMNATION; ETERNAL DAMNATION to the accursed Fiend!!

RICHARD OASTLER.

R. Oastler. *Damnation, Eternal Damnation* (1837), frontispiece

(see page 114.)

_____

27 G. R. W. Baxter   Anti Poor Law Tales

G. R. Wythen Baxter's *The Book of the Bastiles* was a scissors and paste compilation, mainly from newspaper reports, of Anti Poor Law demonstrations and speeches, together with lurid accounts of the cruelties practised on pauper inmates by sadistic workhouse masters. The brutal master of the Rochester Union workhouse was in fact prosecuted and found guilty of assaulting workhouse inmates. The book contains several extracts from reports of his trial, which doubtless served to titillate its readers' imagination as well as to persuade them of the frequency of such occurrences.

_____

"Harriet Decoster Rushworth, twenty years old, with her

H

DAMNATION!

ETERNAL DAMNATION

TO THE FIEND-BEGOTTEN,

"COARSER FOOD"

NEW POOR LAW.

𝔄 Speech

BY RICHARD OASTLER.

The Lord will abhor the bloody and deceitful man.—DAVID.

The Poor Law Commissioners are *bloody and deceitful men.*—TRUTH.

Minister.—Cursed is he that removeth his neighbour's Landmark.
Answer.—Amen.

Minister.—Cursed is he that maketh the blind to go out of his way.
Answer.—Amen.—   THE COMMINATION SERVICE.

Then the Poor Law Commissioners are cursed of God and of Man.
     TRUTH.

LONDON:

H. HETHERINGTON, 126, STRAND, AND ALL BOOKSELLERS.

—

1837.

daughter, an infant *nine months* old, were placed in the workhouse of St. George's-in-the-East. *Her baby was taken from her? and two other babies were put for her to suckle.* This was done the very day she went in."—*Oastler's Letter to Lord John Russell*, March 3, 1838.

"A little boy having been separated from his mother in Nottingham Union, raged in all the agony of despair, and actually tore off his own hair by handsful."—*Ibid.*

"It was stated at Icklesham, that a little child had been heard crying in the Union workhouse, in violent grief. 'Let me out—let me out—I want to see my daddy—I must go to my daddy.' "—*Letter from Mr. John Perceval to Mr. Oastler*, dated from Hastings, May, 11, 1838.

"One of the aged paupers said, 'that he was afraid to say all he knew, but he *doubted* if all that died, got fair burial."—*Ibid.*

"Upwards of half-a-dozen girls in the Hoo workhouse, some of them verging on *womanhood*, have at times had their persons exposed in the most brutal and indecent manner, by the Master, for the purpose of inflicting on them cruel floggings; and the same girls, at other times, have, in a scarcely less indecent manner, been compelled by him to strip the upper parts of their persons naked, to allow him to scourge them with birch rods on their bare shoulders and waists, and which, from more than one of the statements from the lips of the sufferers, appears to have been inflicted without mercy. One girl says, 'My back was marked with blood.' Another, a witness, who had not herself been punished, says, 'We women were called to hold one of the girls while the Master flogged her; but we went down in the yard out of the way, because we could not bear the sight; afterwards we got ointment out of the sick ward to rub her back, for it was *all cut to pieces.*' Again, 'One Sunday the Master flogged little Jemmy (a pauper's illegitimate child, then two years of age) with a birch rod, so that the *child carried the marks a month*, because it cried for its mother, who was gone to church, and for its little brother, who was that day put into breeches, and taken away from the children's ward.' "—*Rochester Correspondent* to the "*Times*," Dec. 26, 1840. G. R. W. Baxter. *The Book of the Bastiles* (1841), 128–9, 156

---

28 'Marcus on Populousness'

The origin of this famous piece of Anti Poor Law propaganda lay in two obscure pamphlets, *An Essay on Populousness Printed for Private Circulation* (1838), and, *On the Possibility of Limiting Populousness by 'Marcus'* (1838). Both of these discuss the possible use of infanticide for dealing with the population explosion, the former suggesting painless extinction by *gaz*. Couched in extremely turgid language, they were probably the work of some Neo-Malthusian crank. They were publicised widely by Joseph Rayner Stephens, however, and by two leading Chartist newspapers, Augustus Beaumont's *Northern Liberator* and Feargus O'Connor's *Northern Star*. It was alleged that they were the work of the Poor Law Commissioners or their associates, who were known to hold Malthusian views on population. Claiming that the original pamphlet had been suppressed, the Anti Poor Law Movement produced a *People's Edition*, which they embellished with the title *The Book of Murder*.

We see that our exposure of this shocking publication has done its work, and that the country rings with execrations of it and of its author or authors.

The Rev. Mr. Stephens amongst others, our readers will see, has made good use of it. The hack-slave *Globe* half denies its existence and then says "even if it be a bad joke, the author should be punished." We repeat WE HAVE the murder pamphlet; we quoted it verbatim et liberatim in our dissection of it; and it is NO JOKE!!

It is a bona-fide, grave, earnest, scientific proposal to murder every third infant (with a few exceptions) by "painless extinction", by means of (carbonic acid) "gas". Who may be *Marcus* its author, we know not. Certain it is that it cannot have been written by any Christian, nor by any infidel who admits the

THE

BOOK OF MURDER!

A VADE-MECUM

FOR THE

COMMISSIONERS AND GUARDIANS

OF THE

New Poor Law

THROUGHOUT GREAT BRITAIN AND IRELAND,

BEING AN EXACT REPRINT OF

The Infamous Essay

ON THE

POSSIBILITY OF
Limiting Populousness,

BY MARCUS,
ONE OF THE THREE.

WITH A REFUTATION OF THE MALTHUSIAN
DOCTRINE.

Oh! grief, then, grief and shame! If in this
Flourishing Land there should be dwellings where
The new-born babe doth bring unto its
Parents' soul, no joy! where squallied Poverty
Receives it at the birth, and, on her withered knees,
Gives it the scanty bread of discontent.—SOUTHEY.

"Rachael weeping for her children and would not be comforted, because they were not."

PRINTED BY JOHN HILL, BLACK HORSE COURT, FLEET ST.,

And now Re-printed for the Instruction of the Labourer,

BY WILLIAM DUGDALE, NO. 37, HOLYWELL STREET, STRAND.

PRICE THREE-PENCE.

1839.

beautiful morality of the New and much of the Old Testament; nor by any person unhardened by doctrines subversive of humanity as well as charity. By a Malthusian it MUST have been written. Now Lord Brougham is a defender of Malthus to the uttermost horrors of his doctrine. Lord Howick is the same. Mr. Place, the drawer up of the horrid bill, is the same. The villainous Commissioners are their agents to carry out these execrable doctrines with effect. Amongst THE GANG then, the authorship rests. We are well read in "styles"; and we say that *Marcus* whoever he be, has read Jeremy Bentham's works much; and that the style is tinged with that of the Malthusian sage. *Northern Liberator* (12 January 1839)

29 G. Tinker   The State of the Huddersfield Union

In the Huddersfield Union, the board of guardians, many of whom were members of the Anti Poor Law Movement, obstructed the New Poor Law by refusing to elect a Union Clerk, without whom no business could be transacted. Some of the guardians favourable to the new system, of whom George Tinker, the author of this letter to the Poor Law Commission, was one, felt that the local magistrates as ex-officio members of the board were sympathising with the Anti Poor Law faction and failing to use their influence to control them or to protect the board from the threat of mob violence.

Gentlemen,

I take the liberty of addressing you for the purpose of calling your attention to the peculiar circumstances in which I, together with several others of the Guardians of the Poor in the Huddersfield Union are situated. You are probably aware of the excitement prevailing in this district respecting the Poor Law Amendment Act, and of some of the means which have been taken to provoke and continue that excitement—such as the recent West Riding meeting. But I believe you cannot be aware of the perfect state of organisation into which the district has been put and the violent and unprincipled measures which are in operation to defeat your intentions.

The peoples' feelings have been worked up to a state of madness by gross mistatements. An Association is formed having for its avowed object direct opposition to the law. Delegates are appointed and contributions levied for the purpose of paying the wages of itinerant agitators and for securing the return of Guardians pledged to oppose your orders. It has so far succeeded as to secure the return of a majority of the Guardians who communicate with and act according to its instructions. In the present alarming state of the district it will be dangerous to put the Law into operation.

At a meeting held on Monday the 5th inst. the proceedings of which I suppose will be communicated to you, the mob amounting to 6 or 8 thousand persons, led on by the notorious Oastler, broke open the gates of the workhouse and threatened to pull down the building if the Guardians did not immediately break up their meeting. It was with difficulty and by a very small majority that the meeting was adjourned to another place in the town, a motion having been made and strongly supported that it should be adjourned to the 1st Monday in April 1838. On the way to our second place of meeting, the guardians who were known to be favourable to the Law were repeatedly surrounded by the mob, and their lives threatened if they attempted to carry it into effect. The magistrate present, R. Battye, Esq. placed us under the merciful protection of Rchd. Oastler, and refused to read the Riot Act, notwithstanding that the heads of several of the constables had been broken and the windows of the room demolished with stones thrown by the mob. The opposition guardians during the meeting, regularly communicated its proceedings to the mob outside by haranguing them out at the windows and by writing. Only eleven out of thirty nine guardians present voted for electing a Clerk, and those who had the manliness to do so were individualized and the mob was promised that they should be afterwards acquainted with their names.

Being a sincere advocate of the Poor Law Amendment Act I am particularised by the opposition guardians, put in bodily fear by the threats of the mob and prevented from following my usual avocations.

This Gentlemen you will perceive is the peculiar and dangerous situation in which some of the Guardians are placed—called upon by one portion of the Executive to administer a certain Act—refused the protection and support of another portion and subjected if honestly performing our duties to the violence of thousands of irritated persons who are under the command of *One* individual whose avowed object is, direct opposition to the established law of the country. I therefore most humbly request on behalf of myself and fellow Guardians your advice and protection.

I have the honour to be, Gentlemen,

Your Obedient Servant,

Geo. Tinker

Guardian for the Township of Hepworth.

Scholes, nr. Huddersfield,

June 8, 1837.

PRO, MH12/15063

30 Poor Law Commission   Poor Relief Regulations

This section from the *Orders and Regulations—for the Guidance and Government of the Boards of Guardians of the several Unions in Lancashire and the West Riding of Yorkshire* shows the Poor Law Commission in face of the disturbed state of these areas, allowing their boards of guardians to continue to give relief as under the old system. In this, the regulation differed markedly from that issued to boards of guardians in southern England (21).

Relief.

21. The guardians shall administer relief according to the provisions of the statute 43 Eliz. cap. 2, and all other statutes relating to the relief of the poor which are or shall be at any

time in force and subsisting; and they shall assume the administration of relief in the several townships and places in the Union, at such times respectively, and in such order as they shall deem fitting and convenient, and shall give due notice thereof to the overseers of the poor of the said several townships respectively; and until the receipt of such notice the overseers of the poor of each township shall continue in the administration of relief to the poor as heretofore, . . . Poor Law Commission. *Fourth Annual Report*, Appendix A, No 7 (1838)

THE FALL OF THE POOR LAW COMMISSION

Despite the absorption of the northern Anti Poor Law Movement into Chartism, the Poor Law Commission still found itself the target of hostility. Boards of guardians, particularly in northern England and in Wales, regarded every action of the Commissioners and their Assistants with suspicion. The 'Three Bashaws of Somerset House' were continually sniped at in Parliament and in the press, particularly in *The Times*. Many of these attacks concentrated on the issue of centralisation: the Poor Law Commission was alleged to be attempting to extend its authority into every sphere of local government, and thus to be undermining one of the most sacred principles of the English constitution. Allegations of inefficiency and corruption at Somerset House were rife.

By 1839 the Poor Law Commission was in a weak position. The Act of 1834 had limited its life to five years, and such was the opposition to it by the time that period expired that the government would only renew its powers annually until 1842, when it was granted a further five-year term.

Although the 1842 Act removed some of the uncertainty surrounding the Commission's future, it further weakened the central authority's power by reducing the number of its Assistant Commissioners from twelve to nine. Each Assistant was now charged with the impossible task of supervising the activities of boards of guardians in more than seventy Unions. Overwork brought a rapid deterioration in the morale of the Assistant

Commissioners, who felt that they were being made scapegoats for the New Poor Law in the localities, while the Poor Law Commissioners, though chiding and sometimes dismissing them for alleged shortcomings, often failed to back them in struggles with local guardians or ignored their advice on how to deal with particular problems (31).

The disgruntled Assistant Commissioners found a ready ally in the Commission's secretary, Edwin Chadwick. His attempt to influence the Commission's decisions had been quickly thwarted by Frankland Lewis, with whom Chadwick soon quarrelled bitterly. Frankland Lewis's resignation in 1839 only increased internal dissension since, to Chadwick's fury, he was succeeded by his son, George Cornewall Lewis. Increasingly Chadwick turned away from poor-law matters to public health work. Thus externally attacked and internally divided, the Poor Law Commission staggered on with too little power and too small a staff to make effective what power it had. Boards of guardians were frequently able to continue to give relief in the old way. Local officials went unsupervised, and abuses unchecked. In 1845 it was revealed that a workhouse master at Andover had so reduced the diet of the able-bodied inmates under his charge that they had gnawed at the rotten bones they were set to crush as a work task.

The Poor Law Commission's enemies descended on this scandal with delight, and forced a Parliamentary Select Committee to enquire into the state of the Andover Union; which committee soon found that it had to extend its terms of reference beyond the bone gnawing at Andover (33). The Committee's Report, which was strongly critical of the Poor Law Commission, ensured that its powers would not be further renewed.

In 1847, the Home Secretary, Sir George Grey, announced that the Poor Law Commission was to be wound up (34). But the idea of a central authority for poor-law administration was not abandoned. The place of the Poor Law Commission was to be taken by a Poor Law Board, whose President was to be a member of the Government with a seat in Parliament. The experiment of 1834 was acknowledged to have failed, and the poor law was now brought directly into the sphere of politics. But the English poor law of the mid-Victorian era was to prove a bitter disappointment to the reformers of 1834.

31 William Day The Difficulties of an Assistant Commissioner

William Day (1798–1849) was a Sussex country gentleman, and a JP in that county. He took a keen interest in local government, particularly in poor-law administration, and submitted a report on poor-law reform to the Royal Commission of 1832–4. In 1835 he was appointed an assistant poor-law commissioner, and put in charge of forming Unions in Shropshire and North Wales. In 1840 he was appointed to inspect the whole of Wales, together with parts of Cheshire, Shropshire and Herefordshire. In January 1844 he was asked to resign by the Poor Law Commission on the grounds that a minor accident he had suffered prevented him from carrying out his duties properly. Bitterly offended, Day, who felt he was being made a scapegoat for the Rebecca Riots that had broken out in his area, wrote a long letter of resignation to the Commissioners in which he justified his conduct in Wales.

Day's case was taken up by Chadwick and used in his attack on the Commissioners before the committee enquiring into the Andover affair. The report of this enquiry strongly condemned the Poor Law Commission for dismissing Day unjustly.

Shrewsbury, 22nd January, 1844.

Gentlemen,

In compliance with Mr. Nicholls's communication, I resign into your hands my appointment as Assistant Commissioner, which I now transmit—an appointment which was originally unsought by myself—accepted at the solicitation of your own colleagues—and for which I sacrificed other arrangements and advantages, which had I then pursued, would have found me now in a very different position to that in which your decision will leave me.

After a faithful service of eight years, against which Calumny itself has never dared to breathe a charge, I am dismissed at a moment's warning—without the slightest previous hint that my conduct was unsatisfactory—without any opportunity of alteration if it were desired—and without even a chance of vindicating myself, if I have been belied.

With reference to the necessity for the frequency of attendance on Boards of Guardians, as regards South Wales, I have to offer the following observations:—The power of accomplishing with success what Mr. Nicholls points out, is controlled by the relative position of the Unions, and the cycle in which their days of meeting succeed. Then, again, in these parts the state of the roads is a material element in the question, where, even with a light carriage and post horses, I have *sometimes* accomplished not even more than four miles an hour.

Inspection of a Workhouse on a Board day is next to useless. The master is almost sure to be prepared, even from the expectation of the Guardians alone. It is only on unexpected visits that its real state can be discovered.

But I offer these observations as no excuse. I deny that at the period of my accident there was any remissness on my part, and the facts shall speak for themselves.

I will not confine myself to the quarter during which my unfortunate accident happened. I will commence with the previous one, and how stand the facts? From the termination of the Lady-day quarter to the 19th of August, the date of my fall, was a period of twenty weeks. During that period (counting adjournments to successive days as separate visits) I transacted business in the different Unions in my district on 111 different occasions. Of these, 47 were either on Board days, or on special investigations. The remainder were confined to the ordinary inspection of the Houses, and inquiries of the officers.

During this period I travelled a distance of 2596 miles, two-thirds of it with my own horses, thereby effecting a saving of one-fourth in my travelling expenses to the Commission, and with none of the facilities of transit which occasionally exist in other parts.

I conducted, during this period, without the assistance of a clerk, which I have never had or even asked of the Commission, the necessary correspondence and office business of my district, and I appeal to yourselves whether I have not conducted it fully and punctually.

The discretion as to the distribution of his visits must necessarily vest in the Assistant Commissioner. There is often as much tact in abstaining, as in forcing one's self upon the deliberations of the Guardians. On a late occasion, when Mr. Weale attended a special meeting at Aberayron for me, the Guardians were disgusted at the interference of the Commission, they herded together in knots at the bottom of the table, venting their indignation at the supposed dictation, and proposed ejecting him from the room. This passed in Welsh, and Mr. Weale was not aware of it. It was from the clerk, on the occasion of a subsequent visit, that I had the statement.

Another circumstance also has operated very materially against me; a circumstance over which I had no controul, but of which the consequences have fallen upon myself.

In South Wales the Workhouses were scarcely dry, when the Prohibitory Order[1] was instantly issued. The transition from a state of uncontrolled license in the administration of relief to the stringent provisions of that regulation, was by a single step—no breathing time was given, but it was brought at once into operation upon a population which was not prepared for it. The intention of cutting off relief in aid of wages, was to cause wages to rise by all that difference. Such, under ordinary circumstances, will *eventually* be the case, but not at once, and the interval is an interval of intense trial.

[1] The order from the Poor Law Commission prohibiting outdoor relief to able-bodied men (37A).

But what was the result in South Wales of this precipitancy? The people refused to acquiesce, and though compelled to submit to the law, took every advantage of evading it. Hence though the law has been carried out to the *letter*, it has been paralysed as to the *spirit*, and the abuse of medical certificates has rendered the order a nullity. This is an abuse I have reported over and over again to yourselves—but you have been unable to suggest a remedy.

This evasion of the law is one of the points upon which a member of the Commission of Inquiry expressed to me that its administration was unsatisfactory. But is this a matter which I can counteract? If the practice have grown out of the terms of your own order, how can I controul it? If the law is unpopular from causes in existence before I came into the district, or from seasons or circumstances which I could not command, why am I to bear the blame? Not the whole Commission, situated as I have been, could have prevented it.

Is then the *only* test of the efficiency of an officer, the success and the popularity of the measures he is called upon to administer? Would you yourselves be content to abide by the same judgement? Why then should I be condemned by it?

Acting upon this impression, therefore, I deem it due to myself to transmit a copy of these observations to Sir James Graham,[1] that if I am correct, I may at least have the satisfaction of offering such a vindication as the absence of a more specific knowledge of the errors I may be charged with enables me to present.

> I remain, Gentlemen,
>> Your obedient Servant,
>>> WILLIAM DAY.

The Poor Law Commissioners.
William Day Esq. *Correspondence with the Poor Law Commissioners* (1844), 23-9

---

[1] The Home Secretary.

32 Poor Law Commission Indoor and Outdoor Relief

The high hopes which the Poor Law Commission had entertained in its early years of effecting a drastic reduction in the cost of poor relief, and of abolishing or severely restricting outdoor relief to the able-bodied poor, had been severely dashed by 1847. Relief costs rose during the economic depression of 1842-3 and proved difficult to reduce to their former level, while the number of indoor paupers remained a small and fairly constant fraction of the whole. (See pp 128-9.)

33 Select Committee on the Andover Union Chadwick's Quarrel with the Poor Law Commissioners

The Parliamentary Select Committee established initially in 1846 to inquire into the specific charges of maladministration in the Andover Union soon found itself being turned into a sounding board for all the grievances that had been building up within the Poor Law Commission. These turned particularly on the disagreements between Edwin Chadwick and the Lewises—Thomas Frankland and his son, George Cornewall. In their evidence before the committee, Chadwick and Lewis were unsparing in their attacks on each other.

(a) Edwin Chadwick:

These conversations and conversational proceedings at casual meetings of the Commissioners, without minutes, or of single Commissioners without minutes, or sittings without regularity, are not regular or in accordance with the intention of the Act, or of the Legislature; and so far an irregularity attaches to the mode in which this business of the dismissal of an Assistant Commissioner was conducted. It would have followed had the deliberations been common, by minutes of the fact of deliberations and in courtesy, that the Assistant Commissioner should have been present to give his explanation at the joint meeting.

STATEMENT showing the Amount of Money expended for
and Out-Door Paupers relieved in England and Wales
together with the estimated Population for each Year,
of the Number of Paupers relieved on the Population, and

Years ended Lady-Day.	Expenditure.					Average Price of Wheat per Quarter in each Year.		Rate per Head of Expenditure for In-Maintenance
	In-Maintenance.	Proportion per Cent. to Total.	Out-Relief.	Proportion per Cent. to Total.	Total In-Maintenance and Out-Relief.			
	£.		£.		£.	s. d.		s.
1840	808,151	22	2,931,263	78	3,739,414	68 6		4
1841	890,883	23	2,995,330	77	3,886,213	65 3		4 1
1842	934,158	23	3,090,884	77	4,025,042	64 0		5
1843	958,057	22	3,321,508	78	4,279,565	54 4		5
1844	833,856	21	3,223,618	79	4,057,474	51 5		4 1
1845	844,816	21	3,272,629	79	4,117,445	49 2		4 1
1846	804,101	20	3,207,819	80	4,011,920	53 3		4
1847	899,095	21	3,467,960	79	4,367,055	59 0		5

* These numbers are for the Quarter ended Lady-Day in each Yea

NOTE.—The above expenditure is for In-Maintenance and Out-R
charges, or workhouse loans repaid. An estimate is made for places not u

The information as regards Pauperism and Expenditure was extra
the several Unions.

Poor Law Commission. *Fourteenth Annual Report*, Appendi
No 2 (1848)

intenance and Out-Relief, and the Number of In-Door
h of the Years ended at Lady-Day, 1840 to 1847, inclusive;
te per head of such Expenditure, and the Ratio per Cent.
rage price of Wheat per Quarter in each Year.

Population for each Year estimated according to the ratio of Increase.	Number of Paupers relieved (including Children).					Ratio per Cent. of Total Number of Paupers relieved to Population.
	In-Door.	Proportion per Cent. to Total.	Out-Door.	Proportion per Cent. to Total.	*Total In-Door and Out-Door.	
5,562,000	169,232	14	1,030,297	86	1,199,529	7·7
5,770,000	192,106	15	1,106,942	85	1,299,048	8·2
5,981,000	222,642	16	1,204,545	84	1,427,187	8·9
5,194,000	238,560	15	1,300,930	85	1,539,490	9·5
5,410,000	230,818	16	1,246,743	84	1,477,561	9·0
5,629,000	215,325	15	1,255,645	85	1,470,970	8·8
5,851,000	200,270	15	1,131,819	85	1,332,089	7·9
7,076,000	265,037	15	1,456,313	85	1,721,350	10·1

, and does not include salaries to paid officers and other establishment
Poor Law Amendment Act.

ı the Quarterly Abstracts received from the Clerks to the Guardians of

19182. Sir *J. Pakington.*] Is it your opinion that is the course which justice required, or the course which the Act prescribes?— I think it is the course the Act requires; a joint proceeding, a regular and stated proceeding.

19183. *Chairman.*] You have used the words "casual meetings;" in what way did you apply the word "casual" to any of the meetings that have reference to Mr. Parker's resignation; do you mean that it was a fortuitous and accidental circumstance of the two gentlemen meeting together?—I think Sir Edmund Head[1] going into Mr. Lewis's room, and Mr. Lewis going into Sir Edmund Head's room, not at any settled time, or with any order of procedure of business, or regulations for taking that business in an orderly and methodical manner, would not meet my conception of the intentions of the Legislature, or conceptions governed by ordinary proceedings of regular Boards, or what was intended to be the proceedings of a Board. In the second section of the Act it is prescribed that "the said Commissioners, or any two of them, may sit from time to time, as they deem it expedient, as a Board." Now by sitting as a Board is always, to my mind, implied order of fixed proceedings, which would not attach to these meetings in a room without order, or minutes made at the time.

(*b*) *Thomas Frankland Lewis:*

22502. Was any statement then made to him?—Yes, by me. I stated to Mr. Chadwick, "I have been greatly surprised at the claim which you have communicated to us through Mr. Lefevre. I have served on a great many Boards, and have seen a great many secretaries, and I never in my life thought of the possibility of there existing on the part of a secretary, a claim of right to be present at the Board, therefore I cannot admit it in your case; and I tell you fairly that I never shall be able to admit it; it is against my entire conviction on the subject." I took the Act of

---

[1] Sir Edmund Head, an Assistant Poor Law Commissioner since 1836, had been appointed a Poor Law Commissioner on the retirement of Shaw Lefevre in 1841. He was a close friend of G. C. Lewis.

Parliament, and read to him the clause which enables us to dismiss the secretary. I said to him, "Mr. Chadwick, we have authority to dismiss you, and I put it to your own judgment, do you suppose it possible, in the nature of things, if we had to deliberate among one another upon the subject of dismissing you, you could have a right to sit there, and hear the reasons we urged with one another on the subject? The thing appears to be impossible;" and with that I believe I closed it, because I did not pretend to give him anything more than my own opinion, which I was prepared to act upon if necessary.

22620. Am I right in supposing that on the whole you thought Mr. Chadwick a dangerous man?—I think if I had trusted the business of the office to Mr. Chadwick's guidance and management, he would have got me into innumerable difficulties.

22620. (*sic*) That is no answer to my question?—Well, then, if you will have it you must. Mr. Chadwick was an able man, but I thought him as unscrupulous and as dangerous an officer as I ever saw within the walls of an office.

22621. Having expressed to us that opinion of Mr. Chadwick, can you explain your having remained Chief Poor-law Commissioner for four years, with the power of removing him, and having allowed him for that time to remain Secretary?—Because I thought, by the arrangements of the business, I had kept it in my own hands, and taken it out of his, and that I was secure by having so done; and I assure the Committee that whatever might have been my dread of Mr. Chadwick, from the apprehension of the mischief he might lead me into by the stringency of his views upon Poor-law administration, and by his laxity in the administration in the conduct of business, I never said a word to any living soul that could injure his reputation, or lower his estimation with any human creature. I upheld the business of the office as well as I could, contending against such difficulties as I was exposed to; but as you have extracted from me that opinion of Mr. Chadwick, I abide by it. Select Committee on the Andover Union. V, Parts I & II, *Evidence of E. Chad-*

wick Q 19181-183. Evidence of T. F. Lewis Q 22502, 22620-21
(1846)

---

34 Sir George Grey   The Poor Law Board

Sir George Grey, Home Secretary in the Whig Government,
announced in this speech in the House of Commons in May
1847 the end of the Poor Law Commission and its replacement
by a new central authority, the Poor Law Board, which, it
was hoped, would not suffer from the constitutional weaknesses of its predecessor.

We have felt that we ought to maintain the principle of the
administration of the Poor Law established in the year 1834,
which was that of combining local administration with a general
superintending and central authority. But though that principle
was recognised, the question for us to consider was in what
manner the central authority invested with discretionary power,
could most advantageously be composed. In the year 1834,
when an extensive change was made in the law, it was thought
that the persons who were to be invested with the discretionary
powers to be exercised by a central authority ought not to form
any part of the Executive Government; that they should remain
free from that popular influence which must necessarily operate
in a greater or less degree upon all public men—upon all who
take part in carrying on the government of the country. It was
at that time thought better, also, that no political changes should
be allowed to affect those who were to be entrusted with these
powers. Upon these grounds, the Poor Law Commission was
separated from the Executive Government; and doubtless there
was at the time much to be urged in favour of such an arrangement; but we must consider it now in the light of experience.
Looking to the results of that arrangement, and appealing to
that experience by which alone it can be tried, I think I may
assert that it has not been as successful as was anticipated. The
responsibility of the Poor Law Commissioners to Parliament was
indirect and imperfect. The power they exercised was free from

that check which is imposed upon those public functionaries who are obliged to listen in this House to charges made against them, either by Members of Parliament, or suggested by other parties; and, on the other hand, they were not enabled to explain their official conduct in this House—they were not enabled to answer their accusers face to face, and their vindication has been for this reason necessarily incomplete. They have laboured under a manifest disadvantage in this respect. When complaints as to any of the ordinary departments of the Government are made, the representative of that department is familiar with the details of the subject to which the complaint relates: he has followed them, step by step; he knows the correspondence relating to it, and remembers the reasons which led to the course that has been pursued; and, therefore, he is able to state fully the grounds of his vindication, and to offer, if not a satisfactory, at least a full and complete explanation of the conduct of the department which he represents. But, under the existing Poor Law Commission, what really happens? Complaints are made, and questions asked of the Home Secretary respecting some matter connected with the administration of the Poor Law. The Home Secretary is expected to give an answer; and his first answer almost necessarily is, that he is entirely ignorant of the matter, but that he will inquire into the facts of the case, and come down on a future day and give a reply; and, consequently, either by personal conversation, or written communication, he obtains an explanation from the Commissioners; but still without a knowledge of all the circumstances which led to the act in question; and in this state he is expected to give full information to the House on the subject. This, unquestionably, leads to great inconvenience; and the administration of the law has been, to a certain degree, prejudiced by it. The principle, therefore, of the Bill which I have to propose is in accordance with what fell from my noble Friend at the head of the Government at the beginning of the Session, namely, that there shall be a general superintending authority immediately responsible to Parliament. My general proposition is, that the existing powers shall be transferred to a new Board, which in its constitution will be similar to the Board of Control.[1] The chief Member of the Board will be called the President, and he will be responsible for the ordinary administration of the law. But associated with the President of the Board there will be certain Members of the Cabinet, *ex-officio* members of the Board, namely, the President of the Council, the Lord Privy Seal, one of the Secretaries of State, and the Chancellor of the Exchequer. There will also be two Secretaries to the Board, and it is proposed that the President and one of the Secretaries shall be allowed to have seats in Parliament. I do not say that they both shall have seats in the House; but it is essential that the Board shall be directly represented in this House either by the President or Secretary.

Hansard. *Parlt Debates*, 3rd Series, Vol XCII, Cols 341-3

---

[1] For India.

PART THREE

The Poor Law
in Operation, 1834-71

The Poor Law Board took over from the Poor Law Commission as the central authority for poor-law administration in England and Wales on 17 December 1847. In 1871 it was absorbed into the new Local Government Board, and in 1919 control of the poor-law system passed to the Ministry of Health.

THE CENTRAL AUTHORITY AND THE BOARDS OF GUARDIANS

Throughout these changes, local poor relief remained in the hands of the boards of guardians, who continued to exercise power until they were dissolved by the Local Government Act of 1929 (96). The majority of guardians were elected annually, each parish in the Union electing one or more guardians in proportion to its population. Unless some local controversy happened to be agitating the ratepayers, there was massive public apathy towards the elections, and many small parishes returned the same representative to the board year after year, without even the formality of a contest. Voting, when it took place, was by open ballot. Voting papers were delivered to the houses of those eligible to vote, and collected later by the parish overseer and his assistants. Corrupt practices were thus made easy, and there were frequent allegations of rigged elections, some of which were substantiated.

There was usually little need to resort to underhand means to gain election to a board of guardians. Such was the unpopularity of the office that there were frequent complaints that persons of social standing were refusing to offer themselves for election, and even those who were *ex officio* members of their local board because they were justices of the peace were said to be infrequent in their attendance at the weekly, or fortnightly, board meetings. The composition of most boards of guardians came to be weighted heavily in favour of the lower middle classes, urban parishes being frequently represented by shopkeepers or publicans, and rural ones by small farmers. Such men earned the contempt of contemporaries and later historians as being self-interested to the point of corruption, hard-hearted and guardians of the rates rather than of the poor (35). Such conduct was inevitable where men of limited education and with all too little time to spare from their own concerns were called upon to perform an unpleasant and often difficult public duty. Some boards, particularly those in the big cities, were conscientious, and others seem to have treated applicants for relief with a rough but genuine kindness (36).

The guardians' chief duties were the appointment of salaried officers, the relieving officer and the workhouse master being the most important; settling relief applications brought before them by the relieving officer; the supervision of the workhouse; and the expenditure, though not the collection, of the poor rate. In performing these tasks, the board often divided into committees, such as the visiting committee responsible for making regular inspections of the workhouse. Relief applications were frequently heard by small committees rather than by the full board, despite the disapproval of the central authority, which feared such a practice might presage a return to a parochial system of relief.

Although relations with the central authority became less strained than they had been in the early years of the New Poor Law, the local authorities remained suspicious of the activities of the Poor Law Commissioners and their successors at the Poor Law Board. By the late 1840s, Somerset House and its overworked inspectorate were coming to learn that more could be achieved by tactful advice and persuasion than by administrative fiat. Even so boards of guardians often did all in their power to evade inconvenient regulations and protested strongly at any interference with their powers of discretion in giving relief (38).

35 Joseph Rogers   A Corrupt Guardian

Joseph Rogers, a brother of the economist Thorold Rogers, began his medical practice in London in 1844. In 1856 he was appointed medical officer to the Strand Union, but was later dismissed by the board of guardians. He was later appointed medical officer to the Westminster Union, was suspended by the guardians, but reinstated in 1883 after appealing to the Local Government Board. He was a strong advocate of work-house reform, particularly for the sick, and was a founder member of the Poor Law Medical Officers' Association.

Here let me remark that there is no occupation that can be followed at which so much money can be made as by the system adopted by some speculators of taking houses in poor localities and letting them out in single rooms to the humbler classes. To get therefrom all the benefit possible you must be absolutely heartless and unprincipled. If the wretched tenants do not pay their rent weekly, they must go out—and do go! Having, after their weekly collections, much spare time on their hands, these men often get on to Boards of Guardians and frequently on to the District Boards[1] as well: at the first they are always present when outdoor relief is given, which they strongly advocate as a means whereby the rent may be more readily secured; secondly, on the District Boards, where they are always at hand when the Inspector of Nuisances and of insanitary tenement houses makes his report. They generally try to be on the best of terms with this latter official, their scheme being to minimize the character of their reports, and to minimize what is required to be done, as it saves their pockets. One of these persons, who had some three

[1] Local boards of health established under the Public Health Act of 1848.

hundred of these houses, was fined by the magistrate for neglect-
ing to keep his houses in a sanitary condition. I had the honour
of his permanent hostility. He was, at the time of being fined,
not only a member of the Board, but of the Health Committee
also. When I was a member of the Strand Board of Works I
carried a resolution that the name of the owner of these tenements
should be always included in the Inspector's Report. In my
deliberate judgment, all persons of this class should be disqualified from sitting on a Board of Guardians, or on any
District Board. The same class of middlemen are to be found in
all large towns; they are the most dangerous members of the
body politic, and should be rigorously treated as such. The
person I have before referred to, was not only a member of the
Strand Board of Guardians but a member of the District Board
also. He was also on that of St. Giles, and St. Pancras. In all
these places, and districts, he had tenement houses. Joseph
Rogers. *Reminiscences of a Medical Officer* (1889), 78–9

36 R. A. Arnold   A Board of Guardians at Work, 1862

R. A. Arnold, a civil servant, journalist and later Liberal MP
for Salford, wrote his account of the Cotton Famine from
experience gained during a three-year tour of duty in Lancashire as an inspector of public works under the 1863 Act (43).
Here he repeats an account of a board of guardians interview-
ing applicants for relief which had first appeared in a Manchester newspaper in June 1862. The reporter obviously made
a clear distinction between the deserving and undeserving
poor, and the guardians' attitude was doubtless conditioned
by the unusual economic circumstances of a period in which
they had been urged to be generous.

The following extract from one of the letters of the correspondent of the *Manchester Examiner*, depicts a scene not unfamiliar
to those who, through business or curiosity, were present at the
meetings of the boards of guardians:—

A clean, old, decrepit man presented himself. 'What's brought you here, Joseph?' said the chairman. 'Why; aw've nought to do,—nor nought to tak to.' 'What's your daughter, Ellen, doing, Joseph?' 'Hoo's eawt o' wark.' 'An' what's your wife doing?' 'Hoo's bin bed-fast aboon five year.' The old man was relieved at once; but, as he walked away, he looked hard at his ticket, as if it wasn't exactly the kind of thing; and, turning round, he said, 'Couldn't yo let me be a sweeper i' th' streets, istid, Mr. Eccles?' A clean old woman came up, with a snow-white night-cap on her head. 'Well, Mary, what do you want?' 'Aw could like yo to gi mo a bit o' summat, Mr. Eccles,—for aw need it.' 'Well, but you've some lodgers, haven't you, Mary?' 'Yigh, aw've three.' 'Well; what do they pay you?' 'They pay'n mo nought. They'n no wark,—an' one connot turn 'em eawt.' This was all quite true. 'Well, but you live with your son don't you?' continued the chairman. 'Nay,' replied the old woman, '*he* lives wi' *me;* an' he's eawt o' wark, too. Aw could like yo to do a bit o' summat for us. We're hard put to't.' 'Don't you think she would be better in the workhouse?' said one of the guardians. 'Oh, no,' replied another, 'don't send th' owd woman there. Let her keep her own little place together, if she can.' Another old woman presented herself, with a threadbare shawl drawn closely round her grey head. 'Well, Ann,' said the chairman, 'there's nobody but yourself and your John, is there?' 'Naw.' What age are you?' 'Aw'm seventy.' 'Seventy!' 'Aye, aw am.' 'Well, and what age is your John?' 'He's gooin' i' scvcnty-four.' 'Where is he, Ann?' 'Well, aw laft him deawn i' th' street yon, gettin' a load o' coals in.' There was a murmur of approbation around the board; and the old woman was sent away relieved and thankful. There were many of all ages, clean in person, and bashful in manner, with their poor clothing put into the tidiest possible trim; others were dirty, and sluttish, and noisy of speech, as in the case of one woman, who, after receiving her ticket for relief, partly in money and partly in kind, whipped a pair of worn clogs from under her shawl, and cried out, 'Aw mun ha' some clogs afore aw go, too; look at thoose. They're a shame to be sin!' Clogs were freely given; and, in several cases, they were all that was asked for. One decent-looking old body, with a starved face, applied. The chairman said, 'Why what's your son doing now? Has he catched no rabbits lately?' 'Nay, aw dunnot know at he does. Aw get nought, an' it's *me* at want's summat, Mr. Eccles,' replied the old woman, in a tremulous tone, with the water rising in her eyes. 'Well, come; we mustn't punish th' owd woman for her son,' said one of the guardians. R. A. Arnold. *History of the Cotton Famine* (1864), 150-53

OUTDOOR RELIEF

Although it began to issue orders for the distribution of relief as soon as the first Unions were formed in 1835, the Poor Law Commission issued no General Order on the subject until 1841. All previous orders took the form of 'Particular Orders' issued separately to one union or parish at a time and therefore not subject, as General Rules were, to being submitted to the Home Secretary and laid before Parliament. By the time its career ended in 1847, however, the Poor Law Commission had issued two General Orders on the subject of relief. The strictest of these was the Outdoor Relief Prohibitory Order, issued in its final form in 1844 (37A). This laid down that relief to able-bodied men and women and their families was to be given only in the work-house, subject to certain exceptions. Large-scale unemployment together with the determined resistance to the New Poor Law in the manufacturing areas of the country, particularly in Lan-cashire and the West Riding, had shown the Poor Law Com-missioners that the issue of such an Order to Unions in these areas would be both ineffective and hazardous. Most of these Unions were therefore subjected to the less stringent Outdoor Labour Test Order of 1842 (37B), which stated that able-bodied men were not to receive relief unless they performed a task of work set them by the board of guardians. Such task work was to be of a monotonous and unpleasant nature, and thus to take the place of the workhouse in maintaining the principle of 'less eligibility' (39).

On taking office in 1847 the Poor Law Board found a large number of Unions in which relief, even to the able bodied, was subject only to the loosest of controls by the central authority. To remedy this situation, they issued a third General Order, the Outdoor Relief Regulation Order, in 1852. In its original form, this Order was intended to control the conditions under which relief was given, not only to the able bodied, but also to the sick and aged (37C). A storm of protest greeted the publication of the Order, and indignant boards of guardians protested to Somerset House at this unwarranted interference with their cherished powers of discretion (38). The Poor Law Board retreated before the storm and amended their Order to cover mostly able-bodied males. The usual exceptions were listed and the Instructional Letter accompanying the Order further weakened its conditions particularly in its prohibition of relief in aid of wages to able-bodied men (37C).

Given the exceptions listed in the Orders, and the lack of any hard and fast definition of such terms as 'able bodied', most boards of guardians found themselves left with considerable latitude in the granting of outdoor relief. Guardians, particularly those in urban industrial areas, much preferred to give outdoor relief than an order for the workhouse. In part their preference was dictated by common sense and humanity. Entry into the workhouse meant breaking up a family. If confined in a workhouse, an unemployed man would be unable to find another job quickly. Outdoor relief was cheaper, for the ratepayers would be forced to bear the full cost of maintaining an applicant and his family if they were taken into the workhouse. A grant of outdoor relief, however, could be augmented by small earnings and receipts from private charity. Boards of guardians and relieving officers openly admitted that the few shillings they gave applicants for outdoor relief were inadequate for their maintenance and would have to be supplemented from other sources which were rarely investigated (40). Relief in aid of wages continued, in some cases to able-bodied men, particularly those in casual work or declining handicraft trades, in many more to widows and old people, who were not included in the prohibitions laid down in the Relief Regulation Order (41).

This practice of uncontrolled inadequate outdoor relief came under increasing criticism in the 1860s. Alarm was particularly expressed about the rapid growth of charitable agencies which were often helping those already relieved by the boards of guardians. Such practices, it was feared, were creating an army of paupers in the great cities, specially in London. A Select Committee that carried out a detailed investigation of the state of poor relief between 1861 and 1864 condemned the practice in its final report. In 1869, the President of the Poor Law Board, G. J. Goschen, further condemned charitable supplements to poor relief and appealed for co-operation between private and public relief agencies to prevent overlapping. The growing desire for such co-ordinated action led to the foundation of the Charity Organisation Society (66).

A further challenge to the relief policies of the Poor Law Board and the boards of guardians in the 1860s came as a result of the Lancashire Cotton Famine. One of the arguments frequently put forward by guardians in the industrial Unions of Lancashire and the West Riding for allowing them the fullest discretion in relief matters had been that, in periods of economic distress, respectable working men who were genuinely unemployed ought to be relieved separately from the idle or dissolute paupers. The Cotton Famine threw large numbers of such respectable artisans out of work, and faced them with the possibility of having to apply for poor relief. The Poor Law Board urged boards of guardians in Lancashire to be generous in their distribution of relief to unemployed operatives. Subscriptions were raised by private charities and distributed by local relief committees in order to provide workers with an honourable alternative to the poor relief they scorned. Yet several critics argued that, in such an emergency, both poor-law and private charity were inadequate to save the workers' self-respect. The situation, in their view, called for extraordinary action by the Government (42). This demand was partly met by the Public Works Act of 1863, which gave powers to local authorities to borrow money at a low rate of interest from the Public Works Loan Commissioners in order to finance town improvement schemes and give employment (43). Although too late and too little to have any great practical effect, the Act was important in that it showed that the established poor-law system was inadequate to cope with the problems of mass unemployment. In later years this was to prove one of the most telling arguments against the English poor law.

37A Poor Law Commission   Outdoor Relief Prohibitory Order, December 1844

This was the strictest of the Orders, and prohibited outdoor relief to both able-bodied men and women, though in exceptional circumstances the Guardians might legally depart from the order.

ARTICLE I.—Every able-bodied person, male or female, requiring relief from any Parish within any of the said Unions, shall be relieved wholly in the Workhouse of the Union, together with such of the family of every such able-bodied person as may be resident with him or her, and may not be in employment, and together with the wife of every such able-bodied male person, if he be a married man, and if she be resident with him; save and except in the following cases:—

  1st. Where such person shall require relief on account of sudden and urgent necessity.
  2d. Where such person shall require relief on account of any sickness, accident, or bodily or mental infirmity affecting such person, or any of his or her family.
  3d. Where such person shall require relief for the purpose of defraying the expenses, either wholly or in part, of the burial of any of his or her family.
  4th. Where such person, being a widow, shall be in the first six months of her widowhood.

5th. Where such person shall be a widow, and have a legitimate child or legitimate children dependent upon her, and incapable of earning his, her, or their livelihood, and have no illegitimate child born after the commencement of her widowhood.

6th. Where such person shall be confined in any gaol or place of safe custody.

7th. Where such person shall be the wife, or child, of any able-bodied man who shall be in the service of Her Majesty as a soldier, sailor, or marine.

8th. Where any able-bodied person, not being a soldier, sailor, or marine, shall not reside within the Union, but the wife, child, or children of such person shall reside within the same, the Board of Guardians of the Union, according to their discretion, may, subject to the regulation contained in Article 4, afford relief in the Workhouse to such wife, child, or children, or may allow out-door relief for any such child or children being within the age of nurture, and resident with the mother within the Union.

Art. 5.—It shall not be lawful for the Guardians, or any of their Officers, or for the Overseer or Overseers of any Parish in the Union, to pay, wholly or in part, the rent of the house or lodging of any pauper, or to apply any portion of the relief ordered to be given to any pauper in payment of any such rent, or to retain any portion of such relief for the purpose of directly or indirectly discharging such rent, in full or in part, for any such pauper.

Art. 6.—Provided always, that in case the Guardians of any of the said Unions depart in any particular instance from any of the regulations hereinbefore contained, and within fifteen days after such departure report the same, and the grounds thereof, to the Poor Law Commissioners, and the Poor Law Commissioners approve of such departure, then the relief granted in such particular instance shall, if otherwise lawful, not be deemed to be unlawful, or be subject to be disallowed. W. C. Glen.

General Orders of the Poor Law Commissioners (1852), 309-12, 317-18

37B Poor Law Commission   Outdoor Labour Test Order, April 1842

This Order was intended mainly for Unions in industrial areas where economic circumstances and often the attitude of the board of guardians made a workhouse test impossible. It covered only able-bodied males, and was subject to the same exceptions as the Prohibitory Order. In some cases, the Order was issued to Unions where the Prohibitory Order was in force, thus giving the Guardians the alternative of offering the workhouse or the work test to able-bodied male paupers.

ART. I.—Every able-bodied male pauper receiving relief from any Parish within the Union, and not relieved in the workhouse, shall be relieved in the following manner: that is to say,—

Half at least of the relief given to such pauper shall be given in food, clothing, and other articles of necessity.

No such pauper shall receive relief from the Guardians of the Union, or any of their Officers, or any Overseer of any Parish in the Union, while he is employed for wages or other hire or remuneration by any person; but every such pauper so relieved shall be set to work by the Guardians.

ART. 2.—The place or places at which able-bodied male paupers shall be so set to work in the Union; the sort or sorts of work in which they or any of them shall be employed, the times and mode of work, and all other matters relating to the employment of such able-bodied paupers, shall be fixed and regulated in such manner as the Poor Law Commissioners shall direct, upon a report being made to them by the Guardians respecting the employment of such able-bodied paupers; which report the Guardians shall transmit to the said Commissioners within fourteen days after the day when this Order shall come into force.

K

W. C. Glen. *General Orders of the Poor Law Commissioners* (1852), 364–5.

37C Poor Law Board Outdoor Relief Regulation Orders, 1852

The original Order of August 1852 (*a*) covered the sick, aged and widows as well as able-bodied men and women. The amended order of December 1852 (*b*) was restricted to able-bodied men; the prohibition on relief in aid of wages, Article 5, remained, but it was subject to numerous exceptions. In addition, the Instructional Letter (*c*) issued with the December Order made it even easier for guardians to avoid interpreting Article 5 too strictly.

(*a*) *August 1852:*

Article 1. Whenever the Guardians shall allow relief to any indigent poor person, out of the Workhouse, *one third* at least of such relief allowed to any person who shall be indigent and helpless from age, sickness, accident, or bodily or mental infirmity, or who shall be a widow having a child or children dependent on her incapable of working, and *one half* at least of the relief allowed to any able-bodied person, other than such widow as aforesaid, shall be given in articles of food or fuel, or in other articles of absolute necessity.

Article 2. In any case in which the Guardians allow relief for a longer period than one week to an indigent poor person, without requiring that such person shall be received into the Workhouse, such relief shall be given or administered weekly.

(*b*) *December 1852:*

ARTICLE 1. Whenever the Guardians allow relief to any able-bodied male person, out of the workhouse, one half at least of the relief so allowed shall be given in articles of food or fuel, or in other articles of absolute necessity.

ARTICLE 2. In any case in which the Guardians allow relief

for a longer period than one week to an indigent poor person, resident within their Union or Parish respectively, without re-quiring that such person shall be received into the workhouse, such relief shall be given or administered weekly, or at such more frequent periods as they may deem expedient.

ARTICLE 3. It shall not be lawful for the Guardians or their officers—

To establish any applicant for relief in trade or business;

Nor to redeem from pawn for any such applicant any tools, implements, or other articles;

Nor to purchase and give to such applicant any tools, imple-ments, or other articles, except articles of clothing or bedding where urgently needed, and such articles as are herein-before referred to in Art. 1.;

Nor to pay, wholly or in part, the rent of the house or lodging of any pauper, nor to apply any portion of the relief ordered to be given to any pauper in payment of any such rent, nor to retain any portion of such relief for the purpose of directly or indirectly discharging such rent, in full or in part, for any such pauper;

Article 5. No relief shall be given to any able-bodied male person while he is employed for wages or other hire or remunera-tion by any person.

Article 6. Every able-bodied male person, if relieved out of the workhouse, shall be set to work by the Guardians, and be kept employed under their direction and superintendence so long as he continues to receive relief.

(c) *Instructional Letter, December 1852:*

Article 5 prohibits the giving relief to able-bodied male paupers while employed for wages. The evils of such a system of relief have been found so great in practice as to be almost universally admitted, and are prominently indicated by the

Legislature in the 4 & 5 William 4. cap. 76. s. 52. as forming the principal ground on which the Poor Law Commissioners were by that Act invested with the power and charged with the duty of making regulations for the due administration of relief to able-bodied persons. The Board desire, however, to point out, that what it is intended actually to prohibit is the giving relief at the same identical time as that at which the person receiving it is in actual employment, and in the receipt of wages, (unless he falls within any of the exceptions afterwards set forth), and that relief given in any other case, as, for instance, in that of a man working for wages on one day and being without work the next, or working half the week and being unemployed during the remainder, and being then in need of relief, is not prohibited by this Article.

Article 6 is framed to meet an ordinary state of circumstances, and the Board must remark with satisfaction, that there appears to be nothing in the existing state of things to prevent its being carried into full operation. If, however, owing to any commercial pressure or general depression of trade, large masses of people should hereafter be thrown out of employment, the Board admit that great difficulty would exist in giving full effect to the provisions of the Article. In such an emergency, instances of which have occurred in former years, the Board would, upon the representation of the Guardians, be prepared at once, as on former occasions, to take such steps, by temporary suspension of this Article or otherwise, as might be expedient to meet satisfactorily and effectually the difficulty experienced. As a general rule, however, applicable to all ordinary circumstances, the Board believe that this Article is both practicable and well calculated to aid in securing a due administration of relief to the able-bodied male poor. Poor Law Board. *Fifth Annual Report*, Appendices 1 & 3 (1852)

---

38 Blackburn Union   A Protest against the Relief Regulation Order

These resolutions passed by the Blackburn (Lancs) board of

guardians were among many received by the Poor Law Board as a result of their issuing the Relief Regulation Order of August 1852. Most of the protests came from guardians in Lancashire, the West Riding, and London—complaining of interference with their discretionary powers over relief, particularly with regard to that given to the sick and aged poor and to the supplementary relief given to handicraft workers to tide them over a period of low earnings.

RESOLUTIONS unanimously passed at a Meeting of the Guardians of the Poor of this Union, held the 9th day of October 1852.

1st. That the carrying into effect of the various provisions of this Order would, in many cases, involve the infliction of extreme hardship upon poor and deserving persons who are, or may be compelled to apply to the local Poor Law authorities for relief.

2d. That although it is important and advantageous to make a distinction in the nature of the relief to be given to indigent and deserving poor persons above a certain age (the age of 60 years, for instance), as compared with that given to younger and able-bodied persons; yet the recent Order draws no such distinction, and the same rule is applied in all cases to the relief of the indigent and helpless out-door poor, whether rendered necessary by age, sickness, accident, bodily or mental infirmity, and without any power of modification being reserved to the local authorities.

3d. That it would be extremely difficult for Guardians to determine (especially for aged and sick poor), what kind of food or articles should be given, and the means to be adopted for obtaining them, so satisfactorily and economically as the poor themselves can provide them, and that, in the opinion of the Guardians, a greater amount of relief would be required to meet the same degree of indigence.

4th. That, in reference to the Article No. 5, the Guardians are of opinion, that (so far as it is intelligible from the wording thereof), it is quite incapable of being carried out; and that, if it is meant to apply to the case, for instance, of a poor hand-loom weaver, who at his regular employment is unable to earn more than 8*s.* per week, and out of this pittance must either support a wife and five or six small children, or submit to leave his regular trade, and go to the workhouse, at a ruinous cost to his township, it is wholly inconsistent with the meaning and provisions of the Statute 43 Elizabeth, c. 2 (the basis of all our system of poor laws), and is calculated to produce an alarming increase of pauperism.

5th. That, in reference to the other Articles of the Order, the Board are of opinion that they become mischievous and impracticable, on account of their entirely prohibiting character, and that the principles being acquiesced in to a certain extent, the discretionary application thereof should have been left to the experience and humanity of the Guardians.

6th. That, considering the respectability of Boards of Guardians, and the attention and economy with which they devote themselves to the fulfilment of their gratuitous duties, a full discretionary power might safely be entrusted to them, and would not only imply a wise and courteous acknowledgment of their arduous services, but would be attended with increased comforts to the poor at a less outlay to the ratepayers.

Also resolved unanimously, That the clerk be directed to forward a copy of the foregoing Resolutions to the Poor Law Board, respectfully soliciting attention thereto, in the hope to induce the Board to reconsider the conditions of the Order, with a view to rescind the same. *Parlt Papers*, LXXXIV (1852-3), 28-9

39 Poplar Union   A Labour Test

As an alternative to the workhouse, the labour test was supposed to maintain the principles of 'less eligibility'. The central authority insisted that the work should be hard, monotonous and unprofitable, stone breaking and oakum-picking (separating the fibres of old ropes) being the most usual. Guardians were not encouraged to develop more interesting types of work, such as farm labour; and some who tried to hire out pauper labour to railway contractors in the 1840s were warned against interfering with the labour market.

POPLAR UNION.

Regulations to be observed in the Stone Yard at the Workhouse of this Union.

1. The hours of labour to be from 9 A.M. to 12 noon, and from 1 to 5 P.M.

2. The gates of the yard to be opened at a quarter before the hour of commencing work, and no labourer will be admitted after half past 9 A.M. or half past 1 P.M.

3. The superintendent of labour shall employ every man sent into the yard by the relieving officers to the utmost of his ability, either in stone-breaking, oakum-picking, or other work in connexion therewith, as may be best suited to his age, strength, and capacity.

4. Each man employed at stone-breaking shall be required to break 5 bushels of granite per day, and each man employed at oakum-picking shall be required to pick 4 lbs. of beaten oakum or 2 lbs. of unbeaten oakum per day.

5. At 4 o'clock the superintendent of labour is to proceed to measure or weigh the tasks performed, and to fill up the tickets for the workers.

6. Where any worker has performed less than his task, but the superintendent of labour shall be of opinion that he has used his best endeavours to do so, the superintendent of labour shall note on the back of the ticket "has worked to the best of his ability all day," the relieving officer will then grant relief as if the task had been performed, and report the case to the Board at their next meeting.

7. Where any worker has not performed his task, and has not, in the opinion of the superintendent of labour, worked to the best of his ability, the superintendent of labour shall note the same on the back of the ticket, and the relieving officer will then grant such relief as the case may require, and report the circumstances to the Board at their next meeting.

8. The superintendent of labour shall report to the Board of Guardians at their weekly meeting the name of any person whom he considers able to perform a greater task than is herein mentioned.

9. The following shall be the scale of relief for those working in the yard during the whole week, a proportion whereof shall be given each day, but the amount will be reduced where any worker has been absent any part of the working hours without having performed the task set him, or without special leave from the Board of Guardians, the relieving officer, or the superintendent of labour.

SCALE OF RELIEF.

Bread.

4-lb. loaves per week.

For a man with a wife and 1 child - 3 ⎫
     ,,   ,,   2 children 4 ⎪
     ,,   ,,   3 ,, 5 ⎪
     ,,   ,,   4 ,, 6 ⎬ With 6*d*. per day in
     ,,   ,,   5 ,, 7 ⎪ money for 6 days.
     ,,   ,,   6 ,, 8 ⎪
     ,,   ,,   7 ,, 9 ⎪
     ,,   ,,   8 ,, 10 ⎭

For a single man - - - 3 And 3*d*. per day for
                                      6 days.

A widower with children will be allowed the same relief as if he had a wife.

By Order,

JAMES RIPLEY COLLINS,

Board Room, 9th July 1867.   Clerk.

Poor Law Board. *Twentieth Annual Report* (1867–8), Appendix, 122

---

40 Rev C. H. Carr   Inadequate Relief

The Rev C. H. Carr, Vicar of St John's, Limehouse, and chaplain of the Stepney Union, gave evidence before the Select Committee of 1861 on the practice of giving small amounts of relief in the expectation that these would be made up from other sources.

___

3725. With respect to those instances which you have given of persons who received inadequate relief, do you think that the guardians have any knowledge of their having any other source of income, except private charity?—I do not think that they have any other source of income, and I do not think that the guardians are aware of their having any other source of income.

3726. Do you think, then, that the guardians in your parish systematically give to the poor people a less amount of relief than is sufficient to keep them alive?—Certainly.

3727. You think that the operation of the pressure on the ratepayers upon the minds of your guardians is such, that in the distribution of relief they systematically do not give enough to keep their poor people alive?—Certainly.

3728. Have you ever taken any steps to have so appalling a state of things brought under the attention of the guardians of your parish?—I believe that the guardians are aware of it, and as has been already stated, they do not profess to give out-door relief sufficient to sustain life. I have the very striking case of Mrs. Richardson, who supports a bed-ridden sister who cannot do anything at all; she receives from the Board 1s. 6d. a week, and off and on half a pound of meat a day, which is not continued, excepting that it has just been put on; occasionally, it is given her. By her needlework she makes 1s. 6d. to 2s. 9d. a week, and her rent varies from 1s. 6d. to 2s. 3d., according as she can get her house full of lodgers. She receives 1s. 6d. a week, and she makes 2s. 9d., that is 4s. 3d., and she pays at the lowest rate 1s. 6d. for rent; that leaves 2s. 9d. for the week to live upon. I believe that that is a perfectly true case, and that the guardians are aware of it; the half pound of meat a day was put on last week; it has been off for some time; I do not know why. Select Committee on Poor Relief (England). IX, *1st Report, Evidence of Rev C. H. Carr* (1861)

See *No 41*, p 156

To
   The Poor Law Board.

NAME	AGE	CALLING	WHERE CHARGEABLE
James Hartley	33	Power Weaver	Barnoldswi
Margaret, his wife	33	House work	,,
Hartley ..	12	None	,,
James ..Bastards	10	,,	,,
Richard..	8	,,	,,
Ann	3	,,	,,
William	1½	,,	,,
Christopher Starkie	38	Hand Loom Weaver	Barnoldswi
Mary Ann his Wife	39	,,	,,
Jabez	13	None, had Rheumatic Fever and not able to work	,,
Thurza	11	None	,,
O'Connor	7	,,	,,
Sarah Ann	6	,,	,,
John	4	,,	,,
Ezra	2	,,	,,
Mark Starkie	28	Hand Loom Weaver & House Work	Barnoldswi
Mary his Wife	28	Power Weaver	,,
Mary Ann	8	None	,,
Sarah	6	,,	,,
Elizabeth	5	,,	,,
Margaret	3	,,	,,
John William	1	,,	,,

'Union Clerk, Skipton, to Poor Law Board', PRO, MH 12/15515

RNINGS	RELIEF ORDERED	PERIOD	CAUSE OF SEEKING RELIEF	REASON FOR ASKING CONSENT OF POOR LAW BOARD TO OUT RELIEF
. o.	2. o.	3 weeks	Insufficiency of income	Small wages which are average for district
. o.	3. o.	3 weeks	Insufficiency of income	Same as above
. 6.				Son only poorly
. o.	2. o.	3 weeks	Insufficiency of income	Small wages which are average for the District
. o.				

41 Skipton Union   Relief in Aid of Wages

Despite the fierce attack the reformers of 1834 had launched
on the 'Speenhamland System', relief in aid of small wages or
earnings continued, particularly in Unions like Skipton in the
West Riding of Yorkshire, which was inhabited by a considerable number of distressed handloom weavers.

Skipton. 22nd Jany 1853.

My Lords and Gentlemen,
  I beg to enclose a Report of Cases in which the Guardians
think that Out Relief should be given. They chiefly arise from
the families being so large that they are unable to support them
out of their earnings. There is no want of application or industry
nor are their wages below the usual rate. The Guardians desire
that the orders which they have made should be extended so
long as their circumstances remain the same.
  I am,
    My Lords and Gent^m.
      Your most obed^t. Servt.
        Thomas Brown.   (See pp 154–5.)

---

42 W. M. Torrens   Poor Relief and the Cotton Famine

William MacCullagh Torrens (1813–94), a Dublin-born bar-
rister and Liberal politician, had gained some experience of
the poor law by serving as an assistant commissioner to the
commission on the proposed Irish poor law of 1835. As MP
for Finsbury after 1865 he took a keen interest in social reform,
his best known achievement being the Artisans Dwelling Act,
the 'Torrens Act', of 1868, which gave local authorities powers
to force improvement on owners of slum property.
  Torrens was critical of the policy pursued by the Poor Law
Board in face of the Lancashire Cotton Famine, and he expressed his criticism in an open letter to the Board's President,
C. P. Villiers, from which these passages are taken. Torrens
was strongly opposed to the Board's allowing guardians in

Lancashire to depart from the central authority's regulations when giving relief. He argued that poor relief should have been continued under the same strict conditions as before. Cotton operatives and the deserving unemployed, however, should never have been brought to the degradation of having to apply for relief. The Government should have stepped in at the earliest possible opportunity and helped local authorities to launch public works schemes in order to create alternative employment.

This notion of giving those thrown out of work by trade depression some alternative to poor relief was to be repeated later in the Chamberlain Circular and the Unemployed Workmen Act of 1905 (77).

Even if it could be shown to demonstration, that all the factory hands might have been carefully fed and comfortably clothed, during the suspension of mill-work, as paupers, that was not the method of relief which ought to have been preferred. Its superiority to all others in uniformity, discipline, and the prevention of fraud hardly admits of dispute: but there is something else to be considered, that, fairly set in the balance of social benefits, may well be thought to outweigh even these great considerations. Morally and industrially, it is a sad, nay, even a terrible thing, to tell a sober, intelligent, laborious, and orderly community, who have hitherto decently paid their way, kept house with modest hospitality, and brought up children in habits of industry and thrift,—that from and after a given day they and their little ones shall be flung down from the level on which they have dwelt, into the bare cold yard of destitution, there to be classed with the depraved, the idle, and the incorrigible; with tramps, and thieves, and strumpets, and all whom the law classes under the general name of vagabonds, of every degree; and all this for no fault of their own, nor from the lack of any forethought of theirs, whereby individually or collectively, they could have averted their sudden destitution for a day. To me it seems, I own, that such a sacrifice is one which society ought not to require,—that the humiliating condition precedent of relief is one which, putting aside all questions of abstract justice, it is not wise or expedient that society should impose. And what I deplore, in looking back through the annals of the last three years, is chiefly this—that while the old system of Relief out of Rates was disfavoured and almost denounced as inhumane and inopportune—whereby the benefits of order and economy were lost—the best men were nevertheless subjected to the humiliation of having to apply for aid in pauper guise, and to accept of pauper fare.

I am far from advocating the use of public money, whether as gift or loan, to constitute a permanent source of employment, at wages likely to detach men from other pursuits. That, I am sure, would be unadvisable. I plead for a temporary shelter, not a permanent home, for industry; but I am convinced that during the period of suspense or transition, use might be made of the time and of the labour of the rescued, to render good service and substantial benefit to the whole of the community. Is there not such a thing as spare work to be done as well as spare labour? Do not the disclosures of the last twelve months in Lancashire prove (if any proof were wanting) that there is abundance of necessary and useful work to be done in our great towns and cities, which nevertheless remains undone so long as trade is brisk and wages high? Will anyone who knows how the mass of the labouring population live, and in what sort of dens and styes they are condemned to dwell during the most prosperous times, deny that there is abundance of work to be done, were it only for sanitary purposes, over and above that for which we can reasonably expect highly-taxed ratepayers spontaneously to pay? W. M. Torrens. *Lancashire's Lesson* (1864), 36–8, 159–60

---

43 Robert Rawlinson   The Public Works Act
Robert Rawlinson (1810–98), a civil engineer, had been appointed a Government inspector under the Public Health Act

of 1848. In 1863 he was appointed inspecting engineer to supervise the sanitary and other works of improvement being carried out in Lancashire under the Public Works Act of that year. He proved to be a staunch defender of the Act against its many critics.

———

The borrowing powers given to Boards of Guardians, and of which they have readily availed themselves, as far as practicable, for the execution of works under the provisions of these Acts, have rendered most valuable assistance in removing one great difficulty which had been experienced; namely, providing labour for the able-bodied poor. The prevention of pauperism, through the medium of these works, has, I am informed, been at the least to an extent of three times the number of men actually employed upon them; and, besides providing wages for the sustenance of from 30,000 to 50,000 persons, the value of the public works in preserving the health, energy, and independence of those employed, and, more indirectly, in fixing the attention even of those who were unemployed, has been and is very considerable.

The public works in Lancashire have served to prove that willing and intelligent men can soon learn a new occupation, when stern necessity forces them to it, and a fair opportunity is afforded them. It was said previous to this great trial that cotton factory workers were entirely unfitted for any other sort of labour than that of attending to machines, in heated factories, or of working at the loom. It was also asserted, that using the pick and the spade would ruin their hands and fingers, by destroying that delicacy of touch required in manipulating cotton thread. Experience, however, teaches the contrary, and further shows that, in a month or six weeks, the cotton worker's hands harden to rough out-of-door work, and breathing fresh air, under the excitement of a new exercise, helps to set the muscles, and speedily to strengthen both the appetite and the man's bodily frame. It must, however, be remembered, that this is not true of all factory workers, but only of a portion of them, and these the best, morally and physically. The public works executed in Lancashire have been in a great degree undertaken by volunteers from amongst the distressed factory operatives. That is, by men willing and wishful to escape from dependence on either the dole of charity or the taint of pauperism. The work has not been "test-work," and yet it has proved the most effective form of test. Willing men have accepted the work so soon as it has been offered to them, and they have striven to the uttermost of their ability to earn an honest and independent living at it. Unwilling men have moved away to some other district, or have managed to do without this form of labour, and thus the Local Relief Committees and the Poor Law Guardians were, for the most part, as effectually relieved from their presence as if they had remained at work. Poor Law Board. *Seventeenth Annual Report*, Appendix No 3 (1864–5)

THE WORKHOUSE

Although the grim workhouse building with its wretched inhabitants is often seen as the symbol of the poor law, it must be remembered that only 10–20 per cent of paupers in the mid-nineteenth century ever saw its inside. The inmates tended to get a larger share of the attention of poor-law critics and reformers than did the far greater number on outdoor relief. Despite the deterrent function the 1834 reformers had intended for it, the inmates of a newly constructed Union workhouse might find themselves better off in accommodation and diet than those who had to eke out an existence on a meagre dole of out relief and such scraps as they might obtain from the charitable (44). The worst conditions were generally found in the old parish workhouses which some boards of guardians still clung to despite their confined situations in town centres and their ill-planned overcrowded interiors. Nevertheless, workhouses both old and new were sources of terror for the poor (45). The monotony of their routine and the prison-like nature of their discipline were repellent; and the ignorance of many of the workhouse staff, together with the infrequent and often perfunctory inspections by both local and central authorities, undoubtedly meant that cruelties were practised on those too feeble to resist or complain (46).

One of the worst features of the New Poor Law, as the Webbs pointed out, was the emergence after 1834 of the 'general mixed workhouse', instead of the separate institutions for different categories of pauper which Edwin Chadwick had recommended. Thus the able bodied were thrust together with the orphaned, the aged and the sick in body and mind into one institution. It became increasingly apparent that most of the workhouse inmates were drawn not from the able bodied, but from the young, the infirm and the elderly. To submit such classes to the rigidities of 'less eligibility' would not only be cruel in the extreme but would serve no useful purpose. In fact such inmates probably suffered more from the indiscipline of many workhouses than they would have done in the ideally 'well regulated workhouse' of the 1834 planners' dreams.

From the first days of the New Poor Law, the Poor Law Commissioners and their assistants had urged that children ought not to be subject to the doctrine of 'less eligibility' and should wherever possible be separated from the morally contaminating atmosphere of the workhouse. By the late 1850s, increasing concern was being expressed for another class of unfortunates in the workhouse, the chronic sick. It had never been intended that sick people should be admitted to the workhouse, its infirmaries being designed only for inmates who were taken ill while in the workhouse. Inevitably, however, the poor who fell sick and had no one to care for them had to be admitted. Voluntary hospitals were reluctant to take chronic cases, those suffering from TB or dropsy for example; and wretched persons of this type came to form a large proportion of workhouse inmates, particularly in the large towns. Workhouse medical officers, often with their own grievances against the guardians, began to expose the terrible condition of the sick wards (46). In 1865 the deaths of two paupers in London workhouses aroused public indignation. The *Lancet* commissioned its own investiga-

L

tion into the sick wards of London workhouses, and published the findings (47). In the following year, an Association for the Improvement of Workhouse Infirmaries was formed, with six peers including Lord Shaftesbury and Viscount Cranborne on its executive committee. The Press, with *The Times* and *Punch* to the fore, leapt into the campaign. Under such pressure, the Poor Law Board was compelled to take action. In 1865 it issued a circular to boards of guardians urging them to improve the state of their sick wards, and, in particular, to appoint trained nurses in place of the pauper inmates who had previously performed such duties. In 1866 a medical inspector, Dr Edward Smith, was appointed to the staff of the Poor Law Board. In 1867, Parliament passed the Metropolitan Poor Act (30 & 31 Vic, c 6), which gave the central authority the power to order the provision of separate asylums for the care of the sick, insane or infirm poor in the Metropolitan area. Unions and parishes in this area could be grouped together into asylum districts to provide such institutions, which were to be controlled by a board of managers elected by the guardians. The Act also established a common poor fund for the whole Metropolitan area to which Unions and parishes contributed according to their rateable value. From this fund, Unions could claim the cost of maintaining lunatics, and smallpox and fever patients in asylums, and also any expenditure incurred in supplying medicine to the poor. The Poor Law Board urged provincial boards of guardians to separate their sick wards from the rest of the workhouse, and to improve conditions within them (48). The principle had been established that the sick poor required specialist treatment. The evolution from workhouse infirmary to municipal hospital had begun, though medical relief carried with it the stigma of pauperism until 1885.

44A Poor Law Commission   Workhouse Diets

One important aspect of the workhouse system was the feeding of the inmates. In view of the need to maintain the 'less eligibility' principle, the workhouse diet should have been

inferior to that of the local independent labourer. Because of
the poor living standards of many lower paid workers at this
period, however, such a rigid definition of less eligibility was
impossible. The Poor Law Commission in 1836 issued six
dietaries (of which three are shown here) from which boards
of guardians were to choose according to the dietary standards of their district. Thus guardians in the manufacturing
districts tended to choose the more generous diets, with meat
dishes on three or more days, while, in rural workhouses,
bread, cheese and bacon bulked large.

CIRCULAR LETTER relative to WORKHOUSE DIETARIES.
Sir,

THE following dietaries, numbered 1, 2, 3, 4, 5 and 6, have
been used in different parts of England, and all of them have
been proved to be sufficient in quantity, and perfectly un-
exceptionable as to the nature of the provisions specified in
each. (Only three diets are given here).

These dietaries are now offered to boards of guardians, to
select from them that one which appears to be the best adapted
for each particular Union.

In making this selection, especial reference must be had to
the usual mode of living of the independent labourers of the
district in which the Union is situated, and on no account must
the dietary of the workhouse be superior or equal to the ordinary
mode of subsistence of the labouring classes of the neighbourhood.

Want of attention to this essential point has been the cause of
much evil, by too frequently exhibiting the pauper inmates of
a workhouse as fed, lodged and clothed in a way superior to
individuals subsisting by their own honest industry, thereby
lessening the stimulus to exertion, and holding out an induce-
ment to idle and improvident habits.

The board of guardians, after they have made a selection of
the dietary most suitable to the circumstances of their Union,
will notify the fact to the Poor Law Commissioners, specifying

the number of the dietary so selected, and the Commissioners will then issue the same under seal, and thus render its observance imperative.

By order of the Board,

(Cont pp 165–7.)   *Edwin Chadwick*, Secretary.

44B Dr Edward Smith   Survey of Workhouse Diets
In 1866 the Poor Law Board commissioned their medical inspector, Dr Edward Smith, to carry out a survey of workhouse diets. Smith, an expert physiologist with a great interest in dietetics, carried out a detailed and critical examination. His remarks reveal the extent to which the doctrine of 'less eligibility' was coming to be modified in view of the fact that few workhouse inmates fell into the able bodied category. Smith's survey constituted a far more scientific approach to the problem of workhouse feeding than had previously been attempted.

THE PROPER DIETARIES IN WORKHOUSES.
Preliminary Considerations.

On proceeding to consider the subject of workhouse dietaries generally, I would premise a fundamental guiding principle—one of rigid utilitarianism—viz., that the inmates of workhouses should be fed in a manner the most consistent with economy and the maintenance of growth, health, and strength. It has always been desired that the arrangements of a workhouse should not be such as would entice able-bodied men to abandon employment and their own homes in order to enter the workhouse, and so far as the well-conducted portion of the community is concerned it has effected its object; but there are ill-conducted persons who are indisposed to earn their own living, and also honest and laborious men who at certain periods are unable to earn their living, to whom any place of shelter with warmth and food would offer inducements to them to enter, and between whom and the principle laid down there is a degree of antagonism.

No. 1.—DIETARY for ABLE-BODIED MEN and WOMEN.

		BREAKFAST		DINNER					SUPPER	
		Bread.	Gruel.	Cooked Meat.	Potatoes.	Soup.	Suet, or Rice Pudding.	Bread.	Cheese.	Broth.
		oz.	pints.	oz.	lbs.	pints.	oz.	oz.	oz.	pints.
Sunday	Men -	6	1½	5	½	-	-	6	-	1½
	Women -	5	1½	5	½	-	-	5	-	1½
Monday	Men -	6	1½	-	-	1½	-	6	2	-
	Women -	5	1½	-	-	1½	-	5	2	-
Tuesday	Men -	6	1½	5	½	-	-	6	-	1½
	Women -	5	1½	5	½	-	-	5	-	1½
Wednesday	Men -	6	1½	-	-	1½	-	6	2	-
	Women -	5	1½	-	-	1½	-	5	2	-
Thursday	Men -	6	1½	5	½	-	-	6	-	1½
	Women -	5	1½	5	½	-	-	5	-	1½
Friday	Men -	6	1½	-	-	-	14	6	2	-
	Women -	5	1½	-	-	-	12	5	2	-
Saturday	Men -	6	1½	-	-	1½	-	6	2	-
	Women -	5	1½	-	-	1½	-	5	2	-

Old people of 60 years of age and upwards may be allowed one ounce of tea, five ounces of butter and seven ounces of sugar per week, in lieu of gruel for breakfast, if deemed expedient to make this change.

Children under nine years of age to be dieted at discretion; above nine, to be allowed the same quantities as women.

Sick to be dieted by the medical officer.

No. 2.—GENERAL DIETARY for the ABLE-BODIED.

		BREAKFAST			DINNER				SUPPER		
		Bread.	Cheese.	Butter.	Meat Pudding, with Vegetables*.	Suet Pudding, with Vegetables*.	Bread.	Cheese.	Bread.	Cheese.	Butter.
		oz.	oz.	oz.	oz.	oz.	oz.	oz.	oz.	oz.	oz.
Sunday -	Men -	6	1	-	16	-	-	-	6	1	-
	Women -	5	-	½	10	-	-	-	5	-	½
Monday -	Men -	6	1	-	-	-	7	1	6	1	-
	Women -	5	-	½	-	-	7	1	5	-	½
Tuesday -	Men -	6	1	-	-	16	-	-	6	1	-
	Women -	5	-	½	-	10	-	-	5	-	½
Wednesday,	Men -	6	1	-	-	-	7	1	6	1	-
	Women -	5	-	½	-	-	7	1	5	-	½
Thursday -	Men -	6	1	-	-	-	7	1	6	1	-
	Women -	5	-	½	-	-	7	1	5	-	½
Friday -	Men -	6	1	-	-	16	-	-	6	1	-
	Women -	5	-	½	-	10	-	-	5	-	½
Saturday -	Men -	6	1	-	-	-	7	1	6	1	-
	Women -	5	-	½	-	-	7	1	5	-	½

Old people, being all 60 years of age and upwards: the weekly addition of one ounce of tea, and milk or sugar; also an additional meat pudding dinner on Thursday in each week, in lieu of bread and cheese, to those for whose age and infirmities it may be deemed requisite.

Children under nine years of age: bread and milk for their breakfast and supper, or gruel when milk cannot be obtained; also such proportions of the dinner diet as may be requisite for their respective ages.

Sick: whatever is ordered for them by the medical officer.

		BREAKFAST			DINNER					SUPPER	
		Bread.	Gruel.	Cooked Meat.	Cooked Meat.	Potatoes or other Vegetables.	Soup.	Bread.	Cheese.	Bread.	Cheese.
		oz.	pints.	oz.	oz.	lb.	pints.	oz.	oz.	oz.	oz.
Sunday	Men	8	1½	-	-	-	-	7	2	6	1½
	Women	6	1½	-	-	-	-	6	1½	5	1½
Monday	Men	8	1½	-	-	-	-	7	2	6	1½
	Women	6	1½	-	-	-	-	6	1½	5	1½
Tuesday	Men	8	1½	8	-	¾	-	-	-	6	1½
	Women	6	1½	6	-	¾	-	-	-	5	1½
Wednesday	Men	8	1½	-	-	-	-	7	2	6	1½
	Women	6	1½	-	-	-	-	6	1½	5	1½
Thursday	Men	8	1½	-	-	-	1½	6	-	6	1½
	Women	6	1½	-	-	-	1½	5	-	5	1½
Friday	Men	8	1½	-	-	-	-	7	2	6	1½
	Women	6	1½	-	-	-	-	6	1½	5	1½
Saturday	Men	8	1½	Bacon. 5	-	¾	-	-	-	6	1½
	Women	6	1½	4	-	¾	-	-	-	5	1½

Old people of 60 years of age and upwards may be allowed one ounce of tea, five ounces of butter, and seven ounces of sugar per week, in lieu of gruel for breakfast, if deemed expedient to make this change.

Children under nine years of age to be dieted at discretion; above nine, to be allowed the same quantities as women.

Sick to be dieted as directed by the medical officer.

Poor Law Commission. *Second Annual Report*, Appendix A, No 7

There can be no doubt, however, that the object for which workhouses have been established is more fully attained now than it has been at any former period. Able-bodied people are now scarcely at all found in them during the greater part of the year (only in winter when labour for the working classes is deficient is there any considerable number of this class), and so much is this the case that the officers can scarcely find enough inmates to keep the house and linen clean. At present those who enjoy the advantages of these institutions are almost solely such as may fittingly receive them, viz., the aged and infirm, the destitute sick, and children. Workhouses are now asylums and infirmaries, and not places where work is necessarily exacted in return for food, clothing, and shelter; and so generally is this appreciated, that the very term "workhouse" has fallen into disuse, and the word "union" has been familiarly substituted for it. This has resulted probably from the general prosperity of the country in recent years, by which labour, and a fair remuneration for it, have been more uniformly obtained, and the improved moral tone and greater thrift of the population generally; and although some of these causes cannot be permanent, there is some reason to hope that workhouses will not be again filled with the class of persons whom it is desirable to exclude.

Whilst, therefore, there is now as strong a necessity as formerly for laying down the principle of rigid economy in the dietaries, as in the general management of workhouses, there is much less reason than heretofore to fear that the comforts which such institutions, when managed under the control of the State, must necessarily afford will be abused.

I have already limited the extent to which economy in the dietary may be carried by the physical requirements of the persons to be fed, since humanity as imperatively requires that the health and strength of those whom the State thus undertakes to protect shall be maintained to a fair standard, as that a sense of justice and propriety demands that nothing superfluous shall be provided, and that nothing shall be wasted. It is not, therefore, simply a duty to find that amount of food which has the cheapest market value, and that quantity which will just sustain life, but that kind of food which will yield the largest amount of nourishment at the least cost; those conditions which will enable the food to be the most perfectly digested, and the body to obtain the greatest possible amount of nourishment from it, and that amount which shall maintain growth, health, and strength. Dr Edward Smith. *Report to the Poor Law Board on Dietaries of Inmates of Workhouses* (1866), 19–25

45 H. Taine   A Manchester Workhouse

Hippolyte Taine (1828–93), the French philosopher and critic, paid a number of visits to England in the 1860s. His notes were not published until 1871, though he claimed that most of them were made in 1861 and 1862.

Our friend, the merchant, took us to a large workhouse outside the city. There is another in the city containing 1,200 paupers; this one, however, can accommodate 1,900, but at present it contains 350 only. It cost £75,000; the annual expenses of the two amount to £55,000 raised by the poor-rate; the master's salary is £200, the doctor's £170. Each superintendent receives £20, exclusive of board, lodging, and washing; a master shoe-maker receives £1 a week for teaching his trade. The guardians give their services gratuitously. The building is spacious, perfectly clean, well kept; it has large courts, gardens are attached to it, looks upon fields and stately trees; it has a chapel, and rooms of which the ceilings are twenty feet high. It is evident that the founders and managers had made it a matter of conscience to produce a work which should be beautiful, correct, and useful. There is no smell anywhere; the beds are almost white, and are furnished with figured coverlets; the most aged and feeble women have white caps and new clothes. Everything has been considered and arranged to maintain a pleasing effect. One room is set apart for the lunatics, another for the female idiots; the latter do needle work for some hours daily; during

the period of recreation they dance together to the sounds of a
fiddle. They make strange grimaces, yet they all seem healthy
and not at all sad. In another room the children are taught
their lessons, one of the elder children acting as monitor. The
kitchen is monumental. Eight or ten cauldrons are set in solid
masonry, some to cook the oatmeal gruel, which is the principal
article of food. The daily ration of each inmate consists of two
pounds of this oatmeal and a pound and a half of potatoes; four
times a week the allowance is increased by four ounces of pie or
of meat without bone. The drink is water, except during illness.
We were astounded; this was a palace compared with the
kennels in which the poor dwell. One of us seriously asked our
friend to reserve a place for him here during his old age.
Recollect that a Manchester or Liverpool labourer can scarcely
procure meat once a week by working ten hours a day! Here an
able-bodied pauper works about six hours, has newspapers, the
Bible, and some good books and reviews to read, lives in a
wholesome air, and enjoys the sight of trees. Nevertheless there
is not an able-bodied inmate of this workhouse at this moment;
it is almost empty, and will not be filled till the winter. When
a working man out of employment applies for help to the
authorities he is commonly told, "Show us that you wish to
work by entering the workhouse." Nine out of ten decline.
Whence this dislike? To-day at a street-corner I saw an old
woman groping with her skinny hands in a heap of rubbish, and
pulling out scraps of vegetables; probably she would not give up
her drop of spirits. But what of the others? I am informed that
they prefer their home and their freedom at any price, that they
cannot bear being shut up and subjected to discipline. They
prefer to be free and to starve. But the children, these little
ones, with their white skulls sprinkled with flaxen hair, crowded
in a room around a pale mother; how is their father able to
witness such a spectacle? He does support the sight; he will not
separate himself from those of his household, abandon his position as head of the family, and be cabined alone in a compart-
ment; he thinks that, if he submitted to this, he would cease to

be a man. The workhouse is regarded as a prison; the poor consider it a point of honour not to go there. Perhaps it must be admitted that the system of administration is foolishly despotic and worrying, that is the fault of every administrative system; the human being becomes a machine; he is treated as if he were devoid of feeling, and insulted quite unconsciously. In "Our Mutual Friend," Dickens has depicted the distaste for the workhouse while siding with the poor. H. Taine. *Notes on England*, translated by W. F. Rae (1874), 300-302

46 R. Tatham   A Workhouse Hospital

Robert Tatham, a medical officer in the Huddersfield Union, became involved in a quarrel with the board of guardians over his salary and conditions of work. So embittered did relations become that the guardians ignored his warnings about the poor state of their workhouse sick wards. As a result of an outbreak of typhus in 1847, the wards became grossly overcrowded. The Poor Law Board's attention was drawn to this situation and they ordered their inspector in the area to carry out a full inquiry. The following extract is taken from his report.

Mr. Tatham states,

The beds in the hospital at the time of the Overseers Report were nearly all straw beds with the exception of about three flock beds; the patients complained much of the beds; they became hard after a few nights and the cords of the beds cut their persons; I have seen weals on their bodies the thickness of my finger from lying on these cords: I have also seen beds too short, so that the persons occupying them could not lie at their length without putting their feet out at the bottom.

In April there were two fever patients in one bed; they were men; owing to the contaminated state of the wards, patients who had been convalescent had relapses of fever and have since died; by the contaminated state of the wards I mean the water closet which was completely full for three or four weeks, and in April it overflowed and ran down the walls into the passage below; another cause of contamination was the children who were rubbing in (*sic*) for the itch; there were two idiotic women, and old women with the children; the old woman passed her defections (*sic*) in bed; and I have frequently seen, in about March, a pool of urine under her bed; these two idiots made their filth on the floor in the presence of the children; I have seen them do it; the stench on opening that door was unbearable.

. . . the hospital was extremely filthy, the floors were filthy. I don't think they had been washed down throughout the hospital, from the time of its being opened; marks of uncleanliness presented themselves nearly everywhere; cobwebs hung from the ceilings; the coverings of the beds were very deficient—mere rags some of them; some of the blankets would hardly hold together if you would shake them. . . . For a considerable period Robert Worth was at times the sole nurse in the hospital, and he had to attend to all the patients; the female nurse Susannah Hitchen was ill at different times, it was at these times that Worth was the sole nurse; both Hitchen and Worth were pauper inmates. PRO, MH12/15070 (July 1848)

47 The 'Lancet' Report on Workhouse Infirmaries

As a result of increasing public anxiety about the state of the sick poor in London workhouses, the *Lancet* in April 1865 appointed a team of three doctors to investigate conditions in a number of these workhouses. Their reports appeared in consecutive issues of the *Lancet* and were later published, together with their recommendations for reform, in a separate pamphlet. This investigation forced the Poor Law Board to order an official examination of the infirmaries by two of their inspectors, Dr Edward Smith and Mr H. B. Farnall.

The *Lancet*, founded in 1823, was noted for its crusading zeal on issues of medical reform. Perhaps its most famous

cause was the exposure, in the early 1850s, of the widespread
adulteration of foodstuffs, a campaign which led to the
Adulteration Act of 1860 and the more effective Sale of Food
and Drugs Act of 1875. Its founder was the radical doctor,
coroner and politician, Thomas Wakley (1795-1862), who
devoted his life to the reform of public health and of the
medical profession. Although he died three years before the
workhouse inquiry, its form followed very closely his more
famous *Lancet* Analytical Sanitary Commission on food
adulteration of 1851.

Before proceeding, however, to examine the efficiency of the
infirmaries, we must ask ourselves, first—What are the main
requirements of hospitals in general? and secondly—What are
the special features of the class of patients by whom the workhouse infirmaries are occupied?

As regards hospitals in general, it may be affirmed that the
following are some of the most important desiderata: convenience and salubrity of the site and the surroundings: efficient
arrangements for drainage and water-supply; isolation of the
sick, especially those with contagious diseases, from the comparatively healthy: a construction which admits of free ventila-
tion without chilliness, and of the constant supervision by the
superior officers and superintendent nurses; a nursing staff fully
competent to take advantage of these conveniences; medical
officers in sufficient numbers proportionally to the sick;
proper classification; and an intelligent liberality of management.

Such are the ordinary maxims which govern the administration of hospitals: but there are certain peculiar features in the
class of applicants for workhouse infirmary relief which must be
examined critically. The present workhouse system is a thing of
shreds and patches, which has slowly grown up to its present
form with all manner of miscellaneous additions and alterations
from time to time; and the buildings in which the in-door
paupers are housed, together with all the arrangements for their

care, partake of this patchwork character. Originally, no doubt, the workhouses were designed principally for the custody of sturdy ne'er-do-well vagrants whose pauper tendencies required to be discouraged; and the necessity of providing for the genuinely sick and feeble was an afterthought, an appendage to the main scheme (ignoring the leading feature of providing for the sick and infirm poor). But, whatever may be the case in some country districts, it is undoubtedly the fact that in metropolitan workhouses at present the really able-bodied are enormously inferior in numbers to the sick. For the inmates of the "sick wards" proper form but a small proportion of the diseased persons in every London workhouse. Multitude of sufferers from chronic diseases, chiefly those of premature old age, crowd the so-called "infirm" wards of the houses, and swell the mortality, which is a melancholy characteristic of these establishments. Examples are not uncommon in which the really able-bodied form but a fourth, a sixth, or even an eighth of the total number of inmates. The fate of the "infirm" inmates of crowded workhouses is lamentable in the extreme; they lead a life which would be like that of a vegetable, were it not that it preserves the doubtful privilege of sensibility to pain and mental misery. They are regarded by the officials connected with the establishment as an anomalous but unavoidable nuisance. Their position is ill-defined, and they are constantly experiencing the force of the old proverb, "Between two stools," &c. They get neither the blessings of health nor the immunities and the careful tending which ought to belong to the sick.

The sooner that we frankly acknowledge that these "infirm" persons are in the great majority of instances *patients*, demanding a strict attendance, and not a mere perfunctory medical supervision, the better will it be for society; yes, and even for the ratepayer's pocket. No good ever came, in this world, of mean and cowardly attempts to ignore plain facts, and it would be easy to show that in many ways the inefficiency of the present system recoils with added force upon its maintainers, and inflicts severe penalties for their short-sighted blunders. A very simple illustration of this may be given: A small tradesman contracts a cold, which may pass by neglect into chronic cough and feeble health. A hard winter puts on the finishing stroke; business and health go together. From bad to worse he passes until he finds there is nothing for him but the "house," into which he is admitted, and, not being very acutely ill, the place assigned to him is the "infirm ward." Here he is not necessarily seen daily by the medical officer; and at any rate, such is the constitution of the law and its details that there are hundreds of such cases, and still more numerous cases of chronic rheumatism, which could not be placed under daily medical supervision. Now, in this condition of infirm health the broken-down tradesman may go on for years, and, as such, is a consumer of the rates, a burden on the State, at a cost per week we leave to be cast up by an official.

If, as we assert ought to be the case, all the infirm were medically treated, there would be a very large per-centage of recovery, and consequently, as before stated, an important saving of the rates. The *Lancet* Sanitary Commission for Investigating the State of the Infirmaries of Workhouses. *Report* (1866), 7-9

48 Poor Law Board   Improvement of Sick Wards
Strong pressure for the improvement of workhouse conditions, particularly for the sick, caused the Poor Law Board to issue a number of directives to boards of guardians. Among them was an order detailing the equipment to be provided in workhouses, particularly in sick wards.

FITTINGS of WARDS and MEDICAL APPLIANCES.—CIRCULAR LETTER from the POOR LAW BOARD to BOARDS OF GUARDIANS.
The Poor Law Board, Whitehall, S.W.,
SIR,   13th *June* 1868.
    I AM directed by the Poor Law Board to inform you that they have prepared instructions in reference to the fittings of ordinary and sick wards, and to medical appliances to be pro-

vided in Workhouses, copies of which may be obtained on application at this office.

It appears to the Board to be desirable that there should be a nearer approach to uniformity in the mode in which Workhouses are furnished, and they are of opinion that whilst for the ordinary wards only a few conveniences, and those of a simple character, are required, the sick wards should be more carefully furnished, and all the necessary medical appliances supplied.

They deem it necessary that ordinarily one or more of the articles which are referred to in the instructions should be kept in stock, and in good condition; and that the procuring of them should not be deferred until the moment when the necessity for their use may be urgent.

It is the duty of the medical officer, under the regulations of the Board, to suggest to the Guardians the number of articles that may be required from time to time, and they do not doubt that the Guardians will duly consider such suggestions; or that they will be made by the medical officer with all reasonable discretion, and with due regard to economy.

I am, &c.

To   H. FLEMING,
    The Clerk to the Guardians.   *Secretary.*

E. Sick Wards.

The fittings should be such as are usually provided in the wards of General Hospitals, and amongst them the following:—

28. The bedsteads should be of iron, with iron laths, of modern make and in good order. The length should be 6 feet 2 inches, and the width 2 feet 8 inches, except for the bedridden, the lying-in cases, and women with children, for whom the width should be 3 to 4 feet.

29. A palliasse of straw or other material, or a layer of cocoa fibre matting, to lie upon the laths.

30. The beds, whether of feathers, carded flock, cut straw or chaff, to be properly made, kept in good order, and suffi-

ciently full. In some Unions, however, hair or wool mattresses are found to be better.

31. Two sheets, two or three blankets, and a cheerful-looking rug.
32. One half the number of bedsteads to have a raising rack.
33. Separate bed rests.
34. Spittoons.
35. A pottery urinal to each bed and special pottery urinary bottles for the use of bed-ridden men.
36. Medicine glasses and feeding bottles.
37. Stone or metallic feet and chest warmers.
38. Air or water beds.
39. Mackintosh sheeting to be used to all lying-in beds.
40. The same with funnels for dirty cases.
41. Square and round mackintosh cushions with depression in the centre to prevent bed sores.
42. Mackintosh urinals to be worn by men who pass their urine involuntarily.
43. A locker with shelves for the use of two inmates, or a bed-table similar to that recommended by Dr. Acland of Oxford, an example of which may be seen at the office of the Poor Law Board.
44. Arm and other chairs for two thirds of the number of sick.
45. Short benches with backs and (for special cases) cushions.
46. Rocking chairs for the lying-in wards.
47. Little arm-chairs and rocking chairs for children's sick wards.
48. Tables.
49. Pottery wash-hand basins for those who are washed in bed.
50. Fixed lavatory basins for others, or washstands with fittings.
51. A sufficient number of roller towels, and one small towel to each person who is usually washed in bed.
52. A proper supply of both combs and hair-brushes, to be kept clean and in good order, in each ward.
53. Sealed night-stools.
54. Gas, where practicable, to remain lit during the night.

M

55. Bells to the nurses room.
56. Jackets with long sleeves, for lunatics.
57. It may be desirable that an inventory of the furniture, fittings, and medical appliances supplied should be fixed in some conspicuous place in each ward.

    Poor Law Board,
        June 1868.

Poor Law Board. *Twenty First Annual Report,* Appendix A, No 5 (1868-9)

PAUPER CHILDREN

About one-third of paupers throughout the nineteenth century were children under 16 years of age. As with the sick and elderly, it was not intended that this class should be subjected to the rigours of 'less eligibility', and the Poor Law Commission was quick to make this point clear to boards of guardians (49). The central authority and its inspectors were aware of the need to remove children on indoor relief as soon as possible from the depressing atmosphere of the workhouse. One method of doing this had been the system of parish apprenticeship, but the central authority looked on this practice with cool disfavour (53). Instead they favoured the idea of pauper schools, separate from the main workhouse, in which not only the three Rs, but also industry and morality could be instilled, in the hope that those who left the school would remain independent of the poor rates for the rest of their lives (50).

Progressive boards of guardians in the larger cities, Leeds and Manchester for example, were also aware of this need and established their own pauper, or industrial, schools at considerable expense in the 1840s (51). Acting under powers obtained in the Poor Law Act of 1844 (7 & 8 Vic, c 101), the Poor Law Commission and Poor Law Board tried to get smaller Unions to combine for the purpose of financing and running district schools for pauper children. Many such schemes foundered, however, on the resistance of the guardians, who preferred to run their own schools, often within the workhouse building, despite the fact that these were generally inferior in both teaching and discipline to the larger institutions. After 1847, a part of the workhouse teacher's salary was paid by the Government, and this had the effect of improving teaching standards, since the size of the grant was dependent upon the efficiency of the teacher.

By the 1860s, however, progressive opinion was turning away from the idea of separate schools for pauper children, or 'barrack schools' as they came to be christened. Children in them, it was argued, were open to bad influences, were generally unhealthy, and were totally unfitted to cope with everyday life when they left the institution. By contrast it was shown that the Scottish system of boarding out pauper children with workers' families tended to avoid all these evils, provided it was done under proper safeguards (52). Some boards of guardians began to experiment with the scheme, and the Poor Law Board gave its somewhat grudging approval in 1870.

Despite continual anxiety over the state of the workhouse child, the condition of the far greater number of children whose parents, usually their widowed mothers, were on outdoor relief was almost completely ignored by the central authority. Attempts by some boards of guardians, at Manchester and Sheffield for example, to promote education for out-relief children at the expense of the rates met with the disapproval of the Poor Law Board. An Act of 1855 (18 & 19 Vic, c 34) did allow boards of guardians to pay the school fees of pauper children, but expressly forbade them to make the children's attendance at school a condition of relief to the parent. Not until 1870 did the guardians obtain this power, and it was the Board schools set up under the Education Act of 1870 rather than the poor-law system which was to reveal to the country the mass of destitution existing amongst its younger citizens.

49 Poor Law Commission   Less Eligibility and Education

Some economy-minded boards of guardians resented spending large sums of money on the education of pauper children, particularly if this meant giving them educational opportunities denied to the children of independent labourers. The Poor Law Commission, however, took a long-term view of the principles of rate economy and less eligibility.

PAPERS on the Subject of the EDUCATION of CHILDREN in the Workhouse.

LETTER from the Clerk to the *Bedford* Union; dated Bedford, 7th February 1836.

THE Guardians of the Bedford Union have directed me to write to inform the Poor Law Commissioners they are desirous of obtaining their sanction to have writing omitted as part of the schoolmaster's instruction in the workhouse, and that he teach *reading only*.

The board do not recommend this on the score of economy, but on that of principle, as they are desirous of avoiding greater advantages to the inmates of the workhouse than to the poor children out of it; withdrawing thereby as much as possible any premium or inducement to the frequenting the workhouse.

The motion that this letter be written to obtain the sanction of the Poor Law Commissioners, was carried, on a division, by 17 against 11.

COMMISSIONERS' Answer to the above Letter.

THE Poor Law Commissioners for England and Wales, in reference to your letter of the 7th instant, and to the application therein made by direction of the Board of Guardians of the Bedford Union, have to inform you, that they think it inconsistent with their duty to give a formal and deliberate sanction to a plan of workhouse instruction to the children who may be inmates, from which instruction in writing shall be systematically excluded.

The principle on which this exclusion is recommended being one of general application, the Commissioners could not recognize and act upon it with respect to Bedford without being prepared to apply it to all other places.

The Commissioners do not under-estimate the weight and importance of the argument that the children of labourers should not be enticed into the workhouse by the prospect of a better education within its walls than they could obtain elsewhere; but they think that this inducement would, to a considerable degree, be counteracted by a distaste for the necessary restraints of workhouse discipline, and the mere fact of its being pauper education.

The Commissioners do not doubt, also, that in all cases there will be schools accessible to the children of independent labourers of such a character as to be more attractive than any schools can be which are accessible only by becoming an inmate of a workhouse.

The Commissioners think it of the greatest importance that the workhouse children should be so taught as to give them the greatest attainable chance of earning an honest and independent maintenance for the remainder of their lives, and they cannot conceal from themselves that the acquisition of the power of writing greatly increases this chance.

They think also, that the workhouse children should not be so treated as to fix upon them any permanent stigma which should be likely to attach to them in after life. All other children who learn to read learn also to write; to have acquired a knowledge of reading, being at the same time altogether ignorant of the art of writing, would become the distinguishing mark of those who had received a workhouse education. Under these circumstances, the Commissioners think it necessary to abide by the rule laid down in the Workhouse Regulations issued for the Bedford Union. Poor Law Commission. *Second Annual Report*, Appendix C, No 8 (1836)

50 J. P. Kay Pauper Schools

Sir James Kay-Shuttleworth (1804-77) was one of the leading educationists of the early nineteenth century. He began his career as a doctor in Manchester, and in 1832 produced an important report on the condition of the working classes in that city. In 1835, he was appointed as an assistant to the Poor Law Commission and was assigned to a number of Unions in East Anglia; he took a particularly close interest in the state of children in Union workhouses, and in 1838 produced the report from which this extract is taken. In 1839, he left poor-law work to become secretary to the new Committee of the Privy Council on Education which had been established to administer the Government grant to voluntary schools. For the next ten years, he developed the system of inspection of schools receiving the grant and worked hard to improve the state of English elementary education, particularly the standard of teaching.

Although rejecting the idea of applying the principle of 'less eligibility' to workhouse children, he stressed that their education should be practical, so as to fit them for their humble role in society.

The great object to be kept in view in regulating any school for the instruction of the children of the labouring class is the rearing of hardy and intelligent working men, whose character and habits may afford the largest amount of security to the property and order of the community. Not only has the training of the children of labourers hitherto been defective, both in the methods of instruction pursued and because it has been confined within the most meagre limits, but because it has failed to inculcate the great practical lesson (for those whose sole dependence for their living is on the labour of their hands) by early habituating them to patient and skilful industry.

An orphan or deserted child, educated from infancy to the age of 12 or 14 in a workhouse, if taught reading, writing, or arithmetic only, is generally unfitted for earning his livelihood by labour. Under such a system he would never have been set to work. He would, therefore, have acquired no skill; he would be effeminate; and, what is worse, the practical lesson in industry, which he would have acquired had he been so fortunate as to live beneath the roof of a frugal and industrious father, would be wanting.

In mingling various kinds of industrial instruction with the plan of training pursued in the model school, it is not proposed to prepare the children for some particular trade or art, so as to supersede the necessity for further instruction; it is chiefly intended that the practical lesson, that they are destined to earn their livelihood by the sweat of their brows, shall be inculcated; to teach them the use of various tools, so that they may be enabled to increase the comfort of their own households by the skill which they have acquired, or to obtain a greater reward for their labour by superior usefulness.

The arrangement of the school routine, and the punctual observance of it, deserve the special attention of the visiting committee. This routine may be variously settled; but it may be useful, in order to facilitate such arrangements, to give a specimen of the succession of employments during a single day in summer, in a rural workhouse school. In this example the industrial training is pursued in the morning, both because work can be more easily performed in the garden at that part of the day, and because the employments of the girls require their absence from school in the morning, while, in a workhouse containing few children, it may be necessary to instruct the boys and girls at the same hours. But the scheme of engagements may easily be modified by transferring these occupations to the afternoon:—

Half-past five, A.M.—Rise, wash, and dress. The monitors are to preserve order.

Six o'clock.—Make beds, scour rooms, light fires, brush shoes, clothes, &c. Preparing the vegetables for the meals, &c.

Twenty minutes past six.—Assemble in the school-room; rolls read by schoolmaster and schoolmistress, each child answering to his or her name; absentees noted. Children inspected, to ensure cleanliness of dress and person.

Half-past six.—The children proceed in an orderly manner to the dining-hall; prayers are read; a hymn sung, in which all the children join. Breakfast.

Quarter-past seven to eight.—Recreation in the yards; gymnastic exercises and healthful games, or exercise on the mast.

Eight to eleven.—In weather suitable for out-door employment, the boys shoulder their tools and proceed to the garden, where they are employed in skilful culture under the instruction of the schoolmaster. At other seasons useful in-door employment (such as making baskets, carpentering, shoemaking, tailoring, whitewashing, and repairing the premises) is pursued; and an effort is made to mend and make all the boys' clothes and shoes in their department of the house.

During the same period the girls ventilate the bed-rooms, make the beds, scour the floors, clean the dining-hall. Certain of the older girls are employed in the wash-house and laundry, or in the kitchen, till noon, or to a later hour.

The children should return to the school-room, carefully wash their hands, arrange themselves in a line to be inspected by the schoolmaster and mistress at eleven.

From eleven to twelve the oldest boys and girls read a chapter in the Bible or Testament; after which the master and mistress ascertain how much they remember of the narrative, &c., read, interrogate them respecting its purport, and instruct them in its relations to the rest of Scripture, and the practical influence it ought to have on their conduct. In such instruction the directions of the chaplain guide the teacher. The younger children meanwhile learn to repeat a hymn, which is read to them for that purpose by a pupil-teacher or monitor.

Twelve.—Children proceed to the hall and dine.

Half-past twelve to two.—Recreation, gymnastic exercises, and games in yards, and exercise on the mast.

Two to five.—The general instruction of the school will proceed; a routine being prepared describing the occupation of each class on every hour in the day and every day in the week. The pupil teachers should likewise have the order of the lessons they impart arranged by the schoolmaster, who should devote two hours every evening to their instruction separately from the rest of the school. The pupil teachers may be so trained as to become as they grow up invaluable assistants to the master, not only in imparting instruction, but ultimately in regulating the moral discipline of the school. The whole instruction should be so regulated as to fit them to become industrious, intelligent, and religious working men. Industry should be associated with all that is cheering, and its intimate connexion with the labours of the intelligence should be made apparent. Our dependence and our hopes should be shown in the light of religion.

Five to six.—The children are all instructed in singing in the dining-hall.

Six o'clock.—Supper. After supper prayers are read, and a hymn is sung by the whole of the assembled inmates.

The children then return to their schools, where the schoolmaster and schoolmistress address any remarks to them which may be suggested by the proceedings of the day. Poor Law Commission. *Report on the Training of Pauper Children* (1841), 33-4, 66-7

---

51 'Household Words'   A Pauper Palace

This account of the Manchester board of guardians' school for pauper children at Swinton, built in the early 1840s, appeared in Charles Dickens's periodical *Household Words* in 1850. Its favourable tone contrasts sharply with the hostile attitude of Dickens to the New Poor Law system in novels like *Oliver Twist* or *Our Mutual Friend*. Later, however, Dickens, like many other humanitarians, began to doubt the wisdom of segregating pauper children in large institutions. An article entitled 'Little Pauper Boarders' in the periodical *All the Year Round* in August 1869 praised the system of boarding out as a welcome alternative to the pauper school.

We went into the play-ground of the junior department, where more than a hundred and fifty children were assembled.

Some were enjoying themselves in the sunshine, some were playing at marbles, others were frisking cheerfully. These children ranged from four to seven years of age. There are some as young as a year and a half in the school. The greater number were congregated at one end of the yard, earnestly watching the proceedings of the master who was giving fresh water to three starlings in cages that stood on the ground. One very young bird was enjoying an airing on the gravel. Two others were perched on a cask. The master informed us it was a part of his system to instruct his charges in kindness to animals by example. He found that the interest which the children took in the animals and in his proceedings towards them, was of service in impressing lessons of benevolence among them towards each other. The practical lessons taught by the master's personal attention to his feathered favourites, outweighed, he thought, the theoretic inconsistency of confining birds in cages.

The play-ground is a training school in another particular. On two sides grew several currant trees, on which the fruit is allowed to ripen without any protection. Though some of the scholars are very young, there do not occur above two or three cases of unlawful plucking per annum. The appropriate punishment of delinquents is for them to sit and see the rest of their school-fellows enjoy, on a day appointed, a treat of fresh ripe fruit, whilst they are debarred from all participation.

The teaching of the juniors is conducted mainly *vivâ voce;* for the mass of them are under six years of age. The class was opened thus:
"What day is this?"
"Monday."
"What sort of a day is it?"
"Very fine."
"Why is it a fine day?"
"Because the sun shines, and it does not rain."
"Is rain a bad thing, then?"
"No."

"What is it useful for?"

"To make the flowers and the fruit grow."

"Who sends rain and sunshine?"

"God."

"What ought we to do in return for his goodness?"

"Praise him!"

"Let us praise him, then," added the master. And the children, all together, repeated and then sung a part of the 149th Psalm.—A lesson on morals succeeded, which evidently interested the children. It was partly in the form of a tale told by the master. A gentleman who was kind to the poor, went to visit in gaol a boy imprisoned for crime. The restraint of the gaol, and the shame of the boy, were so described, as to impress the children with strong interest. Then the boy's crime was traced to disobedience, and the excellence of obedience to teachers and parents was shown. The fact that punishment comes out of, and follows our own actions was enforced by another little story.

By this time some of the very young children showed symptoms of lassitude. One fat little mortal had fallen asleep; and this class was consequently marshalled for dismissal, and as usual marched out singing, to play for a quarter of an hour.

As we descended the steps of the school we scanned the prospect seen from it. The foreground of the landscape was dotted with rural dwellings, interspersed with trees. In the distance rose the spires and tall chimneys of Manchester, brightened by the rays of the evening sun, while a sea of smoke hung like a pall over the great centre of manufacturing activity, and shut out the view beyond. It typified the dark cloud of pauperism which covers so large a portion of the land, and which it is hoped such institutions as the Swinton Industrial Schools are destined to dispel. The centre of manufacturing activity is also the centre of practical and comprehensive education. Why does this activity continue to revolve so near its centre? Why has it not radiated over the length and breadth of the land? The Swinton Institution is a practical illustration of what can be done with even the humblest section of the community; and if it have a disadvantage, that is precisely because it succeeds too well. It places the child-pauper above the child of the industrious. Narrow minds advocate the levelling of the two, by withdrawing the advantage from the former. Let us, however, hope that no effort will relax to bring out, in addition to Pauper Palaces, Educational Palaces for all classes and denominations. *Household Words* (13 July 1850), 362–4

52 Mrs N. Senior   Pauper Schools and Boarding Out

This extract is taken from an influential report by Mrs Jane Elizabeth Senior (1828–77), daughter-in-law of the economist Nassau Senior. Mrs Senior was the first woman to be appointed to the poor-law inspectorate. Her report enormously strengthened the case of those who were arguing for the wider adoption of the Scots system of boarding out pauper children as against the policy of confining them in separate institutions.

CONCLUSION.

It will already have appeared from what I have written of my visits to pauper schools, that I was unfavourably impressed with the effect of thus massing children together in large numbers.

Though I admired, in not a few instances, the pains which had been taken to obviate various evils, and the wise arrangements which had been made for the children's good; yet all the more, considering the amount of money expended and labour bestowed, did I consider the physical condition of the girls in the schools, and their moral condition on coming out of them, disappointing and unsatisfactory.

Impressed with the conviction of the necessary disadvantages of large schools, I wished to ascertain whether, under other conditions, children of the same class appeared to prosper better.

I set out on a tour of inspection in some districts in England and Scotland where the system of boarding-out in families is adopted, and had an opportunity of seeing a large number of pauper children in their cottage homes, and this in various localities.

In the course of this tour I visited several sets of children boarded out in different districts, and under different circumstances. Some boarded out within their own union, some according to rules laid down by the Local Government Board in the boarding-out order. Some boarded out with miners and labourers near large towns, some in Roman Catholic families. Some in an ordinary English village in Buckinghamshire, and some in a remote country district of Scotland.

I received the same impression everywhere, in favour of the free and natural mode of life afforded by cottage homes. I did not see a single case of ringworm or ophthalmia, and the children, almost without exception, looked strong and thriving and happy.

I can imagine that these very advantages might act as an encouragement to the desertion of children, if conferred on those who have parents of their own, morally bound to provide for them; but this objection to boarding out would not hold good in the case of orphans.

It would, in my opinion, be an inestimable benefit to the orphans now being educated at the Metropolitan pauper schools, to be placed under the boarding-out system; provided, of course, that it were properly carried out.

It is alleged, with truth, that boarding out, as at present permitted, may lapse into mere out-relief, granted by Guardians to evade the necessity of providing better accommodation for children in workhouse schools, and with no more effectual supervision of the children than that exercised by the Guardians themselves.

I had rather have no children boarded out, than that the system should be brought into ill repute by the abuses which would be sure to arise, if this irregular system of boarding out is allowed to be practised.

Even where children are boarded out within the Unions to which they belong, the selection of homes, and the supervision of the children placed out, should in all cases be confided by the Guardians to boarding-out committees, such as are indicated in Rule 1. of the Boarding-out Order issued by the Local Government Board.

I believe that it is your intention to make the provisions of that rule binding with regard to all pauper children boarded out in private families.

Another reason has been alleged against the boarding-out system. That it is bad for a labourer, struggling hard to support his family, to see, in the next cottage, a pauper child for whose maintenance a sum is paid, far exceeding what it is in his power to spend on his own child; and that the knowledge that, in case of his death, his children would be equally well done by, will prevent his trying to lay by during his lifetime, for their maintenance, in the event of his death before they can be self supporting.

I think there are two errors in these statements. In the first place, every man, even an uneducated labourer, if he gives the subject a thought, knows what the poor rate means, and is aware that pauper children are supported by the poor rate, at more or less cost.

It is very generally known, even among country people, that a labourer's child living at home, does not cost him what a pauper child, even in the most economical workhouse, costs the rates.

The labourer knows that pauper children must be supported and educated, and the most limited intelligence can understand that 3s. 6d. to board out a child, is less out of the rates than the 4s. or more that the child would cost in the workhouse.

With regard to any jealousy or ill feeling that might arise in the minds of the peasants, who could not spend on their children what was paid for the child boarded out, I do not think that such unworthy feelings, if they exist, should be taken into consideration, and I do not believe that, as a rule, they would be found to exist. The poor are remarkably kind to each other, and full of pity for children deprived of their natural protectors, as any one who knows them well can testify. If they were asked whether a dead neighbour's child should be sent to the work-house, or boarded out at more expense than they can afford for their own children, I well know what the answer would be.

Nor do I believe that a thrifty man would be discouraged in his career of honourable independence, by the knowledge that his children would be provided for out of the workhouse, rather than in it, if he left them unprovided. A worthy man is not thus influenced by unworthy motives, and it is not the sight of a few children boarded out, that would induce the pauper spirit where it did not already exist.

The whole Poor Law system is a necessary evil, and I believe that the time will come when its provisions will be no longer necessary, when education, and improved social arrangements, will have triumphed over pauperism. The enormous buildings that are erected for the reception of pauper children, seem to point to a belief that we are to have an ever-increasing race of paupers throughout the centuries to come. Against such a belief boarding out is a protest. Local Government Board. *Third Annual Report*, Appendix 22 (1873-4), 341-3

SETTLEMENT, REMOVAL AND VAGRANCY

One area of poor-law administration in which the Poor Law Amendment Act of 1834 failed to make any drastic change was the complex law of settlement. Although the Act abolished certain modes of gaining a settlement—by hiring and service for a year or by serving a parish office, for example—it failed to make such provision retrospective, and thus left the law more confused than before. Worse still, since settlement remained on a parochial basis, as did the charge for relieving the poor, parishes within the same Union might become involved in a bitter legal battle over the removal of a pauper, the parish overseers fighting a long drawn out and expensive campaign whilst the board of guardians looked on helplessly. Unscrupulous overseers might resort to underhand means in order to get rid of paupers who had been moved back to their parish (53).

With increasing labour mobility, particularly in industrial areas, it became imperative to mitigate this parochial warfare; and so there had developed, long before 1834, the system of non-resident relief by which the parish of settlement agreed to reimburse the parish in which their paupers were resident for any relief paid to them. This practice continued after 1834 despite the disapproval of the Poor Law Commission, and so, even in periods of economic depression, removal of paupers from manufacturing towns was less extensive than it might otherwise have been.

Rural areas, however, complained that they were subsidising the wealthier industrial towns, who were benefiting from the labour of workers who had migrated from the countryside but did not have to pay the cost of their maintenance when they were out of work, sick or ageing (55). As part of the compensation given to the landed interest after the repeal of the Corn Laws in 1846, an Act (9 & 10 Vic, c 66) was passed making those who had resided in a parish for five years secure against removal to their parish of settlement if they applied for relief, which now had to be paid by the parish they lived in. A proviso in the Act laid down that receipt of poor relief during the five-year residential period disqualified the recipient from acquiring the status of irremovability (56). Unfortunately, the Act was so badly drafted that it was not made clear whether this proviso applied to those relieved before the passing of the Act. The Poor Law Board, acting on legal advice, ruled that it did not apply to the period before 1846; so many of those who had been receiving non-resident relief now became the responsibility of the parishes in which they were resident. Industrial parishes that had attracted large numbers of immigrants from surrounding villages were particularly hard hit (57). Trade depression and an influx of Irish immigrants in 1847 made the situation worse, and poor law administration was seriously disrupted in some areas.

An Act of 1847 (10 & 11 Vic, c 110), passed at the instigation of a private member, W. H. Bodkin, secretary of the Society for the Suppression of Mendicity, helped to relieve the situation by placing the whole cost of relieving the irremovable poor on the common fund of the Union instead of on the individual parishes. Bodkin's Act was a temporary measure, renewed annually. Not until 1865 did a more permanent piece of legislation emerge in the shape of the Union Chargeability Act (28 & 29 Vic, c 79), which placed the whole cost of all relief upon the Union and made that body rather than the parish the area of settlement (59).

The confusion over the Act of 1846 brought criticism of the settlement laws to a head. Numerous Parliamentary Select Committees met to consider the complexities of the problem, and the Poor Law Board commissioned a series of reports on the subject, the most important of which, by George Coode, contained an outspoken condemnation of the laws of settlement and recommended their total abolition (58A). Others were more cautious in their suggestions for reform. Some guardians, while admitting the hardship caused by the Settlement Acts, feared that the abolition of their powers of removal, particularly if extended to the Irish, might saddle their Unions with a large number of applicants for relief (58B). Abolition of settlement might also bring nearer some scheme of national chargeability for the poor, and thus a further weakening of local powers of self-government. So the Settlement Acts remained, amended but unrepealed, to trouble poor-law administrators until 1948.

Closely connected with the problems of settlement and removal was the question of vagrancy. In the early years of the New Poor Law there was no uniform policy on the relief of vagrants. The Poor Law Commission did not regard them as a separate class of pauper. In some areas, they were admitted to Union workhouses, in others they were given relief in kind or tickets entitling them to a night's stay at a common lodging house. Some towns maintained separate night asylums or mendicity offices for the reception of tramps; and sometimes these asylums were under the control of the constable rather than the

N

overseer or the guardians, for vagrancy was still regarded as being in part a police, rather than a poor-law, problem.

The influx of Irish immigrants fleeing from the Great Famine made poor-law authorities think seriously about the problem. The Union workhouse held no terrors for these wretched people, many of whom carried the typhus fever into the overcrowded wards with them. Requests for help and advice on how to deal with this invasion poured into Somerset House. In 1848, Charles Buller, the first President of the Poor Law Board, issued a memorandum urging on boards of guardians the necessity of distinguishing carefully between those tramping in genuine search of work, and those who were idle vagrants (60). The latter, particularly if they were able-bodied men, should be given only the very minimum of aid. Over the next twenty years many Unions built separate vagrant wards at their workhouses. Here food was sparse and sleeping accommodation uncomfortable, consisting of an allowance of bread and gruel and a common sleeping platform where those admitted lay on bare boards covered by a single blanket. In some wards, a bath was a required condition of entry and a task of work one of release (61). Tramps, particularly if young and healthy, were regarded with contempt and suspicion as being part of, or closely related to, the criminal fraternity (62). The 'terror of the tramp' was almost as widespread in Victorian as it has been in Elizabethan England.

53 Bradford Union   An Illegal Removal

Although the quarrel in this case was between the township officers of Idle and the town officers of Sheffield, Bradford guardians stepped in to defend the overseer of one of the constituent parishes in their Union.

Bradford   19th June 1841.

Gentl[n].

Susannah Allott

I am requested by the Board of Guardians of this Union, to

request your interference by way of remonstrance, or otherwise, in the following matter.

A few weeks ago a woman named Susannah Allott with her Family was removed, by a regular removal order, from the Township of Idle in this Union, to the Town of Sheffield, in this County, and to the surprize of the relieving officer of Idle very few Days after her removal had elapsed before she was again an applicant for relief in person at his pay day at Idle.

The Board have had the woman before them, and find that the parish officers of Sheffield, not only persuaded her to return to Idle immediately, but actually paid her coach fare and gave her money to bear her expenses on the road.

This conduct on the part of the Sheffield officers is considered by the Board as highly reprehensible and they therefore request that you will please to cause an inquiry into the matter to be instituted, with a view to prevent the recurrence of such practices.

I have not yet been furnished with the Dates, nor the name of the officers at Sheffield but will send them if necessary, after the next meeting of the Board.

I have the Honor to be Gent^n.

Your most obed^t. S^t.

Jno. Reid Wagstaff.

The Poor Law Commissioners.

PRO, MH12/14721

---

54 Mr Blyth   Close and Open Parishes

One effect of the laws of settlement which many of their critics attacked was their tendency to create 'close' parishes; these were parishes in which all the land and property was in the hands of one or a few landowners. In order to keep down the rate burden in his parish, the owner would refuse to build labourers' cottages and might pull down those already existing when they were vacated. Labourers who worked on farms in such parishes were forced to live some miles away in the nearest 'open' parish, where property was in the hands of several owners who were only too anxious to profit from the demand for cottages by charging high rents for inferior accommodation.

The Union Chargeability Act of 1865, by ending parochial settlement and chargeability, destroyed many of the advantages of the open parish. Although the 1834 Act had given powers to boards of guardians to declare their Union a single area for settlement and rating, the Docking Union was one of the few to take advantage of this permissive clause. This letter was written to the Poor Law Board's Inspector, G. à Beckett, who was carrying out an inquiry into the operation of the laws of settlement in East Anglia.

COMMUNICATION from Mr. BLYTH.

DEAR SIR,   *Sussex Farm, Burnham, July* 8, 1848.

IN compliance with your request that I should relate, in writing, my opinions as to the effect which the present law of settlement has upon the condition of the poor, and the probability that exists as to any improvement to be derived from an alteration of the law, I will refer at once to the reasons which were adopted by the Board of Guardians of the Docking Union for extending the limits of settlement from parishes to Unions, and I will endeavour to show you how those reasons, and the inferences deduced, are supported by practical experience. You will bear this in mind, that the Docking Union comprises a district purely agricultural. It is true that the sea affords occupation for a small portion of the population, but not sufficient to make any impression upon the general character of the poor, their employment, or their subsistence.

First, then, our labourers are located for the most part in villages, lying at considerable distances from each other, and not scattered over the face of the country; the farm-houses, some of them in the villages, many (most) of them situate at distances varying from half a mile to two miles from the village. There are nine (*sic*) parishes, viz., Barnow, Barwick, Broomsthorpe,

Bagthorpe, Houghton, Tring, Burnham Dockdale, Anmer; the exclusive property respectively of one proprietor, residing (either himself or represented by a responsible tenant) on the estate. In each one of these parishes the system has been quietly acted upon, more or less, of avoiding the expenses of maintaining the poor as much as possible by reducing or keeping down the number of cottages. In Barmer, Broomsthorpe, Waterden, there are not more than two cottages each; the labourers required to till the land residing respectively for Barmer in Syderstone, for Broomsthorpe in Rudham, for Waterden in South Creake, in Tring and Burnham Deepdale. I have myself known cottages taken down avowedly to reduce the liability of maintaining the poor. Of Anmer, the proprietor himself stated in our Board-room that he considered his estate to be valuable in proportion as he could keep it free from any increased liability, and therefore he disapproved any measure which might deprive him of the independence in the management of his *own* poor, which he now enjoyed. These are all proofs that the dislike to build or to maintain cottages have in close parishes driven the labourers who till the soil to more distant residences. These residences are found, secondly, in our larger villages or towns, such as Docking, Burnham, Creaknorth, Creaksouth, Snethsham. In these places are small freeholds and copyhold estates, the owners of which have found the building of cottages a most profitable invest-ment; and *that alone* being their object, they have paid no attention to the convenience necessary to make these com-fortable or even healthy residences. In one part of Docking there is a large collection of houses, apparently 20 or 30, built all together, without one bit of garden-ground. Docking is in the hands of two large owners and a few small freeholders. The former have built none; the latter a great number of cottages within my recollection. In Burnham Sutton a small landed proprietor built, a few years ago, several cottages, and attached to each a very good garden. At his death, four years since, these cottages were sold in separate lots, bought by small capitalists, and in several instances these lots, with their garden, have been built upon, and divided into two or even four small tenements. The two principal landowners in Burnham (about 1100 acres each) have not for their labourers more than two cottages each by the respective farmhouses. I mention all these as facts showing the actual state of things. Poor Law Board. *Reports on the Laws of Settlement and Removal of the Poor*, XXVII, Appendix 13 (1850)

55 A. Power   The Burden on Agriculture

Alfred Power, who appeared as a witness before the Select Committee on the Poor Law Amendment Act of 1837, was the assistant commissioner primarily responsible for forming Unions in the West Riding and Lancashire in 1837 and 1838. In this part of the country rural and industrial parishes lay close together and there was a continual drift of labourers from the villages into the industrial towns.

The questioner in this case was John Fielden, the Todmorden cotton manufacturer, who was a strong opponent of the New Poor Law.

2984. Mr. *Fielden.*] You have stated to the Committee, that there is a difference between those employed in agriculture and those in manufacture, in the district you have been in; what is the difference that you alluded to?—The agricultural districts are relieving, to a considerable extent and in a great proportion, poor residing at a distance, who have gone to the manufacturing towns, but they still keep their settlements in the agricultural parishes from which they have migrated; that is not so much the case in the manufacturing parts; for instance, if I were to compare, which I am able to do from documents, the numbers relieved by townships of a particular union who are not resident in that union, as between an agricultural union and a manufacturing union, I should find a much greater proportion in the agricultural union relieved at a distance.

2985. Can you assign a reason for the relief being given to them at a distance in the agricultural unions, prevailing to an extent more than it does in manufacturing unions?—The persons have migrated to manufacturing towns, no doubt, to considerable extent; parties who have been employed there.

2986. Was that alleged as a ground of complaint in those agricultural districts, the poor whom they had to relieve being at a distance?—It has produced great difficulties to the parties managing those townships heretofore, and it continues to produce great difficulties to the boards of guardians who have been substituted.

2987. Were the rates higher on that account in those agricultural unions?—I have no doubt that they would be on that account considerably higher.

2988. Did those whom you met with in the formation of the unions tell you so?—I do not know that I have had that stated to me in direct terms; but I do not feel any doubt in my own mind that they were higher on that account. Select Committee on the Poor Law Amendment Act. *Report*, XVIII, *Evidence of Alfred Power* (1837–8)

------

56 The 1846 Act

As well as rendering all those who had resided in a parish for five years irremovable, subject to certain conditions, the Act prohibited the removal of widows for a year after their husband's death, and of children whose parents were irremovable. Those who had fulfilled the residential qualification did not gain a settlement in the parish, though they could not be removed from it; a new category of pauper was created, that of the 'irremovable'.

------

9 & 10 VICT. CAP. 66.

An Act to amend the Laws relating to the Removal of the
    Poor.   [26th August, 1846.]
"Whereas it is expedient that the laws relating to the removal of the poor should be amended;" Be it enacted by the Queen's most excellent Majesty, by and with the advice and consent of the Lords spiritual and temporal, and Commons, in this present

parliament assembled, and by the authority of the same, that from and after the passing of this Act no person shall be removed, nor shall any warrant be granted for the removal of any person from any parish in which such person shall have resided for five years next before the application for the warrant; Provided always, that the time during which such person shall be a prisoner in a prison or shall be serving Her Majesty as a soldier, marine, or sailor, or reside as an in-pensioner in Greenwich or Chelsea hospitals, or shall be confined in a lunatic asylum, or house duly licensed or hospital registered for the reception of lunatics, or as a patient in a hospital, or during which any such person shall receive relief from any parish, or shall be wholly or in part maintained by any rate or subscription raised in a parish in which such person does not reside, not being a *bonâ fide* charitable gift, shall for all purposes be excluded in the computation of time hereinbefore mentioned, and that the removal of a pauper lunatic to a lunatic asylum, under the provisions of any Act relating to the maintenance and care of pauper lunatics, shall not be deemed a removal within the meaning of this Act: Provided always, that whenever any person shall have a wife or children having no other settlement than his or her own, such wife and children shall be removable whenever he or she is removable, and shall not be removable when he or she is not removable.

II. And be it enacted, that no woman residing in any parish with her husband at the time of his death shall be removed, nor shall any warrant be granted for her removal, from such parish, for twelve calendar months next after his death, if she so long continue a widow.

III. And be it enacted, that no child under the age of sixteen years, whether legitimate or illegitimate, residing in any parish with his or her father or mother, stepfather or stepmother, or reputed father, shall be removed, nor shall any warrant be granted for the removal of such child, from such parish, in any case where such father, mother, stepfather, stepmother, or reputed father may not lawfully be removed from such parish.

IV. And be it enacted, that no warrant shall be granted for the removal of any person becoming chargeable in respect of relief made necessary by sickness or accident, unless the justices granting the warrant shall state in such warrant that they are satisfied that the sickness or accident will produce permanent disability.

V. Provided always, and be it enacted, that no person hereby exempted from liability to be removed shall by reason of such exemption acquire any settlement in any parish. W. C. Glen. *The Statutes in Force Relating to the Poor* (1857), 639-40

57 J. Beckwith and C. Heaps The Effects of the 1846 Act

John Beckwith was clerk to the Leeds board of guardians, and Christopher Heaps was secretary and treasurer to the overseers of the township of Leeds. With a large immigrant population, Leeds was particularly hard hit by the Act, which coincided with a period of economic depression and a large influx of destitute Irish fleeing from the Famine. Both witnesses used the opportunity of their appearance before the Select Committee on Settlement and Poor Removal of 1846 to publicise the drastic effects of the Act on an industrial town like Leeds.

3905. Can you state what has been the effect of the Act of last year upon the numbers of the poor relieved at the expense of Leeds?—I can state that the effect has been to add considerably to the cost of the township of Leeds, and to the burden to be borne by that township.

3908. Upon the whole, how many previously chargeable to you have ceased to be chargeable, and how many have become chargeable that were not chargeable before?—One hundred and eighty-one cases, comprising 341 persons, were chargeable to us being non-resident; and of those 76 families, comprising 149 persons, have now become chargeable to the places where they were resident. On the other hand, of the 447 cases, comprising 710 persons that we were relieving for other unions, we have now to take upon ourselves the burden of 122 cases, comprising 303 persons; but adding also the families relieved by the surrounding townships, and distant townships, who have agents in Leeds to pay their poor, the number thrown upon us is 835 cases, comprising 1,519 persons.

3909. What is the balance?—It would be 759 cases, and 1,270 persons.

3910. Has the expense of maintaining the poor been increased in Leeds from the number of persons applying for relief, who previously would not have applied from fear of removal?—It has been considerably increased; but it is difficult to state precisely the extent.

3911. Many parties previously would not have applied for relief, but in preference would have suffered great hardship?—That was so, I believe.

3912. Therefore, in that respect, this law has proved beneficial to the poor, although increasing the burden upon the ratepayers?—It is certainly a burden to the ratepayers, and so far beneficial to the poor, who would not probably have applied for relief, wishing to avoid removal to their own township.

3913. In fact, there would have been cases of considerable hardship?—Yes; and I may state that a considerable proportion of the increase arises from Irish cases. Some of those have been recent cases; and it is difficult to state, looking at the affairs in Ireland generally, how much of the increase is to be attributed to the alteration in the law, and how much to the influx of the Irish.

3914. Upon the whole, do you think that the Poor-law Removal Act of last year has been beneficial to the poor, or not?—If it had been framed as it was intended to have been framed, I should say that it would have been rather beneficial than otherwise; but from its extreme ambiguity, the poor have been very much pushed from pillar to post, no person choosing to do what they did not see clearly and distinctly that they were bound to do. Select Committee on Settlement and Poor Removal. XI, *6th Report, Evidence of J. Beckwith and C. Heaps, Junior* (1846)

58A George Coode   Reform of the Law of Settlement
George Coode (1807–69) was assistant secretary to the Poor Law Commission until 1846. He was responsible for drafting the Irish Poor Law Act of 1838, and wrote a number of articles on poor-law and local government problems.

VIII.—GENERAL RECAPITULATION, RECOMMENDATIONS, AND CONCLUSION.

We have examined the origin, progress, and bearing of this law, paradoxically called a law of settlement, which denies to every man a settlement in 15,534 parishes, where it makes him an alien, and affects to settle him, whether he will or not, in a single one, making it the interest of himself to escape, and of the whole parish to expel him, even from that.

We have seen that this law originated unexpectedly, was recommended on false pretences, was carried by a local interest, and without discussion.

That it has never operated to the satisfaction of the so-called parish interests, by which it has been alone supported, and has always operated adversely to that of the general population.

That it has always impeded the labourer, and never afforded him an advantage, still less an equivalent, for the restraint on his liberty and prosperity.

That it has always encumbered the agriculture, the production, and the trade of the less progressive parishes, by the idleness it enforced and encouraged, the pauperism it created and made stagnant.

That it has always prevented the supply of a respectable population to the places where fresh hands were wanted, and has allowed them to increase chiefly or only by the addition of the outcast people from other places. It has deteriorated the towns, and made them the less fit to receive a decent population.

That it has made the parish of the settlement a prison, and every other parish a hostile fortress. It has encouraged the refusal, the restriction, or the destruction of habitations where it pretended to give the legal home, and it has denied a home everywhere else, and has often left no alternative but sordid, compulsory, and unprosperous settlement or a vagrant life, for which last it has provided the most specious justifications.

That it has, by destroying the field of the Englishman's employment, allured the Irish, and even afforded them bounties to supply his place where he was wanted.

That it has accumulated the unsettled population in undefended places, which have become filthy nests of wretchedness, pauperism, and crime.

That it has isolated the interests of every parish,—made inter-parochial war their normal state.

That it has never benefited one parish, but by the more than equal injury of another, with the addition of injury to the settler.

That it has, contrary to the main object of law, to remove occasions of dispute, created the occasion for the greatest mass of dispute and litigation ever witnessed in any nation for any equal period of time.

We have seen incessant attempts made at amendment. The law has traversed from the one extreme of universal removability of the poor man only likely to be chargeable,—persevered in till it was as unendurable to other classes as to the poor,—to the nearly opposite result, the prohibition of all removal except of unsettled poor, chargeable, who have not been resident for a defined time or under defined circumstances; a provision, which under the controlling influence of the continuing settlement law, is rapidly producing mischiefs both to parishes and the poor as virulent as the worst of the effects of that fatal system. We have seen nothing but failure in attempts at partial amendments, or, more frequently, the introduction of new and unexpected mischiefs.

On the other hand we have seen instances of pure abolition

or extensive excision of the larger members of this body of law, such as the abolition of the power of removal of all unchargeable people, and the entire abolition of heads of settlement, and we have seen in all such cases that the destruction has been free from mischief, even when frustrated of some of its good effects by the remaining portions of the law of removal.

The apprehended dangers of the entire abolition of the law of removal have been examined in detail, and none will stand the investigation.

Some amendments, proposed with a view to lessen the admitted mischiefs of the law, are shown to involve preponderating mischiefs of their own, and to be less effective for their proposed end than simple and absolute abolition.

We come, then, to the conclusion, that the only course consistent with the public welfare is, TO REPEAL THE POWER OF REMOVAL BY WARRANT. George Coode. *Report to the Poor Law Board on the Law of Settlement and Removal* (1851), 187-9

58B Joseph Ellison   Reform of the Law of Settlement

Joseph Ellison was a former member of the Dewsbury board of guardians and, before that, of the Gomersal select vestry (25). His proposals for the reform of the settlement law reflect the caution of many local administrators in the face of demands for the total abolition of the law made by critics like George Coode.

338. Before we come to your suggestions, are you of opinion that you could altogether do away with the power of removal of the chargeable Irish paupers from England to Ireland?—No.

339. Will you state to the Committee why you think it would not be safe or proper to do away with the power of removal altogether?—I think, if you did away with the power of removal, you would have a vast many more applications for relief than you have now, because the power of removal is the very instrument which prevents a great many parties applying for

relief. They know that if they apply for relief, and are at all likely to become permanent paupers, they will be removed out of the country. Knowing this, rather than be removed they do not apply. I think it would be a very great hardship upon the ratepayers if you were to abolish the law of removal altogether, especially in those districts where the Irish are congregated in numbers.

340. Will you state any other reasons which occur to you for thinking that the taking away of the power of removal altogether is inadvisable?—I would not take it away with regard to the English paupers; I think it would be a piece of very bad policy to do so; if you did that you would encourage vagrancy; they would move about from one township to the other, and I consider vagrancy a very great evil, with children especially; it trains them up to every kind of petty thieving, and I think that you ought by all means, as much as you can, to repress vagrancy. Select Committee on Poor Removal. XIII, *Evidence of Joseph Ellison* (1854–5)

---

59 The Union Chargeability Act

By placing the whole cost of relief on the common fund of the Union and by making the Union instead of the parish the area of settlement, the Act increased the control of the board of guardians over poor-law administration at the expense of the overseers. Section 8 of the Act reduced the period of residence required for irremovability to one year.

UNION CHARGEABILITY ACT, 1865.—AN ACT to provide for the better DISTRIBUTION of the CHARGE for the RELIEF of the POOR in UNIONS [28 & 29 Vict. c. 79., passed 29th June 1865.]

WHEREAS it is expedient to make provision for the better distribution of the charge for the relief of the poor in Unions than is by law now established: Be it therefore enacted by the Queen's most Excellent Majesty, by and with the advice and consent of the Lords Spiritual and Temporal, and Commons, in this present Parliament assembled, and by the authority of the same, as follows:

1. From and after the twenty-fifth day of March one thousand eight hundred and sixty-six, so much of the twenty-sixth section of the fourth and fifth William the Fourth, chapter seventy-six, as requires that each of the Parishes in a Union formed under the authority of that Act shall be separately chargeable with and liable to defray the expense of its own poor, whether relieved in or out of the workhouse of such Union, shall be repealed; and all the cost of the relief to the poor, and the expenses of the burial of the dead body of any poor person, under the direction of the Guardians or any of their officers duly authorized, in such Union, thenceforth incurred, and all charges thenceforth incurred by the Guardians of such Union in respect of vaccination and registration fees and expenses, shall be charged upon the common fund thereof.

2. When any pauper relieved in any such Union shall be settled in any Parish situated in another Union or subject to a Board of Guardians, and shall not be exempt from removal by reason of any provision of the law, the Guardians of the Union to which such pauper shall be chargeable may obtain an order of removal addressed to the Guardians of the Union or Parish, or the overseers of the Parish, as the case may require, in which such pauper shall be settled, and the Guardians of such last-mentioned Union or Parish shall receive such pauper in like manner and subject to the like incidents and consequences as in the case of orders of removals heretofore obtained by overseers, with such modifications as may be necessary to meet the circumstances of the chargeability to the Union instead of the Parish. Poor Law Board. *Eighteenth Annual Report* (1865–6), 27

---

60 Charles Buller   The Buller Minute

Charles Buller (1806–48), the son of an East India Company official, was a keen administrative reformer who had gained experience as chief secretary to the Governor General of

Canada, Lord Durham, and as secretary to the India Board
of Control. He and Gibbon Wakefield wrote most of the
Durham Report of 1839, which advocated self-government
for Canada. His career as first president of the Poor Law
Board was cut short by his sudden death in 1848.

_____

VAGRANCY.—MINUTE of the POOR LAW BOARD.

Poor Law Board, Somerset House,
August 4, 1848.

THE Board have received representations from every part of
England and Wales respecting the continual and rapid increase
of vagrancy. After making due allowance for the influence of
circumstances that have created temporary distress, it is impossible to come to any other conclusion than that the system
which has of late years been adopted in the relief of casual poor,
has been the principal cause of the extension of vagrancy. It is
not difficult to see that a regular provision of food and lodging,
at the public expense, for every person who chooses to demand
them at any place, must diminish the risks and privations of a
vagrant life, and tempt a resort to it on the part of many who
would otherwise have been deterred from adopting it. Experience has shown that the roughness of the lodging and coarseness
of the fare provided, while they inflict undesirable hardship on
the really meritorious and destitute wayfarer, do not counter-
balance the inducements which the certainty of sustenance and
shelter holds out to the dishonest vagrant. The task of work
prescribed and found useful where it has been properly applied,
has, from its being only occasionally enforced, exercised no
general influence as a test; and the laws against vagrancy and
disorderly conduct have failed to produce the effect of re-
pression. The Board are unable to suggest any additional test or
punishment that shall prevent the abuse of relief indiscriminately extended to every stranger who may represent himself as
destitute. A sound and vigilant discrimination in respect of the
objects of relief, and the steady refusal of aid to all who are not
ascertained to be in a state of destitution, are obviously the most

effectual remedies against the continued increase of vagrancy and mendicancy.

The Board cannot close this minute without again impressing on Boards of Guardians the absolute necessity of discriminating by inquiry and investigation between real and simulated destitution. This is no principle of partial applicability or incomplete obligation. It is the undoubted principle of the law, which equally requires the grant of relief to the destitute, and prohibits the misapplication of the public fund to those who are not destitute.

It was found necessary by the late Poor Law Commissioners at one time to remind the various Unions and their officers of the responsibility which would be incurred by refusing relief where it was required. The present state of things renders it necessary that this Board should now impress on them the grievous mischiefs that must arise, and the responsibilities that may be incurred by a too ready distribution of relief to tramps and vagrants not entitled to it. Boards of Guardians and their officers may, in their attempts to restore a more wise and just system, be subjected to some obloquy from prejudices that confound poverty with profligacy; they will, however, be supported by the consciousness of discharging their duty to those whose funds they have to administer, as well as to the deserving poor, and of resisting the extension of a most pernicious and formidable abuse. They may confidently reckon on the support of a public opinion, which the present state of things has aroused and enlightened; and those who are responsible to the Poor Law Board may feel assured that, while no instance of neglect or harshness to the poor will be tolerated, they may look to the Board for a candid construction of their acts and motives, and for a hearty and steadfast support of those who shall exert themselves to guard from the grasp of imposture that fund which should be sacred to the necessities of the poor.

CHARLES BULLER, *President.*

GEO. NICHOLLS, *Secretary.*

O

Poor Law Board. *First Annual Report*, Appendix A, No 7 (1848)

61 Liverpool Parish   Rules for a Vagrant Ward

In 1865 the Poor Law Board reflected the increasing public concern about the problem of vagrancy by asking for reports from its inspectors on the methods used by local authorities to deal with tramps. Inspector U. Corbett reporting on his district of Lancashire, Yorkshire and the North Midlands, appended these rules for the Liverpool vagrant ward.

PARISH OF LIVERPOOL.—REGULATIONS for Guidance of the Superintendent of the Vagrant Department of the Workhouse.

The department to be open for the admission of Vagrants at 5 o'clock p.m. daily, and to continue open until 10 o'clock on the following morning.

All destitute poor persons presenting orders for admission from any of the relieving officers, together with all others applying, who shall appear to the superintendent to be destitute tramps or Vagrants, to be admitted.

The superintendent shall record in a book the names of all persons admitted, and shall prepare weekly abstracts of same.

He shall also record the names of all applicants whom in the exercise of his discretion he shall refuse to admit, with his reasons for every such refusal, and he shall hold himself prepared to account for his conduct in every such case.

He shall call the special attention of the superintendent relieving officer to all cases that have been admitted into the Vagrant wards for three nights in any month.

Vagrants upon admission to be searched and placed in a bath. The temperature of the bath to be fixed daily by the medical officer on duty.

Vagrants capable of doing so, to be required to grind corn, not exceeding 30 lbs. each on the evening of admission, and 30 lbs. before discharge on the following morning; but the officer in charge to have the power of diminishing the quantity according to his discretion in special cases.

Any Vagrant pleading inability to work by reason of illness or any other cause to be excused, unless the medical officer shall certify that such Vagrant is capable of working and performing the task imposed.

Oakum-picking or other lighter work to be provided for those who are not fit for the heavier work of corn-grinding.

Each Vagrant on admission to receive 6 ounces of bread and 1 pint of milk gruel, and before discharge a like allowance.

Vagrants to be discharged on completing morning's task of work, or not later than 10 o'clock a.m. daily.

In all cases of difficulty, the superintendent to apply for instruction and direction to the governor of the workhouse. Poor Law Board. *Reports on Vagrancy*, XXV (1866), 153

62 Andrew Doyle   The 'Terror of the Tramp'

Inspector Andrew Doyle, reporting on vagrancy in his area of the West Midlands and North and Central Wales, was in no doubt that vagrants were a criminal class who posed a considerable threat to society.

If confirmation were wanted of the truth of the representations contained in the preceding letters, as to the character and habits of the vagrant class, it is furnished by themselves in the notices which they usually leave behind them upon the walls and doors of the vagrant wards. These professional "tramps" or "cadgers" "work" particular districts, generally in couples, not unfrequently in small bands of three or four. For the information and guidance of their associates their visits are generally recorded, their destination indicated, and appointments made with their "pals." Here are some of the notices which I have had copied from the vagrant wards of different workhouses:—

"*Private notice.*—Saucy Harry and his moll will be at Chester to eat their Christmas dinner, when they hope Saucer and the fraternity will meet them at the union.—14th November 1865."

"*Notice to our pals.*—Bristol Jack and Burslem was here on the

15th of April, bound for Montgomeryshire for the summer season."

"Notice to Long Cockney, or Cambridge, or any of the fraternity.—Harry the Mark was here from Carmarthen, and if anybody of the Yorkshire tramps wishes to find him he is to be found in South Wales for the next three months.—17th August 1865."

"Spanish Jim, the b—— fool who robbed two poor b—— tramps in Clatterbridge union, was here on the—find it out."

"Taffy, the Sanctus, was here on the 28th of November 1865."

"Yankey Ben, with Hungerford Tom and Stockport Ginger. The oakum was tried to be burned here on 28th October by Messers John Whittington, Joseph Walker, Thos. Pickering, Jas. Hawthornwaite."

"The Flying Dutchman off to Brum for a summer cruise at the back doors or any other door."

"Cockney Harry and Lambeth bound for Brum for jolly rags."

"Beware of the Cheshire tramps, Spanish Jem, Kildare Jem, Dublin Dick, Navvy Jack, Dick Graven, the shrewd Cheshire tramps."

"Wild Scoty the celebrated king of the cadgers, is in Newgate in London, going to be hanged by the neck till he is dead; this is a great fact.—*Written by his mate.*"

"Never be ashamed of cadging. I was worth five hundred pounds once, and now I am glad to cadge for a penny or a piece of bread.—*Lanky Tom.*"

"The Governor of Chester Castle orders all subalterns to meet at Stourbridge."

"If ragtailed Soph stays here (Shiffnal) come on to Stafford."

"Wrexham is head-quarters now."

"Belfast Jack bound for head-quarters, Chester."

"The York Spinner, Dick Blazeaway, Lancashire Crab, Dublin Smasher, and Bob Curly called for one night on their road for the tip at Birmingham."

"Bow street, Long Macclesfield, Welsh Ned, Sailor Jack, the Islington Kid, Wakefield Charley, and an Irish cabinet maker were located here 10th September 1865."

Indications are frequently given as to the character of the relief afforded in different unions. The "bare-boards" of some vagrant wards are carefully distinguished from the "good padding" of others, and warnings are given, that in such and such unions the "tear-ups" will not get new suits. The bad character of the Congleton workhouse (near Sandbach) is thus recorded:—

> "Oh Sandbach, thou art no catch,
>   For like heavy bread, a damned bad batch,
>   A nice new suit for all tear-ups,
>   And stones to crack for refractory pups."

The workhouse of the Seisdon Union (at Trysull) appears to be in rather better odour with the "fraternity,"

> "Dry bread in the morning, ditto at night,
>   Keep up your pecker and make it all right.
>   Certainly the meals are paltry and mean,
>   But the beds are nice and clean;
>   Men, don't tear these beds, sheets, or rugs,
>   For there are neither lice, fleas, or bugs
>   At this little clean union at Trysull.
>   But still at this place there is a drawback,
>   And now I will put you on the right track,
>   For I would as soon lodge here as in Piccadilly
>   If along with the bread they gave a drop of skilly,
>   At this little clean union at Trysull.
>   So I tell you again, treat this place with respect,
>   And instead of abusing, pray do it protect,
>   For to lodge here one night is certainly a treat,
>   At this little clean union at Trysull.—*Bow Street.*"

"Shaver here, bound for Salop to see the Rev. Henry Burton, a most benevolent minister of the Church of England, and may the devil fetch him soon." Poor Law Board. *Reports on Vagrancy*, XXXV (1866), 62-3

FINANCE

One problem to which the Royal Commission of 1832–4 gave little or no consideration was finance. They aimed at reducing the cost of poor relief, but gave no thought to the inadequacies and illogicalities of the existing method of rating. The Act of 1834 left the power of collecting the poor rate in the hands of the parish overseer, and, as has been seen, the cost of relieving its paupers, whether in or out of the workhouse, had to be borne by each parish separately until 1865.

One result of this was a grossly unfair distribution of the burden of poor relief within Unions. Parishes with a large working-class population were forced to pay out heavily in a period of economic depression on the basis of a low rateable value. By contrast, parishes whose inhabitants were wealthier could rate property of a high valuation, out of which they had to relieve only the few paupers belonging to them and pay their share of the common Union expenses (63). In rural areas the division into 'close' and 'open' parishes which the Settlement Act encouraged exacerbated these inequalities (54).

Chafing under these unequal burdens, parishes often delayed paying the amounts levied on them by boards of guardians until the last possible moment. In periods of bad harvest or trade depression some small ratepayers found it impossible to pay their poor rates and had to be excused payment by the magistrates. Thus a Union often found its finances at a low ebb just when demands on them were greatest, and some came perilously close to bankruptcy (64). The Lancashire Cotton Famine exposed the weaknesses of the system, many townships populated by unemployed operatives being quite unable to meet the calls on their rates made by the board of guardians. The crisis forced the pace of reform. In 1861, rateable value, not relief expenditure as previously, was made the basis of each parish's contribution to the common fund of the Union. In the following year, powers of assessment for rating purposes passed from parish overseers to boards of guardians. Finally the Union Chargeability Act of 1865 ended the system of parochial charge-ability and thrust the whole cost of relief upon the common fund of the Union (59). Inequalities between parishes in the same Union were much reduced, but inequalities between Unions remained and were to be a potent source of friction in later years.

Not only were parishes forced to bear unequal portions of the costs of a Union, but ratepayers also complained that the antiquated formula of assessment laid down by the Act of 1601 meant that some of them had to pay an unfair proportion of the poor rate. Landowners and farmers complained that a heavier burden fell on the land, since the poor rate was essentially a tax on real property. Factory owners and merchants were rated in respect of their factory buildings, warehouses and private houses, but their profits and stock remained inviolable from the rate collector. In urban areas, poor rates often had to be collected from a large number of small properties, since it was the occupier and not the landlord who was liable for payment of the rate. Acts of 1850 (13 & 14 Vic, c 99) and of 1869 (32 & 33 Vic, c 41) allowed for the rating of owners instead of occupiers of small tenements, but not all rating authorities took advantage of these Acts. Collection of the rate from a large number of small tenements was a difficult task, particularly as the occupiers of such property frequently moved house and thus escaped payment. Nevertheless a considerable proportion of the rate in many towns fell on the small ratepayer, particularly when wealthier citizens began to move away from the town centre to suburban parishes where paupers were few and the rates low (65). The financial basis of the nineteenth-century poor law stood in urgent need of reform.

63 R. E. Warwick The Inequality of the Poor Rate Parishes

This table, submitted to the Select Committee on Parochial Assessments of 1850 by R. E. Warwick, a guardian of one of the poorer parishes in the City of London Union, reveals how wealthy parishes escaped with a far lower rate than poorer ones with large numbers of paupers to relieve.

DISTRIBUTION of the POOR RATE for the Year ending 25 March 1849.

1 Parish, no rate required.
26 Parishes –   –   not exceeding 1s. in pound per annum.
18   „   exceeding 1s.   „   1s. 6d.   „
19   „   „   1s. 6d. „   2s.   „
15   „   „   2s.   „   3s.   „
 6   „   „   3s.   „   4s.   „
 6   „   „   4s.   „   5s.   „
 4   „   „   5s.   „   8s.   „
 3   „   no Return.
__
98   „

Lowest amount of rate levied, 3½d. in pound per annum.
Highest   „   „   8s.   „   „

FOURTEEN PARISHES with Large RENTALS; Small EXPENDITURE.

PARISHES.	RENTAL.	RATE.	
	£.	s.	d.
St. Mildred, Bread-street - - -	2,476	nil.	
St. Christopher-le-Stock - - -	3,027	–	3½
St. Andrew Undershaft - - -	15,400	1	2
St. Helen, Bishopsgate - - -	11,865	1	4
St. Michael, Cornhill - - - -	20,513	1	–
St. Michael, Bassishaw - - -	11,218	1	–
St. Olave, Hart-street - - - -	13,041	1	6
St. Bartholomew by Exchange - -	16,131	–	8
St. Lawrence, Jewry - - - -	12,606	–	9
St. Mary Woolnoth - - - -	11,066	–	9
St. Michael, Crooked-lane - - -	7,271	1	–
St. Dunstan in the East - - -	17,358	1	6
St. Margaret, Lothbury - - -	9,993	1	–
St. Peter, Cornhill - - - -	14,656	1	6
TOTALS - - £.	166,625	13	5½

FOURTEEN PARISHES with Small RENTALS; Large EXPENDITURE.

PARISHES.	RENTAL.	RATE.	
	£.	s.	d.
St. Nicholas Olave - - - -	1,507	8	–
St. Nicholas Cole Abbey - - -	1,613	3	3
St. Olave, Silver-street - - -	3,203	5	–
Holy Trinity-the-Less - - -	2,494	6	4
St. Mary Magdalen, Old Fish-street -	3,020	5	–
St. Alphage - - - - -	3,527	4	1
St. James, Garlickhithe - - -	4,762	5	3
St. Bennet, Paul's Wharf - - -	4,700	4	3
Whitefriars Precinct - - - -	5,403	4	–
St. James, Duke's-place - - -	3,343	3	8
St. Thomas Apostle - - - -	3,287	3	–
St. Mary Mounthaw - - - -	973	4	3
St. Michael, Queenhithe - - -	3,541	3	3
St. Ann, Blackfriars - - - -	13,978	4	3
TOTALS - - £.	55,352	63	7

ROB. E. WARWICK,
Guardian, St. Ann, Blackfriars.
Select Committee on Parochial Assessments. *Report*, XVI (1850),
140–41

___

64 William Day   Poor-law Union Finance

William Day, in his letter of complaint to the Poor Law
Commissioners on the difficulties of an Assistant Commissioner (31), also pointed to the very great problems under
which boards of guardians laboured in matters of finance.

___

The orders of the Commissioners require the Guardians to
levy contributions from time to time on the different Parishes of
their Union, to meet the necessary demands for the relief of
their respective Poor. When so levied they are paid into a Joint

Stock Fund with the Treasurer, in whose hands the parochial contributions cease to be separately distinguished. The Relieving Officers, however, receive their cheques for the relief of their poor upon the general fund, and neither know nor inquire from the assets of what particular parish they are cashed. So long as the Union accounts present a credit balance with the Treasurer, the cheques are answered, and no question raised.

If the calls of the Guardians were accurately calculated, and punctually paid up, no material inconvenience would probably arise. Under ordinary circumstances the prospective expenditure might be correctly estimated, and for contingent and unexpected emergencies, extraordinary levies would be required.

During the whole period, however, that I was connected with the Commission, I was never fortunate enough to find in the majority of parishes that convenient season when orders were received with favour, and paid with punctuality. Excuses are never wanting. If the harvest is bad there is no corn to exchange for money—if good, there is no money to be got for corn. If there are restrictions on trade, the manufacturers languish, and cease to be customers; if restrictions are diminished or removed, then the foreigner is in the market, and undersells the home producer. Be the state of circumstances what they may, there is always a reason for payment in arrear.

The practical result is this—that each Parish in an Union struggles to be the last to pay, and speculates upon the Treasurer's funds being replenished by its neighbours. The other parishes play the same game, until the Union becomes bankrupt, and the relief of the poor is suddenly stopped. In one of my Unions, the Guardians adjourned indefinitely for want of funds, and in too many others the Poor have gone unrelieved for weeks and weeks together.

Bad as is this state of things, even this is not the worst. Not only do the parishes not pay up their quotas for the relief of their poor, but they exhaust those funds which have been actually provided by other parishes for the same purpose. I have already explained that the Relieving Officer's cheques are answered by the Treasurer so long as he has funds, let them belong to what parish they may; and thus the Union at large may be living upon the rates of the single township of A, until their whole credit is exhausted, and the system recommenced at the other end of the alphabet.

The short fact is this:—In every poor country, especially such as Wales, where the rate-payers themselves are on the very verge of pauperism, the Overseers will neither make nor collect rates, except upon compulsion. The Guardians are themselves rate-payers generally in arrear, and will not proceed against those officers whose very first step would be to lay informations against themselves. I have thus known in one Union, when the clerk reported the failure of funds in the hands of the Treasurer, a motion made and carried, that the question of fresh calls upon the different parishes should be adjourned for six months. In fact, my experience has taught me that the power of *self taxation*, when accompanied by practical irresponsibility, is the most dangerous that can be committed to a fluctuating and *ungraspable* body. There is *no* responsibility where the members of the Corporation in whom it professes to be vested, are indeterminate, and where the modus operandi fixes nothing of personality on any of its proceedings. William Day. *Correspondence with the Poor Law Commissioners* (1844), 9–10

65 William Rathbone   The Inequality of the Poor-rate Ratepayers

William Rathbone (1819–1902), a member of an old established and wealthy Liverpool merchant family, was MP for Liverpool 1868–80, and later for Caernarvonshire. He was an active philanthropist in his native city, perhaps his most famous work being the establishment of a system of district nursing in Liverpool.

In this published version of a speech he made in the House of Commons in June 1869 he was sharply critical of those members of his own class who were dodging their full share of the burden of the poor rate and also their duty to serve the community as poor-law guardians.

The principal wealth of our large towns is the commercial, manufacturing, and trading capital, and yet it is exactly this capital which does not contribute, except incidentally, to local taxation. I maintain that the classes who possess this property do not contribute their fair share towards the rates levied to support, in sickness, accident, or poverty, those without whose labour their wealth would never have been created. Nay, more, as their wealth has increased, as the large towns have expanded, and as the burden of supporting the poor in the large towns has become heavier, the proportionate contribution of this class towards local taxation has actually diminished. They do not contribute upon their capital, because their capital consisting chiefly of personalty is, as a rule, exempted from liability. They do not contribute upon their domestic expenditure as they used to do, because the rich merchant, broker, or banker, instead of living as he formerly did, and as his fathers had done, on the spot where his business was carried on, and in the midst of those whom he employed, now lives out of town and beyond the area of its taxation. The amount, consequently, which he contributes to its poor rate is insignificant, if compared with his means. And I would ask whether it is unreasonable to suppose that this has something to do with the withdrawal of that class from the most important part of the duties of a good citizen—the guardianship of the poor. It is no slight evil that the class whose experience, from their having had to deal with expenditure on a large scale and with economy on a large scale, would be peculiarly valuable, should have almost entirely withdrawn themselves from parochial work.

After much inquiry into this subject, I find that, broadly speaking, the per-centage of his income that a man pays to the poor rates is often in the inverse ratio to the amount of his income. The wealthier he is the smaller the per-centage he pays. Take the case of a man doing a large business with only a moderately large office and warehouse. He only pays on the rent of his office or warehouse, whatever his profits may be. I know the case of merchants who have made the calculation, and find that their rates vary from $\frac{1}{2}$ to 2 per cent. on their incomes, while the average per-centage of the rates of the porters in their employ amounts to $3\frac{3}{4}$ per cent. on their incomes. In other words, the labourers pay from twice to seven times as much in proportion to their incomes as do their employers, the merchants and brokers alluded to. And if you take the case of the shopkeepers, the inequality becomes even more apparent. The proportion of their income which two of the most prosperous shopkeepers in Liverpool pay to the poor rate amounts to 5 per cent., and if this is the case with these wealthy and prosperous tradesmen, how heavy must be the burden upon the men who are striving hard, and who barely succeed in gaining sufficient to maintain and educate their families. Upon this class of small tradesmen the pressure of the poor rate must indeed be very oppressive.

I repeat, therefore, that in the large towns, and I have no doubt the same is the case in other places, the poorer class contributes to the poor rate a larger proportion of its income than the richer, and the poorer in each class contribute a larger proportion of their income than the richer. No one, I presume, will for a moment contend that such a state of things is just or defensible. William Rathbone. *Local Taxation and Poor Law Administration in Great Cities* (1869)

PART FOUR

The Poor Law
under Attack 1870-1914

During the 1860s, the inadequacies of the poor-law system had been increasingly exposed. The Lancashire Cotton Famine had shown its futility in the face of mass industrial unemployment; the *Lancet* inquiries of 1865 had revealed the wretched state of the sick poor in the workhouses; and the 'barrack schools' for pauper children were being subjected to increasing criticism. Most alarming of all, as far as many poor-law administrators were concerned, was the realisation that the allowance system of relief in aid of earnings was far from dead. In the big cities, in particular, many boards of guardians were doling out small amounts of cash relief to able-bodied paupers, and leaving them to bring these inadequate allowances up to subsistence level by begging, stealing, or working at ill-paid jobs.

THE CAMPAIGN AGAINST OUTDOOR RELIEF

The appointment of G. J. Goschen as President of the Poor Law Board in the Gladstone Administration of 1868, and the replacement of the Poor Law Board by a new central authority, the Local Government Board, brought with them a sterner attitude towards the administration of poor relief. Goschen's minute on poor relief in London in 1869 (66) condemned the practice of giving out relief in aid of earnings and suggested greater co-operation between boards of guardians and charit-

able agencies in the giving of aid. Goschen's successor at the
Local Government Board, James Stansfeld, shared his anxieties
about the lax system of outdoor relief, and in 1871 the Board
issued a circular on the subject to its inspectors (67). Although
this made no change in the Orders regulating poor relief, it did
require inspectors to impress upon boards of guardians the need
for a much stricter adherence to the regulations, and thus a
reduction in the number of applicants to whom out relief was
granted. This request was readily acceded to by the inspectorate, several of whose members had been pressing the central
authority for this very reform. Some boards of guardians also
showed themselves willing (68). Attempts were made at Poplar
and Kensington in London, and later in Birmingham, Manchester and Sheffield to implement the 1834 Poor Law by
establishing separate 'test' workhouses to which the able-bodied
poor could be sent and where they would be subjected to strict
discipline and irksome labour. Although great claims were made
for the success of these institutions in reducing the number of
applications for relief, none of them seem to have lasted for
more than ten years before, in the Webbs' phrase, they
'reverted to type' and became general mixed workhouses once
more.

   The growing concern about indiscriminate grants of outdoor
relief in the 1860s was matched by a fear that similar practices
were being followed by the administrators of private charities.
Mid-Victorian England spawned a great mass of charitable
institutions, which vied with each other for funds and the favour
of wealthy, preferably titled, patrons; but many of them gave
too little thought to the objects for which they were established.
Aid was given to the poor without any inquiry as to whether it
was sufficient or suited to the nature of the case. There was
little co-operation between charities instituted for the same
purpose. The Select Committee on Poor Relief of 1864 strongly
criticised the indiscriminate way in which voluntary agencies
had tried to supplement the inadequate doles granted by boards
of guardians in London. The Goschen Minute of 1869 asked for

greater co-ordination between voluntary and poor-law relieving agencies.

Models for a better organised scheme of charitable relief were not lacking. In Glasgow in the 1820s the Rev Thomas Chalmers had divided a large parish into a number of districts each under a deacon whose duty it was to visit the poor, assess their needs and find the best method of helping them, without, if possible, calling on parish funds. A similar system of district visitors had been developed after 1853 in the German city of Elberfeld, though under this system the expenses of relief were met from public funds. In London the Board of Jewish Guardians adopted Chalmers's method of visiting those who called on them for aid.

Such examples were not lost on would-be charity reformers. William Rathbone, inspired by a visit to Elberfeld, was prominent in establishing a Central Relief Society in Liverpool in 1863. This body attempted to unite the various charities in the city and persuade them to conduct their operations in a more business-like fashion. Visitors were paid by the Society to investigate cases of need.

Five years later a body calling itself the London Association for the Prevention of Pauperism and Crime was formed. In 1870 this clumsy title was discarded in favour of the Charity Organisation Society. The Society, led by its energetic secretary, Charles Stewart Loch, was to be a major influence in the shaping of social policy in the later nineteenth century. Its attitude to poverty was moralistic and individualistic. COS members firmly believed that a distinction could be made between the deserving and undeserving poor: the former should, after careful investigation, be given charitable relief of the type most likely to set them on their feet and inspire them to stay there by their own efforts; the latter—the workshy, the backsliders, the drunkards—should be denied the aid of private charity and left to the none too tender mercies of the poor relief system, operating along strict 'less eligibility' lines. Despite these forbidding attitudes, the COS was not entirely reactionary.

It stressed the fact that mere almsgiving was not enough: the wealthier classes must get to know the circumstances of the poor by visiting them or even by living among them; those who wished to act as visitors must be properly trained for the task; and methodical casework was the only way to discover the requirements of the deserving pauper—and once discovered these must be met regardless of cost.

In order to carry out its plans, the COS encouraged co-ordination not only between various charitable agencies but also between those agencies and boards of guardians. Thus there developed in some Unions a system of close co-operation between relieving officers and COS visitors (69). By its insistence on a methodical system of relief, its hostility to indiscriminate alms, and its desire for a stricter poor law system, the COS endeared itself to the inspectors and permanent officials of the Local Government Board. Between them, these two bodies constituted a formidable pressure group for a return to those 'principles of 1834' which many boards of guardians seemed to have forgotten.

66 G. J. Goschen   The Goschen Minute

George Joachim Goschen (1831–1907) was the son of a London merchant. Educated at Rugby and Oriel College, Oxford, he was made a director of the Bank of England at the age of 27, and in 1863 was elected as MP for the City of London. In the first Gladstone administration of 1868–74, he held the posts of President of the Poor Law Board (1868–71) and First Lord of the Admiralty (1871–4). After 1880 he became increasingly suspicious of the Radical elements in the Liberal Party, and was a founder member of the Unionist group that broke away from the Liberals over the question of Irish Home Rule in 1886. Goschen later held office as Chancellor of the Exchequer and as First Lord of the Admiralty in Lord Salisbury's Conservative Administrations of 1886–92 and 1895–1902.

P

RELIEF to the POOR in the METROPOLIS.—MINUTE of the
POOR LAW BOARD.

THE published statements of Metropolitan pauperism have
for some weeks past shown a considerable increase in the
number of the out-door poor, not only as compared with previous weeks, but as compared with the high totals of 1867 and
1868. At the same time it has come to the knowledge of the
Board that many persons (especially in the East End of London)
who two winters ago were most eager in soliciting charitable
contributions have now expressed the opinion that the large
sums spent then in charity tended to attract pauperism to those
districts where money flowed most freely, and that they depre-
cate a repetition of the system then pursued. Under these circumstances the Board consider it equally important to guard on
the one hand against any alarm which might arise on the part
of the public, and result in an indiscriminate distribution of
charitable funds, and on the other hand to take such precautions and make such preparations as may enable Boards of
Guardians and charitable agencies to work with effect and
rapidity if any emergency should arise. And, indeed, without
considering the question of an increase in the numbers of the
out-door poor, and looking simply to the present expenditure on
poor relief, it appears to be a matter of essential importance
that an attempt should be made to bring the authorities administering the Poor Laws and those who administer charitable funds to as clear an understanding as possible, so as to
avoid the double distribution of relief to the same persons, and
at the same time to secure that the most effective use should
be made of the large sums habitually contributed by the
public towards relieving such cases as the Poor Law can
scarcely reach.

The question arises, how far it is possible to mark out the
separate limits of the Poor Law and of charity respectively,
and how it is possible to secure joint action between the
two.

One of the most recognized principles in our Poor Law is,

that relief should be given only to the actually destitute, and not in aid of wages. In the case of widows with families, where it is often manifestly impossible that the earnings of the woman can support the family, the rule is frequently departed from, but, as a general principle, it lies at the root of the present system of relief. In innumerable cases its application appears to be harsh for the moment, and it might also be held to be an aggravation of an existing difficulty to insist that, so long as a person is in employment, and wages are earned, though such wages may be insufficient, the Poor Law authorities ought to hold aloof and refuse to supplement the receipts of the family, actually offering in preference to take upon themselves the entire cost of their maintenance. Still it is certain that no system could be more dangerous, both to the working classes and to the ratepayers, than to supplement insufficiency of wages by the expenditure of public money.

The fundamental doctrine of the English Poor Laws, in which they differ from those of most other countries, is that relief is given, not as a matter of charity but of legal obligation, and to extend this legal obligation beyond the class to which it now applies, namely, the actually destitute, to a further and much larger class, namely, those in receipt of insufficient wages, would be not only to increase to an unlimited extent the present enormous expenditure, but to allow the belief in a legal claim to public money in every emergency to supplant, in a further portion of the population, the full recognition of the necessity for self-reliance and thrift.

It is clear, therefore, that the Poor Law authorities could not be allowed without public danger to extend their operations beyond those persons who are actually destitute, and for whom they are at present legally bound to provide. It would seem to follow that charitable organizations, whose alms could in no case be claimed as a right, would find their most appropriate sphere in assisting those who have some, but insufficient means, and who, though on the verge of pauperism, are not actual paupers, leaving to the operation of the general law the provision for the totally destitute. Poor Law Board. *Twenty Second Annual Report*, Appendix A, No 4 (1869–70)

67 Local Government Board Circular on Outdoor Relief (1871)

Although this document did not alter the regulations controlling the giving of outdoor relief, its whole tone condemned the out-relief system. Guardians were discouraged from granting outdoor relief to able-bodied women, and, in the numerous cases of widows with dependent children, were asked to consider taking one or more of the children into the workhouse as a suitable mode of relief. Even the aged and sick, the Board advised, should have their applications for relief carefully scrutinised.

OUT-DOOR RELIEF.—CIRCULAR from the LOCAL GOVERNMENT BOARD to the POOR LAW INSPECTORS.

Local Government Board, Whitehall, S.W.,
SIR,   *2nd December* 1871.

THE large increase which has within the last few years taken place in the amount of out-door relief has been regarded by the Local Government Board with much anxiety, and has led them to institute special inquiries in the metropolis, and in the counties of Berks, Cornwall, Devon, Dorset, Gloucester, Kent, Somerset, Southampton, Surrey, Sussex, and Wilts.

In addition to these inquiries, the Board have, as you are aware, instructed their Inspectors to report upon the state of out-door relief in their several districts.

Many causes have doubtless contributed to the increase in out-door relief which has taken place; but the Board believe, from the information before them, that it is not to any considerable extent attributable to defects in the law or orders which regulate out-door relief. So far, therefore, as the increase is attributable to defective management or administration of the law, the remedy is in the hands of its local administrators, the Guardians, and may be at once applied by them.

The Board trust that you will take as early an opportunity as your engagements will permit, to bring this subject before the several Boards of Guardians in the district under your supervision. Your own knowledge of the circumstances of particular Unions will enable you to urge upon Guardians the special suggestions that may be applicable to each Union. But the Board desire to submit to you some facts and considerations that may assist in obtaining considerable general improvement, as well as greater uniformity, in the administration of relief throughout the country.

The cost of out-door relief in England and Wales in the year 1860 amounted to £2,862,753, whilst the out-door relief for the year 1870 amounted to £3,633,051, being an increase of £770,308.

The ratio of out-door paupers to the population was, in 1860, 1 in every 27, and, in 1870, 1 in every 25.

Making every allowance for the increase of population, stagnation in trades, and temporary disturbances in the labour market, variations in the seasons, and other causes which necessarily influence Poor Law relief generally, the increase in the cost of out-door relief is so great, as to excite apprehension; and to suggest that measures should be taken, not only to check any further increase, but to diminish the present amount.

Against all the causes which tend to an increased expenditure of the rates in the form of out-door relief, it is impossible effectually to guard; but it ought to be possible to guard, for the future, against such expenditure as may arise from a too lax or indiscriminate system of administration.

The inquiries which have been made by the Board show conclusively,—

1. That out-door relief is in many cases granted by the Guardians too readily and without sufficient inquiry, and that they give it also in numerous instances in which it would be more judicious to apply the workhouse test, and to adhere more

strictly to the provisions of the orders and regulations in force in regard to out-door relief.

2. That there is a great diversity of practice in the administration of out-door relief and that a marked contrast is shown in the numbers relieved, and in the amount of the relief granted in the Unions in which the Guardians adhere strictly to the law, and in those in which they more or less disregard it.

3. It has been shown that in numerous instances the Guardians disregard the advantages which result not only to the ratepayers but to the poor themselves from the offer of in-door in preference to out-door relief. A certainty of obtaining out-door relief in his own home whenever he may ask for it extinguishes in the mind of the labourer all motive for husbanding his resources, and induces him to rely exclusively upon the rates instead of upon his own savings for such relief as he may require. It removes every incentive to self-reliance and prudent forethought on his part, and induces him, moreover, to apply for relief on occasions when the circumstances are not such as to render him absolutely in need of it. Local Government Board. *First Annual Report*, Appendix A, No 20 (1871–2)

68 Manchester Guardians Regulations on Outdoor Relief (1875)

The Circular on Outdoor Relief caused the Manchester board of guardians, which prided itself on its strict administration, to tighten its regulations yet further, particularly those on outdoor relief to women.

1. Out-door relief shall not be granted or allowed by the Relief Committees, except in case of sickness, to applicants of any of the following classes:—
   (*a.*) Single able-bodied men.
   (*b.*) Single able-bodied women.
   (*c.*) Able-bodied widows without children, or having only one child to support.

(*d.*) Married women (with or without families) whose husbands, having been convicted of crime, are undergoing a term of imprisonment.

(*e.*) Married women (with or without families) deserted by their husbands.

(*f.*) Married women (with or without families) left destitute through their husbands having joined the militia, and being called up for training.

(*g.*) Persons residing with relatives, where the united income of the family is sufficient for the support of all its members, whether such relatives are liable by law to support the applicant or not.

2. Out-door relief shall not be granted in any case for a longer period than thirteen weeks at a time.

3. Out-door relief shall not be granted to any able-bodied person for a longer period than six weeks at a time.

4. Out-door relief shall not be granted, on account of the sickness of the applicant, or any of his family, for a longer period than two weeks at a time, unless such sickness shall be certified in writing by the district medical officer as being likely to be of long duration, or to be of a permanent character.

5. Where relief is allowed to a parent through the admission of a child or children into the Swinton schools or the workhouse, such relief shall not be granted for a longer period than six months at a time; and if at the expiration of such period a continuance of the relief is required, the relieving officer shall visit and inquire into the circumstances of the parent, and bring the case up for re-consideration by the Relief Committee, in the same manner as if it were a case of out-door relief. Local Government Board. *Fifth Annual Report*, Appendix B, No 18 (1875–6)

69 Dr P. F. Aschrott   The COS at Work

Dr P. F. Aschrott, a famous German jurist and political economist, first published his work *Das Englische Armen-Wesen* in 1886. On the suggestion of Professor Henry Sidgwick it was

translated into English and this extract is taken from the
second edition of 1902. The book itself consists of a detailed
and legalistic account of the history and existing organisation
of the English Poor Law system. Dr Aschcrott was an admirer
of the work of the Charity Organisation Society, and gave a
detailed account of its work in an appendix.

Aschcrott's examples, however, exaggerate the extent to
which the Charity Organisation Society was able to achieve
its original purpose of co-ordinating poor relief and private
charity. Many boards of guardians ignored it and other
philanthropic organisations regarded it jealously as a poten-
tial rival. Thus many of its district committees were forced to
work alone.

Marylebone was one district in which the Society did have
some initial success in its task of co-ordination. Much of the
credit for this was due to Octavia Hill (1838–1912), grand-
daughter of the sanitary reformer Dr Southwood Smith.
Although best known for her work on working-class housing,
Octavia Hill was a prominent member of the Society and a
firm believer in its principles.

The organization takes place in the following fashion. The
district committees of the society act for areas corresponding
with the poor law unions and parishes of the metropolis. There
are at present 40 district committees. It is desired, whenever
possible, to obtain the election of members of the district committees as guardians, in order to establish relations with the
administration of poor law relief. This has been effected in
certain districts, and in these it becomes possible to arrange
that such cases brought before the guardians as are fit objects of
private charity should be referred to the district committee, and
that such cases as on investigation by the district committee are
recognized as suitable for parochial relief, should be referred to
the guardians.

This co-operation of the district committees with the boards
of guardians, wherever established, results in a reasonable divi-

sion of labour without waste of strength, and answers admirably. For example, in the half-year ending Lady-day, 1901, the board of guardians of the Whitechapel union referred 80 persons, after relieving them temporarily, to the district committee, from whom all received suitable help, of a kind which could not, according to the rigid rules of the Whitechapel union, have been afforded under the poor law.

The co-operation of the Charity Organization Society with the guardians is, to a large extent, effected through the relieving officers. The relieving officer is asked to inform the district committee of all cases which appear suitable for private charity; on the other hand, the relieving officer is made acquainted with each case applying to the district committee. In this way it is possible to prevent relief from being given simultaneously to one and the same person, both from the poor law and from private charity, without the knowledge of the administrators of each class of relief. Persons assisted by the guardians do not, unless their cases are exceptional, receive help from private charity, though in cases in which the guardians give outdoor relief in continuous weekly allowances, in some parts of London relief is also given not infrequently from church charities.

At each district committee there is an honorary or paid secretary (or sometimes both) and an agent or enquiry officer. Members of the committee and their friends take an active personal share in the committee's work. They take part in the daily business of the office, in obtaining information on the spot as to applications to the Charity Organization Society in acting as almoners in pension and other cases, and to assist in other ways. Help is also given by district visitors and other local workers. Searching enquiries, by which full details are obtained as to the cause of poverty, are absolutely necessary, in order to distinguish charitable from poor law cases, and to settle the proper means of relief to the former. Such inquiries are for the most part made by the paid officers of the Society.

For this reason, among others, the Charity Organization Society has laid the greatest stress on the importance of educating and training district visitors, and has in this matter received the special support of Miss Octavia Hill, a lady who has displayed extraordinary capacity for organization and admirable devotion to the work which she has undertaken in various branches of philanthropy. In the poorer districts, where efficient district visitors are seldom numerous, it has been necessary to attract to the committee visitors living in other districts, with the result of some inconvenience in the matter of distance.

The agent or visitor of the committee has to fill up a form as to the case under enquiry. The following particulars have to be ascertained: Age? Family? If children, at what school? Occupation? Where now or last employed? At what wages? Other sources of income? If out of employment, reason for leaving last place? Since when unemployed, and how long employed in the last year? How many rooms does he occupy? At what rent? Arrears of rent? Pawntickets? Other debts? If member of a Friendly Society or Trades Union? Any relief already obtained from private individuals or charitable institutions, or from the guardians? Can assistance be obtained from these or other sources (relations, trade unions, benefit societies, &c.)? Present and previous residence? In what way he thinks he can be permanently benefited?

Each answer must show from whom the information is received. In order to obtain it, the visitor is to have recourse to the relieving officer, the present and previous employer, the clergyman, and if necessary the schoolmaster. Dr P. F. Aschcrott. *The English Poor Law System*, Appendix No 1 (2nd Edition 1902)

THE INADEQUACIES OF THE POOR LAW

Although the desire of the Local Government Board's inspectorate and the COS was largely unrealised, their criticisms of the existing poor-law system had shown that most boards of guardians had no informed or constructive policy for meeting the needs of paupers. From the 1880s on, the failure of poor-law administrators even to alleviate urban poverty, let alone find any solution to it, was increasingly criticised. The last thirty years of the nineteenth century saw the weakening of that spirit of optimism and self-confidence which had marked mid-Victorian England. The economic and military rivalry of other nations, Germany, France and the United States in particular, led to a questioning of Britain's fitness to meet these challenges. The consciences of the wealthier classes, especially those of its younger members, were uneasy at the fact that mass poverty should exist in the wealthiest and most powerful nation in the world. 'They were conscious of something wrong underneath modern progress, they realised that free trade, reform bills, philanthropic activity and missions had made neither health nor wealth. They were drawn to do something for the poor,' wrote Canon Samuel Barnett in 1898.*

This desire to do something was increased, not only by published revelations of the wretched state of the poor in such works as *The Bitter Cry of Outcast London* (1883) or General William Booth's *In Darkest England and the Way Out* (1890), but also by the pressures of an increasingly organised and coherent labour movement. The mass demonstrations in London in 1886 and 1887, the emergence of trade unions amongst unskilled workers in 1889 and 1890, and the increased working-class electorate created by the Reform Acts of 1867 and 1884 helped to convince many people of the need for a more effective social policy to improve working-class conditions. The fact that much of this working-class organisation and agitation was inspired by Socialist bodies such as the Marxist Social Democratic Federation added a note of urgency to the problem. Thus the 1880s was a decade of Royal Commissions on such topics as Labour, the Housing of the Working Classes, and the Condition of the Aged Poor. Increasingly it was being realised that private philanthropy was not enough; the State must play an increasing and more effective role in improving the conditions of life for the mass of its members.

As one of the institutions that might have played such a role

* S. Barnett in W. H. Reason. *University and Social Settlements* (1898), quoted in K. Woodroofe. *From Charity to Social Work* (1962), 66.

but had singularly failed to do so, the Poor Law was an easy target for the critics. Its alleged inhumanities, particularly those practised in its workhouses, were assailed by Socialist publications like Robert Blatchford's *Clarion* or by philanthropists like William Booth (70). The poor-law system had had to meet such attacks throughout its history, but in this period it also had to meet less passionate but ultimately far more devastating intellectual criticism from economists and social scientists. The studies of poverty conducted by Charles Booth in London between 1886 and 1903 and by Seebohm Rowntree in York in 1899 were far more penetrating than the heart-stirring but fragmentary disclosures like *The Bitter Cry of Outcast London.* Indeed, Booth was inspired to begin his survey of *London Life and Labour* because his rational scientific mind was disturbed by the apparently unsupported allegation in a Socialist pamphlet that a quarter of the population of London were living in poverty. By 1889, Booth and his seven assistants were able to show as a result of methodical research that the pamphlet had erred. Its error was not, however, one of overstatement. Booth showed that 30 per cent of London's population was living in poverty, which he defined as having an income of less than 18s od to 21s od (90–105p) a week to support a family consisting of man, wife and three children. Rowntree's investigation, published in 1901 under the title *Poverty. A Study in Town Life,* showed clearly that Booth's survey was no freakish one based on the exceptional conditions of London's East End; 28 per cent of the population of a relatively prosperous provincial city like York lived in poverty in 1899. At the close of the nineteenth century, a third of the population of England and Wales were living below the bare minimum required to maintain even physical well-being.

More important than these findings, however, was the fact that Booth and Rowntree by their dispassionate scientific enquiries were able to isolate the causes of poverty—low wages, unemployment and old age—over which the individual had little or no control. They showed poverty and its causes to be capable of definition and isolation, and thus seemed to open the way to their cure and prevention, just as the public-health reforms of the nineteenth century had succeeded in eradicating infectious diseases like cholera. Although their work contained no explicit condemnation of the Poor Law, they proved that the central and local authorities for poor relief had made no attempt to tackle the causes of poverty, and raised considerable doubts as to whether the poor law was the proper agency to undertake this task in the future (71).

This was perhaps the most devastating type of attack that the nineteenth-century poor law had to bear: the allegation, not that it was inhumane or inefficient, but that it was irrelevant to the needs of an urban industrial society. Such allegations became increasingly widespread in late Victorian England. The greatest economist of his day, Professor Alfred Marshall, told a Royal Commission in 1895 that he considered the thinking behind the Poor Law to be totally out of touch with the conditions of modern society (72). Canon Samuel Barnett, a former member of the COS, who had broken with the Society over the question of State intervention in 1886, attacked the lack of uniformity in the giving of poor relief, and pleaded for new thinking on the subject (73). Particular criticism was directed at the treatment of old people and children. The Royal Commission on the Aged Poor (1895) condemned the inadequacy and irrelevancy of both outdoor and indoor relief to the aged, though it did not go so far as to recommend State pensions, an idea which was being advocated as a means of removing old people from reliance on poor relief. The plight of children in the slums of the big cities was arousing concern. School boards after 1870 found that many of the children for whom they were providing education were unable to benefit from it because of their wretched physical condition. During the Boer War, recruiting sergeants were forced to reject large numbers of young volunteers from the big cities because of their poor health. Alarm at this situation in a period of increasing international tension led to the appointment of an Interdepartmental Committee on Physical Deterioration, which reported in 1904. Once again poor-law provision for children was shown to be totally inadequate to meet the problem, a fact which its critics were not slow to capitalise on.

In the face of such criticism, poor-law administrators did attempt to improve the system. Many of these attempts were inspired by the fact that some of the sharpest critics of the Poor Law were being elected to boards of guardians. The Local Government Act of 1894 removed both the property qualification for prospective poor-law guardians and plural voting in the exercise of the poor-law franchise. Elections for boards of guardians became more open, and political organisations like the Social Democratic Federation or the Independent Labour Party ran candidates. Working men began to appear on boards of guardians, many of them, like Will Crooks and George Lansbury in Poplar, being convinced Socialists (74). Women were also beginning to force their way into the hitherto male preserve of the board room. The result was often the adoption of a more generous policy of relief despite the disapproval of the central authority and its inspectorate. Suitable alternatives to the workhouse were developed by some boards: the Sheffield Guardians pioneered the idea of 'scattered homes' for pauper children despite the misgivings of the central authority (76).

The Local Government Board itself was forced to modify some of its thinking and to urge less progressive boards of guardians to improve or amend their methods of relief. In 1885 it gave its consent to the Medical Relief Disqualification Act, which allowed those who received only medical aid from the guardians to continue to exercise the franchise, and not lose the right to vote in common with other paupers. The criticisms of the Royal Commission on the Aged Poor and of the Select Committee on the Aged Deserving Poor (1899) led the Local Government Board to recommend to boards of guardians that their aged paupers be treated with greater sympathy (75A). More humane treatment of children was also urged, and by the turn of the century the Board's inspectors were keenly advocating the adoption of the cottage homes or 'scattered homes' systems which they had earlier treated with some suspicion (76). Thus the institutional treatment of children and old people did improve over this period, though in some of the more conservative rural Unions the change was extremely slow (75B).

Welcome though they were, such changes in policy and practice failed to meet the criticism that the poor-law system was not equipped to tackle the problems of an industrialised society. Nowhere was this more clearly shown than in the case of the unemployed. It had long been recognised that the workhouse test was irrelevant in the face of large-scale industrial unemployment. The Lancashire Cotton Famine had shown that. Widespread unemployment during the trade depression of the mid-1880s once again brought the problem to the fore. The President of the Local Government Board, Joseph Chamberlain, issued in 1886 a circular in which he urged town councils to undertake programmes of municipal works in order to provide work for unemployed men who would otherwise have to undergo the degrading experience of applying for poor relief (77A). As far as the poor-law system was concerned, the Chamberlain Circular was a confession of defeat. The Unemployed Workmen Act of 1905 carried the policy of the Circular a stage further (77B); by permitting the establishment of municipal distress committees, it allowed the formation of an alternative body for the relief of the unemployed, despite the fact that the local boards of guardians were given representation on the committees. The solution of the unemployment problem was coming to be seen as beyond the capability of the Poor Law.

70 Robert Blatchford   A Socialist View of the Poor Law

'Nunquam' was the pseudonym used by Robert Blatchford (1851–1943), editor and owner of the popular Socialist paper *The Clarion*. The son of an actor, Blatchford had a mixed career that included apprenticeship to a brush maker, a period of Army service, and a job with the Weaver Navigation Company, before he turned to journalism in 1885. His conversion to Socialism came as a result of his experiences in collecting material in Ireland and in the slums of Manchester for articles in the *Sunday Chronicle*. As a result of his Socialist beliefs, he lost a highly paid job on the *Chronicle* in 1891, and with the help of three friends formed *The Clarion*, which was published in Manchester. Despite his unorthodox ideas, Blatchford's paper proved to be a great success, particularly after the publication of his best-selling work *Merrie England* in 1893.

To prevent mistakes I will, before dealing with the facts, explain as clearly as I can the position of the pauper as it appears to me, and as I think it appears to the average Poor-Law Guardian.

The average Guardian, it seems to me, divides his paupers into two classes.

1. The undeserving wastrels who have "only themselves to blame" for their misfortunes, and on whom kindness is wasted.

2. The "industrious poor," who have become destitute through age or misfortune, and deserve the "charity" of their more successful neighbours.

I accept these two divisions, but have something to say to the description. I take the "wastrels" first.

A man is what nature and circumstances make him. If he is born vicious he is not to blame for that, any more than he is to blame for being born blind or imbecile.

If he becomes vicious from bad training, or evil surroundings, he is no more to blame for that than he is to blame for being taught to eat peas with his knife, or consider pigeon-shooting sport.

We have to consider, then, the relations of this man to society. If all his failings were due to nature and none of them to society, then I say this wastrel is still bone of our bone and flesh of our flesh, and is entitled to our succour and our kindness by virtue of his manhood.

But when we remember the cruelties and injustices of competitive commercial warfare, and when we remember the slums, and the betting dens, and the dram shops, we cannot deny that in most cases, if not in all cases, the loafer, the drunkard, and the criminal are what modern civilisation have made them.

Suppose a pauper is a drunkard. The highest medical and official testimony shows us that the craving for alcohol is greatly due to a disorganised system, and that such disorganisation is mostly caused by over work, bad sanitation, and monotony of life.

Therefore, when we wax virtuously indignant with the wastrel, let us remember who makes him a loafer, a drunkard, a gambler; and who gets rich upon his ruin.

I say, then, that the wastrel is generally a wastrel of our wasting, and that we owe him all the atonement and forbearance it is in our power to give.

We come now to the second class—the industrious poor who are indigent from age or from misfortune, and "through no fault of their own."

Of these I have only to say that they are indigent in their old age after a life of toil because they have been robbed of the fruits of their labour by the class from whom our guardians and magistrates are mostly drawn.

To these men the State is not only a debtor, it is a fraudulent trustee. It is not for the State, then, to speak of "charity" to these men, but of reparation, of reverence, and of honour.

You see, then, where I start from. I insist upon the common manhood of these paupers, and demand that they shall be treated with respect as well as with love. *The Clarion* (17 September 1892)

---

71 B. S. Rowntree   The Investigation of Poverty

Benjamin Seebohm Rowntree (1871–1954) was the son of the York cocoa manufacturer, Joseph Rowntree. His Quaker upbringing instilled in him a strong sense of social responsibility

Q

and this, allied to his enthusiasm for social statistics, proved excellent qualifications for the task of social investigator. Although inspired by the work of the Liverpool shipowner Charles Booth (1840–1916) in the East End of London, Rowntree's survey used new techniques. Thus Rowntree distinguished between 'primary' poverty, caused by the utter insufficiency of the family income, and 'secondary' poverty, caused by the misspending of what, given a rigidly disciplined pattern of expenditure, would have been an adequate income for healthy physical subsistence. Booth made no such distinction. In addition, while Booth with his Poverty Line made a static survey of poverty, Rowntree developed the dynamic concept of the Poverty Cycle, which showed that a working man was liable to fall below the Poverty Line at certain periods of his life. Rowntree, operating in a much smaller community than Booth, was able to make a house-to-house survey of 11,560 working-class families in York, thus avoiding the rather unsatisfactory method of sampling that Booth was forced to adopt. Nevertheless, their inquiries produced remarkably similar results, and each of them acknowledged a debt of gratitude to the other.

On analysing the cases of "primary" poverty in York, we find that they are immediately due to one or other of the above causes in the following proportions (See table on page 243)

The proportion of "primary" poverty, due to various causes, is shown in the diagram on page 244.

The life of a labourer is marked by five alternating periods of want and comparative plenty. During early childhood, unless his father is a skilled worker, he probably will be in poverty; this will last until he, or some of his brothers or sisters, begin to earn money and thus augment their father's wage sufficiently to raise the family above the poverty line. Then follows the period during which he is earning money and living under his parents' roof; for some portion of this period he will be earning more money than is required for lodging, food, and clothes. This is his chance to save money. If he has saved enough to pay for furnishing a cottage, this period of comparative prosperity may continue after marriage until he has two or three children, when poverty will again overtake him. This period of poverty will last perhaps for ten years, *i.e.* until the first child is fourteen years old and begins to earn wages; but if there are more than three children it may last longer. While the children are earning, and before they leave the home to marry, the man enjoys another period of prosperity—possibly, however, only to sink back again into poverty when his children have married and left him, and he himself is too old to work, for his income has never permitted his saving enough for him and his wife to live upon for more than a very short time.

Section.	No. of Households affected.	Immediate Cause of "Primary" Poverty.	No. of Children affected.	No. of Adults affected.	Total Number affected.	Percentage of Total Population living under "Primary" Poverty Line.
1.	403	Death of chief wage-earner . .	460	670	1130	15·63
2.	146	Illness or old age of chief wage-earner . . .	81	289	370	5·11
3.	38	Chief wage-earner out of work . .	78	89	167	2·31
4.	51	Irregularity of work	94	111	205	2·83
5.	187	Largeness of family, *i.e.* more than four children . .	1122	480	1602	22·16
6.	640	In regular work, but at low wages .	2380	1376	3756	51·96
	1439		4215	3015	7230	100·00

A labourer is thus in poverty, and therefore underfed—

(*a*) In childhood—when his constitution is being built up.

(*b*) In early middle life—when he should be in his prime.

(*c*) In old age.

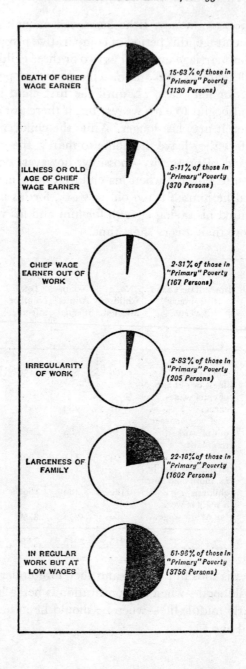

DEATH OF CHIEF WAGE EARNER — 15·63 % of those in "Primary" Poverty (1130 Persons)

ILLNESS OR OLD AGE OF CHIEF WAGE EARNER — 5·11 % of those in "Primary" Poverty (370 Persons)

CHIEF WAGE EARNER OUT OF WORK — 2·31 % of those in "Primary" Poverty (167 Persons)

IRREGULARITY OF WORK — 2·83 % of those in "Primary" Poverty (205 Persons)

LARGENESS OF FAMILY — 22·16% of those in "Primary" Poverty (1602 Persons)

IN REGULAR WORK BUT AT LOW WAGES — 51·96 % of those in "Primary" Poverty (3756 Persons)

The accompanying diagram may serve to illustrate this:—

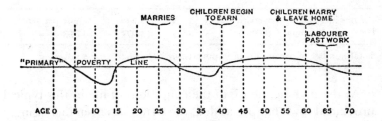

It should be noted that the women are in poverty during the greater part of the period that they are bearing children.

We thus see that the 7230 persons shown by this inquiry to be in a state of "primary" poverty, *represent merely that section who happened to be in one of these poverty periods at the time the inquiry was made.* Many of these will, in course of time, pass on into a period of comparative prosperity; this will take place as soon as the children, now dependent, begin to earn. But their places below the poverty line will be taken by others who are at present living in that prosperous period previous to, or shortly after, marriage. Again, many now classed as above the poverty line were below it until the children began to earn. The proportion of the community who at one period or other of their lives suffer from poverty to the point of physical privation is therefore much greater, and the injurious effects of such a condition are much more widespread than would appear from a consideration of the number who can be shown to be below the poverty line at any given moment.

In this way 20,302 persons, or 27.84 per cent of the total population, were returned as living in poverty. Subtracting those whose poverty is "primary," we arrive at the number living in "secondary" poverty, viz. 13,072, or 17.93 per cent of the total population. The figures will be clearer if shown in tabular form:—

		Proportion of total Population of York.
Persons in 'primary' poverty	7,230	9·91 per cent
Persons in 'secondary' poverty	13,072	17·93 ,,
Total number of persons living in poverty .	20,302	27·84 ,,

As the investigation into the conditions of life in this typical provincial town has proceeded, the writer has been increasingly impressed with the gravity of the facts which have unfolded themselves.

That in this land of abounding wealth, during a time of perhaps unexampled prosperity, probably more than one-fourth of the population are living in poverty, is a fact which may well cause great searchings of heart. There is surely need for a greater concentration of thought by the nation upon the well-being of its own people, for no civilisation can be sound or stable which has at its base this mass of stunted human life. The suffering may be all but voiceless, and we may long remain ignorant of its extent and severity, but when once we realise it we see that social questions of profound importance await solution. What, for instance, are the primary causes of this poverty? How far is it the result of false social and economic conditions? If it be due in part to faults in the national character, what influences can be exerted to impart to that character greater strength and thoughtfulness?

The object of the writer, however, has been to state facts rather than to suggest remedies. He desires, nevertheless, to express his belief that however difficult the path of social progress may be, a way of advance will open out before patient and penetrating thought if inspired by a true human sympathy.

The dark shadow of the Malthusian philosophy has passed away, and no view of the ultimate scheme of things would now be accepted under which multitudes of men and women are doomed by inevitable law to a struggle for existence so severe as necessarily to cripple or destroy the higher parts of their nature.

B. S. Rowntree. *Poverty. A Study of Town Life* (1901), 120–21, 136–8, 298, 304–5

72 Alfred Marshall   Outdated Ideas

Alfred Marshall (1842–1924) had succeeded Henry Fawcett as Professor of Political Economy at Cambridge in 1885. He was a member of the Royal Commission on Labour of 1891–4, and was frequently summoned as a witness to Royal Commissions and Parliamentary Select Committees. He took this role very seriously, and spent a good deal of time in preparing his evidence.

10272. Let us confine ourselves to the question of out-door relief to the aged poor. Do you believe that the giving of out-door relief to the aged poor, without, of course, hedging it round with proper precautions, would have the effect of reducing wages; do not let us go into the future generations, but the present existing state of things?—I am afraid I cannot answer that without reference to the future generation. You see all these statements about wages are repetitions of doctrines that were universal among the economists of the beginning of the century; you have the same phrases, the same tone of thought; you can trace the economic dogmas of present Poor Law litera-ture direct from those times; and the doctrines which they laid down I think were fairly true in their time. The doctrine is that if you tax the rich, and give money to the working classes, the result will be that the working classes will increase in number, and the result will be you will have lowered wages in the next generation; and the grant will not have improved the position of the working classes on the whole. As regards this a change has come, which separates the economics of this generation from the economics of the past; but it seems to me not to have penetrated the Poor Law literature yet; and this is the main thing that I desire to urge. It seems to me that whenever I read Poor Law literature of to-day I am taken back to the beginning of the century; everything that is said about economics has the flavour of that old time. Statements, which were true then, taking account of the condition of the working classes and of the state of wealth, are reproduced and made the basis of arguments which seem to me to be not valid now. I once ventured to say that, as regards the relief of distress, the conditions of 1834 were not substantially the same as at this time; and I was at once told that it was a national calamity that anybody who wrote on economic matters should be so ignorant as not to know that they were substantially the same. That has been repeated more or less emphatically by people of high authority, and I do not think it is true. The particular purpose that made me accept your invitation to come here was that I might submit to cross-examination the statement of my opinion that it is not true. Royal Commission on the Aged Poor. *Report* (Cd 7684–II), XIV, *Evidence of Prof Alfred Marshall* (1895)

73 Samuel Barnett   Lack of Uniformity

Samuel Barnett (1844–1913) was vicar of St Jude's, White-chapel. His experiences in the East End of London made him aware of the need for closer contact between the poor and the wealthier classes. He took a prominent part in establishing Toynbee Hall in Whitechapel, and was its warden from 1884 until 1906. Founded in memory of the young historian, Arnold Toynbee, the Hall was the first of the University settlements to which young graduates of Oxford and Cambridge came to live and work amongst the poor of the East End.

An early member of the COS, Canon Barnett resigned from the Society in 1886 after a dispute about the extent to which the State could usefully intervene in social welfare. Despite his strong feelings about the inadequacy of the poor-law system, Canon Barnett refused to accept a seat on the Royal Commission of 1905.

_____

For the sick the 646 Boards of Guardians are permitted, according to their fancies, to provide workhouse sick-wards, separate infirmaries of general character, specialised hospitals and sanatoria for particular diseases, subsidies to voluntary institutions, dispensaries, and domiciliary treatment, with or without nurses. The result is confusion in the public mind, and unequal treatment to the equally worthy sick poor. There are some infirmaries where skill and love were hourly united for the benefit of each decrepit old pauper; and there are infirmaries where classification is all but absent, and where to be sick is considered as almost a crime.

The widow is equally unable to feel security about her fate. In one Union she is refused out-relief; in others she is given 1s. and a loaf for each child; in another, 5s. for herself, 4s. for the first child, 3s. for the second, and 2s. for each additional member of her family. By some Boards she is made to part with her children and send them to the Union Schools; in others she and all her family are offered only refuge, food, and clothing, within "the House." If any official view has been expressed by the Central Authority on these treatments, the diversity of which almost amounts to cruelty, I have yet to discover it.

If space allowed a full expansion of this aspect of the subject, I could show a similar confusion of policy and inconsistency of practice with regard to the able-bodied, the aged, the imbecile, the infirm, the blind, deaf, dumb, lame, and deformed. For them all different Unions have different methods, from the hard parting of Darby and Joan at the "House" gates, Darby to become one among the rows of corduroy-clad, dreary old men, Joan to join the groups of uniformed old women, whose work-room hands lie idly on their laps, to the alms-houses specially designed and built for "deserving couples," who have paid rates and passed a certain number of years in the parish.

If the principles of 1834 had been repudiated after being carefully tested, the consequences would not have been so disastrous, but the Local Government Board have never either advised their abandonment or enforced their observance. The principle of Less Eligibility will at one time be enforced by degrading labour, such as stone-breaking, and ignored by the dietary table which provides bacon for breakfast, beer and tobacco at Christmas, and expenses for children's excursions. In the same Union one can find efforts to retain the workhouse test, while rendering it null and void by the provision of sentimental luxuries within the workhouse walls.

The principle of National Uniformity has been frankly abandoned, the Central Body contenting itself with keeping control over details which are comparatively unimportant, while allowing wide divergencies of practice to be initiated and continued. Canon and Mrs S. A. Barnett. *Towards Social Reform* (1909), 160-63

74 George Lansbury   A Working-class Guardian

George Lansbury (1859–1940), the son of a railway navvy, became a partner in the small sawmill and veneer works owned by his father-in-law, and settled in Bow, London. In 1890 he was converted to Socialism and joined the Social Democratic Federation; and two years later he was elected to the Poplar board of guardians. As a guardian, he took a leading role in establishing the Hollesley Bay Colony to provide constructive agricultural work for the unemployed. As a member of the Poplar Town Council, he fought to reduce the inequalities of the rating burden in the 1920s (see Part Five). He founded the *Daily Herald* in 1912 and was its editor until 1922. He was MP for Bow from 1910 to 1912, and again from 1922 to 1940, serving as Commissioner of Works in the 1929 Labour Government, and as leader of the Parliamentary Labour Party from 1931 to 1935. A staunch pacifist, feminist and Anglican churchman, Lansbury was a much loved figure in the Labour movement, though its harder-headed members accused him of being too sentimental. 'His bleeding heart', one of them is alleged to have said, 'was always stronger than his bloody head.'

From the first moment I determined to fight for one policy only, and that was decent treatment for the poor outside the workhouse, and hang the rates! This sort of saying brings censure on me and on the movement: it cannot be helped. My view of life places money, property, and privilege on a much lower scale than human life. I am quite aware some people are bad and deceitful. I know this because I know myself. I know people drink, gamble, and are often lazy. I also know that taken in the mass the poor are as decent as any other class, and so when I stood as a Guardian I took as my policy that no widow or orphan, no sick, infirm, or aged person should lack proper provision of the needs of life, and able-bodied people should get work or maintenance. To-day everybody agrees with this policy. I also determined to humanize Poor Law administration: I never could see any difference between outdoor relief and a state pension, or between the pension of a widowed queen and outdoor relief for the wife or mother of a worker. The nonsense about the disgrace of the Poor Law I fought against till at least in London we killed it for good and all.

My daily work was in a sawmill and veneer works: often I had no time to change my clothes or even to wash, because I made it a point to be punctual at all meetings. My knowledge of law was absolutely *nil*, so from the start I followed the line laid down by Parnell and learnt law and rules of procedure by simply breaking them. At the first meeting I arrived collarless and sprinkled with sawdust. Will Crooks and Harry W. Kaye, of the Transport Workers, at that time cashier for the Dockers' Union, and two others were there, making five Labour and Socialist members out of twenty-four. We elected a chairman and then it was proposed to take the minutes as read. Of course, my curiosity was aroused, and I insisted that the clerk should read the whole of the minutes, and after a long struggle this was done. Then came questions and appointment to committees. We five managed to dominate the proceedings and very soon discovered that two or three people who know what they want and are persistent enough can usually get it.

At the close of this first meeting we were all invited to tea. Quite innocently I asked who was going to pay for it. The answer came: "Oh, the chairman always gives a tea on the occasion of his election." I replied, "Well, when you make me chairman you won't get any tea, as it is not in my power to pay for it, so you must excuse me from accepting a free tea at your hands."

This first Board was made up of chemists, doctors, clergy, undertakers, house agents (mostly slum-owners' agents), a representative of the London and India Dock Company, whose business on the Board was to look after the assessment committee and see to it that big properties like the docks and railways were not over-assessed. When the assessment business was taken away from the Guardians and given to the Borough Council, the dock company lost all interest in the Guardians and transferred their official to the Council, where he at once secured election to the assessment committee. Most Guardians were freemasons, and so were many of the officials and all the contractors. I do not think there was any real corruption except that people did look after their friends. You scratch my back and I'll scratch yours was the kind of policy where jobs and contracts were concerned. I have often said the Board was made up of those who reckoned to make a bit out of the poor, and who could play into each others' hands. You see, the slum owner and agent could be depended upon to create conditions which produce disease: the doctor would then get the job of attending the sick, the chemist would be needed to supply drugs, the parson to pray, and when, between them all, the victims died, the undertaker was on hand to bury them. It was a nice kind of family or company arrangement by which it was clearly possible for most of my colleagues to serve God and the devil, at least to their own mutual advantage. George Lansbury. *My Life* (1928), 133–5

BETTER TREATMENT

75A Local Government Board   Advice on Treatment of Old People

The Royal Commission on the Aged Poor had condemned,

in its report of 1895, both the giving of inadequate outdoor relief to old people and the confinement of some of them in unsuitable workhouses, as did a Parliamentary Select Committee on the Aged Deserving Poor in 1899. In face of this criticism, the Local Government Board sent a circular to boards of guardians urging them to give adequate outdoor relief to old people wherever possible, and if they had to be taken into the workhouse to increase their comforts and privileges.

With regard to the treatment of the aged deserving poor, it has been felt that persons who have habitually led decent and deserving lives should, if they require relief in their old age, receive different treatment from those whose previous habits and character have been unsatisfactory and who have failed to exercise thrift in the bringing up of their families or otherwise. The Board consider that aged deserving persons should not be urged to enter the workhouse at all unless there is some cause which renders such a course necessary, such as infirmity of mind or body, the absence of house accommodation or of a suitable person to care for them, or some similar cause, but that they should be relieved by having adequate out-door relief granted to them. The Board are happy to think that it is commonly the practice of boards of guardians to grant outdoor relief in such cases, but they are afraid that too frequently such relief is not adequate in amount. They are desirous of pressing upon the guardians that such relief should when granted be always adequate.

When, however, it is necessary that such persons should receive indoor relief, the Board consider that they might be granted certain privileges which could not be accorded to every inmate of the workhouse.

The Board had intended to issue an Order dealing with this matter, but for the reasons already stated they have been unable to do so at present. They think it may be convenient, however, if they indicate the heads of the regulations which they had in contemplation.

These are as follows:—

1. That the guardians should form a special class of inmates of 65 years of age and upwards with regard to whom the guardians after due enquiries have satisfied themselves that by reason of their moral character or behaviour or previous habits they are sufficiently deserving to be members of the class.

2. That for such inmates extra day-rooms should be provided, which might if thought desirable be available for members of both sexes, in which they would have the opportunity of separation from disreputable inmates, and in which their meals, other than dinner, might be served at hours fixed by the guardians.

3. That sleeping accommodation in separate cubicles should be provided for them.

4. That privileges should be given them as regards the hours of going to bed and rising.

5. That considerably increased liberty should be granted to them, and greater facilities for being visited by their friends.

6. That for each inmate of this class a locker should be provided; the key would be retained by the inmate, but it would be required that the contents of the locker should be open to proper inspection; and

7. That as regards the inmates of this class the provisions in the Orders relating to the supply of tobacco, dry tea and sugar should be made compulsory. Local Government Board. *Thirtieth Annual Report*, Appendix A, No 11 (1900–01)

75B G. Cuttle   Old People in Essex Workhouses

Despite the advice of Royal Commissions, Select Committees and the Local Government Board, aged workhouse inmates often found the improvement of their conditions to be a slow and faltering process, as these reminiscences of poor-law administration in Essex in the early twentieth century show.

The attitude towards aged inmates in 1895 is illustrated by a discussion at Billericay shortly after the election under the new Act.[1] A member called attention to the aimless wanderings of old men about the grounds, and suggested the provision of garden plots to grow small salad stuff as an addition to their meals. Another member remarked that they "had dominoes," the Chairman recalled trouble through their selling things (the trouble probably being connected with beer provided thereby), the Master would prefer not to have such plots in front of the House, and the Inspector said that if they could work it was the Master's duty to employ them for the benefit of the House and not their particular benefit. This incident shows that at Billericay old people were allowed to wander in the grounds. At Chelmsford the 1895 impulse exhausted itself in the purchase of six new seats to replace broken ones in the old men's yard, nor was it until 1905 that they had seats in the grounds, though allowed, in 1901, to walk in the garden up to 5 *p.m.*; old people went to bed by seven at latest. Ongar did not allow use of the garden until 1907; each class took exercise in a yard; whether the yard or yards had walls ten feet high, as at Chelmsford, does not appear; also they had to enter the building at the back. At Maldon use of the garden was obtained in 1895; the Master, probably relying on support from the Chairman, treated questions by a clerical Guardian contemptuously, saying that inmates were allowed there "morning, noon and night," but had to admit that there were no seats; being handled gently by the cleric he thought he could find some, and did, even seats with backs, a "funny" Guardian suggesting awnings to keep off the sun. This clerical Guardian in 1895 presented cushions for the use of old men in the day-room, who probably (as certainly at Dunmow) had only forms against a wall; the new Inspector in 1901 found the "old fellows" so sitting in their day-room, "bolt up-right"; in the same year he suggested purchase at Maldon of 12 Windsor chairs, on which the Board acted, and in 1906 supplied chairs for their bedrooms. Moreover, this Board, having spent £3 on replenishing the library, spent one shilling and

---

[1] The Local Government Act of 1894.

fourpence per month on "periodicals," for which later bound magazines, two halfpenny newspapers and a weekly local paper were substituted; in 1909 a piano was provided by collections made in the parishes. G. Cuttle. *The Legacy of the Rural Guardians* (1934), 40–41

---

76 T. J. Macnamara   Better Treatment for Children

The fate of the child pauper in the workhouse had been a constant source of concern since 1834 (see Part Three). As with aged workhouse inmates, the Local Government Board urged on local boards of guardians the need to humanise conditions in workhouses where children were confined. Most poor-law officials, however, had long believed that children ought to be in separate institutions away from the depressing atmosphere of the general workhouse. Large institutions for children, like the 'barrack schools' of the mid-nineteenth century, were also losing favour (52). Progressive boards of guardians were experimenting with the practice of 'boarding out' children under their care with ordinary families, or with providing smaller institutions like cottage homes where a family atmosphere could be maintained. In 1893, the Sheffield board of guardians pioneered the 'scattered homes' system, which combined the advantages of cottage homes and boarding out: the guardians rented a number of workers' houses in different parts of the city, and put some children into each house under the care of a foster mother; and the children were brought up and educated with the children of the neighbourhood, thus avoiding some of the stigma of pauperism.

Despite its obvious advantages, the scattered homes system was slow to spread. Less imaginative boards of guardians continued to keep children in the workhouse, and only gradually improved their conditions. In 1906 there were still nearly 22,000 children in English workhouses, apart from the large numbers being brought up with the aid of outdoor relief, to whom the poor-law authorities gave little care or attention.

___

i.—The "Cottage Homes" System.

From the point of view of the children themselves, and setting aside questions of cost, the ideal system in my opinion is that of the Cottage Homes. Take the Cottage Homes at Sidcup, provided by the Greenwich Union.—These children have a most beautiful park of 58½ acres. At its entrance is a charming Cottage Receiving Home. Dotted over the park are homes and cottages designed to house from 15 to 53 children. Each cottage is a self-contained household presided over by a foster-mother and father, the latter being also one of the industrial trainers for the boys. Inside the cottage everything is designed on the most natural home lines, and thus the artificiality of institution life is avoided—a most important matter from the point of view of the future of the girls. The park contains of course a first-class elementary school which the children attend, and I can speak of its work as well up to the test of the ordinary Council schools outside. There is a splendid gymnasium and a not less splendid swimming bath. There are also shops for the teaching of woodwork, tailoring, and bootmaking. Everybody concerned, the Superintendent, the Head Mistress, the Drill Instructor, the Bandmaster, the Industrial Trainers and the Foster-Mothers are all to be highly congratulated upon the tone which pervades the whole system of schools and homes. Amid such beautiful surroundings and in receipt of such care and solicitude, the children are healthy and strong, and sickness is rare.

ii.—The "Scattered Homes" Plan.

Side by side with this Cottage Homes system is the Scattered Homes plan. I went into this pretty closely in Camberwell. At Nunhead the Guardians have provided a Receiving Home where the children spend a probationary period—after which they are drafted off to the Scattered Homes. To provide these the Guardians have either bought or are renting a number of

R

small houses, valued at from £35 to £40 a year, in various streets of the locality. I visited a number of these in the Friern Road and the Upland Road, East Dulwich. Each household is in charge of a foster-mother who is assisted by a "working-boy" or "working-girl," as the case may be. The children are plainly and sufficiently fed and clothed and attend the Public Elementary Schools in the locality. The central feature of the system is, as far as possible, to direct the children's lives along precisely the same lines as in an ordinary artisan dwelling. They are all, so far as I could see, happy and bright and speak in grateful terms of the way they are treated both at home and at school. There is nothing "institutional" in the working of the scheme which owes a good deal to the motherly genius and administrative capacity of the Superintendent, Mrs. Abbott. The foster-mothers appear to have been well selected and seem to appreciate the spirit of the experiment. Perhaps if there were more suitably chosen visitors to these little homes the foster-mothers— who do however get a day off a week—would find it easier to keep their hearts young and their spirits fresh. For certainly the work, week in week out, must grow monotonous. Care should be taken I think by the Guardians to see that in outward appearance the Scattered Homes, both as to window decoration and general embellishment, do not fall below the level of the other houses in the street. T. J. Macnamara. *Report on Children under the Poor Law* (3899), XCII (1908), 12–13

77A Joseph Chamberlain   The Chamberlain Circular (1886)

Joseph Chamberlain (1836–1914), a Birmingham screw manufacturer, first became famous in municipal politics. He was Lord Mayor of Birmingham from 1873 to 1876, and entered Parliament as MP for that city in 1876. He was President of the Board of Trade in Gladstone's second ministry (1880–85) and, to his disappointment, President of the Local Government Board in the short-lived third ministry of 1886. In that year he broke with the Gladstonian Liberals over Irish Home Rule, and became a leading member of the Unionist Party. He was Colonial Secretary from 1895 until his resignation in 1903 over the issue of tariff reform. His active political career was ended by a paralytic stroke in 1906.

Despite his short tenure of the post, Chamberlain, with his working knowledge of local government, was well fitted for the presidency of the Local Government Board. Although addressed to the boards of guardians, his circular gave the major role in relieving unemployment to the town councils.

It is not desirable that the working classes should be familiarised with Poor Law relief, and if once the honourable sentiment which now leads them to avoid it is broken down it is probable that recourse will be had to this provision on the slightest occasion.

The Local Government Board have no doubt that the powers which the guardians possess are fully sufficient to enable them to deal with ordinary pauperism, and to meet the demand for relief from the classes who usually seek it.

When the workhouse is full, or when the circumstances are so exceptional that it is desirable to give out-door relief to the able-bodied poor on the ground of want of work, the guardians in the unions which are the great centres of population are authorised to provide a labour test, on the performance of which grants in money and kind may be made, according to the discretion of the guardians. In other unions, where the guardians have not already this power, the necessary order is issued whenever the circumstances appear to require it.

But these provisions do not in all cases meet the emergency. The labour test is usually stone breaking or oakum picking. This work, which is selected as offering the least competition with other labour, presses hardly upon the skilled artisans, and, in some cases, their proficiency in their special trades may be prejudiced by such employment. Spade husbandry is less open to objection, and when facilities offer for adopting work of this character as a labour test the Board will be glad to assist the guardians by authorising the hiring of land for the purpose, when this is necessary. In any case, however, the receipt of relief from the guardians, although accompanied by a task of work, entails the disqualification which by statute attaches to pauperism.

What is required in the endeavour to relieve artisans and others who have hitherto avoided Poor Law assistance, and who are temporarily deprived of employment, is,—

    1. Work which will not involve the stigma of pauperism;

    2. Work which all can perform, whatever may have been their previous avocations;

    3. Work which does not compete with that of other labourers at present in employment;

    And, lastly, work which is not likely to interfere with the resumption of regular employment in their own trades by those who seek it.

The Board have no power to enforce the adoption of any particular proposals, and the object of this circular is to bring the subject generally under the notice of boards of guardians and other local authorities. 'Circular Addressed by the President of the Local Government Board to the Several Boards of Guardians', 15 March 1886. *Parlt Papers* (69), LVI (1886)

77B The Unemployed Workmen Act (1905)

This Act, which was largely the work of the Conservative President of the Local Government Board, Walter Long, and his successor, Gerald Balfour, gave statutory recognition to the policy of the Chamberlain Circular, which the Board had been urging on local authorities without very great success since 1886. In addition, it gave powers to local authorities to set up labour exchanges and to assist the migration and emigration of unemployed persons. The metropolitan organisation of joint committees of guardians and town councillors in each London borough, with a central committee to co-ordinate their work, had in fact been in existence since 1903. This organisation's most successful activities had been the establishment of a network of labour exchanges and the organisation of the farm colony at Hollesley Bay. The 1905 Act gave it statutory recognition and provided for the establishment of similar committees in provincial towns.

In fact, the Act proved difficult to work. Local authorities found it difficult to provide suitable work, and often found themselves swamped by applications for jobs from ill-paid casual labourers. Outside London, few distress committees established labour exchanges. The scheme developed into yet another palliative for unemployment, and found no favour in the eyes of the Royal Commission on the Poor Laws.

CHAPTER 18.

An Act to establish organisation with a view to the provision of Employment or Assistance for Unemployed Workmen in proper cases.　　　　　　　　　　　[11th August 1905.]

1.—(1) For the purposes of this Act there shall be established, by order of the Local Government Board under this Act, a distress committee of the council of every metropolitan borough in London, consisting partly of members of the borough council and partly of members of the board of guardians of every poor law union wholly or partly within the borough and of persons experienced in the relief of distress, and a central body for the whole of the administrative county of London, consisting partly of members of, and selected by, the distress committees and of members of, and selected by, the London County Council, and partly of persons co-opted to be additional members of the body, and partly, if the order so provides, of persons nominated by the Local Government Board, but the number of the persons so co-opted and nominated shall not exceed one-fourth of the total number of the body, every such order shall provide that one member at least of the committee or body established by the order shall be a woman.

(2) The distress committee shall make themselves acquainted

with the conditions of labour within their area, and when required by the central body shall receive, inquire into and discriminate between any applications made to them from persons unemployed:

(3) If the distress committee are satisfied that any applicant is honestly desirous of obtaining work, but is temporarily unable to do so from exceptional causes over which he has no control, and consider that his case is capable of more suitable treatment under this Act than under the poor law, they may endeavour to obtain work for the applicant, or, if they think the case is one for treatment by the central body rather than by themselves, refer the case to the central body, but the distress committee shall have no power to provide, or contribute towards the provision of, work for any unemployed person.

(4) The central body shall superintend and, as far as possible co-ordinate the action of the distress committees, and aid the efforts of those committees by establishing, taking over, or assisting labour exchanges and employment registers, and by the collection of information and otherwise as they think fit.

(5) The central body may, if they think fit, in any case of an unemployed person referred to them by a distress committee, assist that person by aiding the emigration or removal to another area of that person and any of his dependants, or by providing, or contributing towards the provision of, temporary work in such a manner as they think best calculated to put him in a position to obtain regular work or other means of supporting himself.
Public General Acts, 5 Ed VII, c 18 (1903–05), 65–6

THE ROYAL COMMISSION ON THE POOR LAWS

The passing of the Unemployed Workmen Act of 1905 undoubtedly alarmed those officials of the Local Government Board and members of the Charity Organisation Society who were hoping for a stricter system of poor relief. In the early years of the twentieth century, poor-law administration seemed to be drifting further and further from the principles of 1834.

The cost of relief had been rising sharply since the 1890s, partly no doubt because of the better institutional forms of relief offered by boards of guardians, but also, it was feared, because of an increase in the amount of outdoor relief being paid. The number relieved fell sharply after 1870, levelled out after 1890, and tended to rise after 1901 (78). Although the great majority of those relieved were not able bodied, it was noted that an increasing number of able-bodied men were coming forward to claim relief. The 1905 Act seemed, to the believers in the policy of 1834, to encourage this tendency and to open the frightening prospect of State provision of relief and employment.

Thus, though there was no public outcry about the state of the poor laws, pressure was undoubtedly being brought to bear on the Government to take some action to reform them. A prominent source of such pressure was to be found in the Poor Law Division of the Local Government Board, whose permanent secretary, James Stewart Davy, was imbued with the ideals of the inspectorate of the 1870s. The Conservative Government, in its last months of office, yielded to this pressure, and in August 1905 the Prime Minister, Arthur Balfour, announced the appointment of a Royal Commission to inquire not only into the working of the poor laws in England, Scotland and Ireland, but also into the various methods of relieving unemployment that had been developed outside the framework of the Poor Law. The Commission was composed of twenty members, including four senior civil servants, five members of boards of guardians and six members of the Charity Organisation Society. Authorities on social policy such as Charles Booth, Octavia Hill, and Helen Bosanquet accepted invitations to sit on the Commission. Unlike the Commission of 1832 it was a body of experts, many of whom had a close working knowledge of poor-law administration.

Beatrice Webb's diary covers the activities of the Royal Commission thoroughly, and if it is to be believed, the permanent officials of the Local Government Board were planning to

stampede the Royal Commission into a hasty inquiry which
would condemn the existing system of relief and recommend
the establishment of a 'less eligibility' system for the able-bodied
poor along the lines suggested by the Royal Commission of
1832-4 (79). Mrs Webb pressed for a far more searching inquiry, an appeal supported by the COS members of the Commission, who firmly believed in proper investigation. The Royal
Commission took over three years to complete its work: 200
Unions and 400 institutions were visited, 450 witnesses were
heard, 900 statements of written evidence were accepted, and
the evidence when complete filled forty-seven folio volumes.

It soon became apparent, however, that if J. S. Davy had
failed to bend the Commission to the will of the Local Government Board, Beatrice Webb was determined to bend it to hers.
As early as 1906 she was talking of 'my' Royal Commission, and
by the following year was convinced of the need to have a
strong minority report ready for publication. So it was inevitable that when the Commission reported, as it did in February 1909, its members would be divided in their recommendations. The chairman and fourteen Commissioners signed the
Majority Report. Beatrice Webb found three signatures for her
Minority Report—George Lansbury, Francis Chandler, a trade
union official and former chairman of the Chorlton (Manchester) Board of Guardians, and the Rev Russell Wakefield,
the Dean of Norwich. (Charles Booth had resigned from the
Commission on grounds of ill health in 1908, and thus signed
neither Report.)

Despite the division of opinion on the Commission, there was
a considerable amount of agreement in the two Reports. Both
Majority and Minority condemned the existing poor relief
system root and branch. The lax distribution of outdoor relief,
the general mixed workhouses, the apathy and ignorance of
many boards of guardians and their electorates, the overworked
untrained relieving officers, the wasteful overlapping of poor
law and other local authority services, all came in for attack
in both Reports; both desired a new system aimed at pre-

venting and curing poverty, and at stimulating individual self-help; and both advocated the abolition of the boards of guardians.

The major differences between the Reports lay in their constructive suggestions for replacing the old system. The Majority aimed at a major reconstruction of poor relief, which they renamed 'public assistance'. Boards of guardians were to be replaced by borough and county public assistance authorities, whose members were to be appointed by town and county councils. Such bodies would closely resemble the local education authorities established under the Education Act of 1902. These authorities would control funds and institutions, appoint officers, draw up contracts and take all important decisions on relief policy. Subordinate to them would be a number of public assistance committees to attend to the distribution of relief and the varying needs of applicants. The work of the local authorities would be co-ordinated by a Public Assistance Division of the Local Government Board. The COS influence on the Majority Report was revealed by its stress on the important role of voluntary relief organisations in the system; they were to be organised in each area by voluntary aid committees which would co-operate closely with the public assistance authorities (80).

While the Majority Report wanted a complete rebuilding of the poor-law system, the Minority Report wanted to demolish it entirely. Instead of retaining an all-purpose poor-relief or public-assistance authority, the Minority pressed for specialisation of functions. The duties of the present boards of guardians were to be broken up and distributed among the various committees of the town and county councils. Thus the sick poor would be the responsibility of the health committee, children of the education committee, and so on. The system would be co-ordinated by a registrar of public assistance who would sanction grants of outdoor relief, or home aliment, awarded by the committees, and would operate a means test on those using the services provided. The Minority Report dealt with the able-bodied unemployed as an entirely separate problem, capable of solution only on a national scale. They advocated the setting up of a new Ministry of Labour charged with the duty of preventing unemployment by establishing labour exchanges, running training schemes, and planning ten-year programmes of Government works to be put into operation in periods of high cyclical unemployment (81). The Majority Report, though advocating national labour exchanges and an unemployment insurance scheme, was far less radical in its proposals for settling this most difficult of social problems.

Nevertheless the suggestions of the Majority Report were progressive and received a favourable press. Alarmed by this and by the fear that the Government would ignore the Minority Report, Beatrice Webb and her husband Sidney organised a propaganda campaign to spread their ideas for poor-law reform. A society, the National Committee for the Break Up of the Poor Law, which later changed its name to the National Committee for the Prevention of Destitution, was formed, and provincial branches were established. Lectures were organised, pamphlets published, and a monthly magazine, *The Crusade*, launched in February 1910 (82). The campaign made the Minority Report and its proposals famous. The Majority Report by contrast was pushed into obscurity. Its advocates formed their own society, the National Poor Law Reform Association, but it lacked the energy and organisational ability of the NCPD, and it came to be seen increasingly as a mere reactionary defender of the *status quo*.

Yet even the NCPD for all its energy was visibly flagging by 1911. The Webbs soon lost interest in it, preferring the quieter influence exercised from the study and the dinner table to the noisier less reasoned demands of the platform. In 1911 they left England on a world tour, and virtually abandoned the National Committee. In the short run, at least, the campaign had no success. Neither of the Reports was acted upon. The Webbs admitted that the Royal Commission was 'from a constructive standpoint, as big a failure as the Royal Commission of 1832–4 was a success'.[1] Obviously the Royal Commission would have been in a far stronger position had it presented a united report, but even had it done so it is doubtful whether any immediate action would have followed. Powerful vested interests stood in the way of breaking up and restructuring the Poor Law. Boards of guardians were strongly opposed to their own dissolution, and attacked the Royal Commission's Reports at their annual poor-law conferences. The officials of the Local Government Board had little enthusiasm for the suggested reforms. Their President, the erstwhile fiery Socialist John Burns, disliked the Webbs, and was easily persuaded to oppose sweeping reform. The Labour Party and allied working-class organisations were far from enthusiastic about the Minority Report, with its ideas of compulsion by experts. Most working men wanted higher wages rather than more social regulations. The Conservative Opposition was generally hostile to the Minority Report, despite the close friendship of their leader, Arthur Balfour, and the Webbs (83). As for the Government, its Radical members, notably David Lloyd George and Winston Churchill, who were enthusiastic for social reform, were busily hatching schemes of their own. The most ambitious of these, the National Insurance Bill of 1911, was primarily responsible for diverting attention from the campaign to break up the Poor Law. John Burns smugly remarked that it had 'dished the Webbs', while Beatrice fumed over 'Lloyd George's rotten scheme of sickness insurance'.[2]

For all the battering it had received at the hands of the Royal Commission, the nineteenth-century poor-law system stood, only slightly amended, on the eve of the First World War. Yet, though it was not broken up, the Poor Law by 1914 was deeply undermined. The Royal Commission had noted the extent to which other authorities were taking over or duplicating some of the functions of boards of guardians. After 1906, this process increased rapidly. The Education (Provision of Meals) Act of

[1] S. & B. Webb. *English Local Government: English Poor Law History*, Part 2, Vol 2 (reprint 1963), 470.

[2] B. Webb. *Our Partnership* (1948), 475.

1906, the Children Act of 1908, the Old Age Pensions Act of the same year, the Insurance Act of 1911, all reduced to some extent the activities of the local poor-law authorities. In setting up the administrative machinery for these Acts, the existing poor-law system was largely ignored. If the Poor Law was not to be broken up, it seemed that it was to be allowed to crumble.

78 Local Government Board   The Statistics of Pauperism

These statistics published by the Local Government Board in 1909 showed that the steep decline in pauperism had ended in the 1880s and it was even showing a tendency to rise after 1901. Relief costs were shown to be rising almost continuously, the steep rise from 1890 nearly keeping pace with the growth in rateable values. (Cont. pp 269-70.)

79 Beatrice Webb   The Aims of the Royal Commission

As Charles Booth's cousin and his 'industrious apprentice' during his early investigations into poverty in London, Beatrice Webb was well placed to influence him as to the procedure to be adopted by the Royal Commission. Beatrice Potter (1858-1943) was the daughter of a wealthy industrial and railway magnate. Her early friendship with the philosopher Herbert Spencer stimulated her interest in social problems and her work for Charles Booth confirmed her enthusiasm for social inquiry. In 1892 she married the Fabian Socialist Sidney Webb (1859-1947), thus entering upon one of the most famous of academic partnerships, whose crowning glory was probably the eleven-volume history of English local government, which included a three-volume study of the history of the English Poor Law. Although Sidney Webb was not himself a member of the Royal Commission, he played a major part by helping his wife to draft and write the Minority Report.

GRAPH I

PAUPERISM IN ENGLAND AND WALES, SCOTLAND AND IRELAND — YEARS 1850 TO 1908.

AVERAGE DAILY NUMBER OF PAUPERS OF ALL CLASSES RELIEVED PER 1000 OF POPULATION.

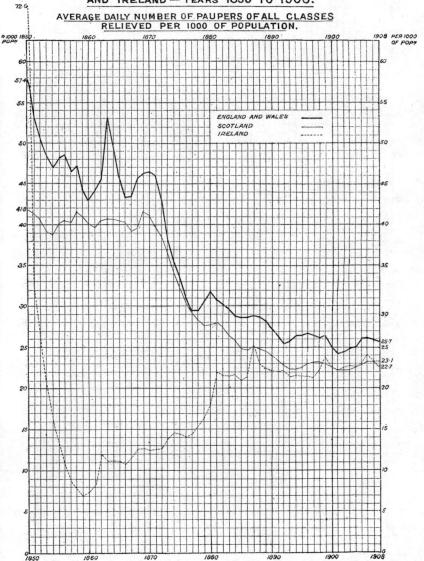

GRAPH 2

Cost of Poor Relief in relation to Rateable Property and Population - England & Wales.

(COST OF RELIEF, RATEABLE VALUE AND POPULATION IN 1850 = 100
FIGURES FOR SUBSEQUENT YEARS IN PERCENTAGES OF 1850 FIGURES.)

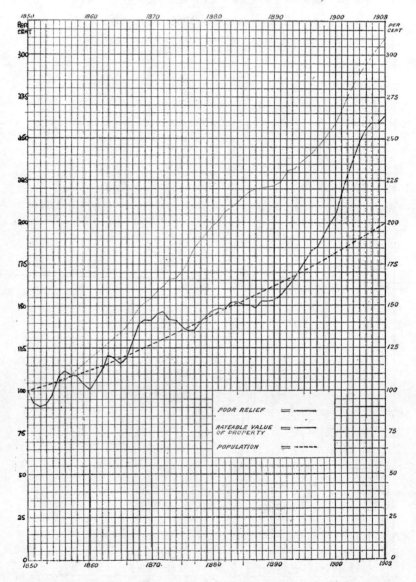

Local Government Board. *Statistical Memoranda on Public Health and Social Conditions*, Section 4 (1909), Cd 4671

December 2nd (1905).—A pleasant visit to Gracedieu colloguing in the old way with Charles Booth as to the proper course of the poor law enquiry. I had extracted from Davy, the assistant secretary of the L.G.B., in a little interview I had had with him, the intention of the L.G.B. officials as to the purpose and procedure they intended to be followed by the Commission. They were going to use us to get certain radical reforms of structure; the boards of guardians were to be swept away, judicial officers appointed and possibly the institutions transferred to the county authorities. With all of which I am inclined to agree. But we were also to recommend reversion to the principles of 1834 as regards policy; to stem the tide of philanthropic impulse that was sweeping away the old embankment of deterrent tests to the receipt of relief. Though I think the exact form in which this impulse has clothed itself is radically wrong and mischievous, yet I believe in the impulse, if it takes the right forms. It is just this vital question of what and which forms are right that I want to discover and this Commission to investigate. Having settled the conclusions to which we are to be led, the L.G.B. officials (on and off the Commission) have predetermined the procedure. We were to be spoon-fed by evidence carefully selected and prepared; they were to draft the circular to the board of guardians; they were to select the inspectors who were to give evidence; they were virtually to select the guardians to be called in support of this evidence. Assistant commissioners were to be appointed who were to collect evidence illustrative of these theories. And above all we were to be given *opinions* and not *facts*. Charles Booth and I consulted what line we should take. To-day at lunch I put Lansbury (the working-man on the Commission) on his guard against this policy. Beatrice Webb. *Our Partnership* (1948), 322

80 Royal Commission   The Majority Report
While thoroughly condemning the existing system of poor relief and recommending the abolition of the boards of guardians, the majority of the Royal Commissioners, strongly in-

fluenced by those of their colleagues who were members of the COS, urged the importance of organised voluntary charity in any new scheme of public welfare.

----

(38). Conclusion.

167. The proposals we make cover a large field of administration, will conflict with many old traditions, and will take time before they can come into really effective operation. But the evils we have had to describe are so widespread and deeprooted, and form so integral a part of the social life of the country, that no remedies less in scope or in force would in our judgment be sufficient.

168. But great as are the administrative changes which we propose, and costly as some of the new establishments may be, we feel strongly that the pauperism and distress we have described can never be successfully combated by administration and expenditure. The causes of distress are not only economic and industrial; in their origin and character they are largely moral. Government by itself cannot correct or remove such influences. Something more is required. The co-operation, spontaneous and whole-hearted, of the community at large, and especially of those sections of it which are well to-do and free from the pressure of poverty, is indispensable. There is evidence from many quarters to show that the weak part of our system is not want of public spirit or benevolence, or lack of funds or of social workers, or of the material out of which these can be made. Its weakness is lack of organisation, of method, and of confidence in those who administer the system. We have so framed the new system as to invite and bring into positions of authority the best talent and experience that the locality can provide. In addition to those vested with such authority we have left a place in the new system for all capable and willing social workers; but they must work in accord, under guidance, and in the sphere allotted to them.

169. Great Britain is the home of voluntary effort, and its triumphs and successes constitute in themselves much of the

history of the country. But voluntary effort when attacking a common and ubiquitous evil must be disciplined and led. We have here to learn a lesson from foreign countries whose charitable and social organisations, notably in France, Germany, Belgium, and Holland, work under official guidance with efficacy, promptitude, and success. Looking at the voluntary resources and societies at our disposal there is every reason to believe that we can vie with and surpass any results obtained abroad. To this end it is organisation we need, and this organisation we now suggest.

173. "Land of Hope and Glory" is a popular and patriotic lyric sung each year with rapture by thousands of voices. The enthusiasm is partly evoked by the beauty of the idea itself, but more by the belief that Great Britain does, above other countries, merit this eulogium, and that the conditions in existence here are such that the fulfilment of hope and the achievement of glory are more open to the individual than in other and less favoured lands. To certain classes of the community into whose moral and material condition it has been our duty to enquire, these words are a mockery and a falsehood. To many of them, possibly from their own failure and faults, there is in this life but little hope, and to many more "glory" or its realisation is an unknown ideal. Our investigations prove the existence in our midst of a class whose condition and environment are a discredit, and a peril to the whole community. Each and every section of society has a common duty to perform in combating this evil and contracting its area, a duty which can only be performed by united and untiring effort to convert useless and costly inefficients into self-sustaining and respectable members of the community. No country, however rich, can permanently hold its own in the race of international competition, if hampered by an increasing load of this dead weight; or can successfully perform the role of sovereignty beyond the seas, if a portion of its own folk at home are sinking below the civilization and aspirations of its subject races abroad. Royal Commission on

s

the Poor Laws and the Relief of Distress. *Majority Report* (Cd 4499), XXXVII, Part IX (1909), 643–4

81 Royal Commission   The Minority Report

The Minority Report was drafted by Sidney Webb and published as a Fabian Society pamphlet under the title *The Break Up of the Poor Law*. As this implies, the Report advocated the total abolition rather than the restructuring of the existing system. Its most striking recommendations lay in its plan for dealing with the able-bodied unemployed. These, it argued, should be dealt with nationally by a new Government department rather than locally and piecemeal by town and county councils.

THE SCHEME OF REFORM.

The state of anarchy and confusion, into which has fallen the whole realm of relief and assistance to the poor and to persons in distress, is so generally recognised that many plans of reform have been submitted to us, each representing a section of public opinion. In fact, throughout the three years of our investigations we have been living under a continuous pressure for a remodelling of the Poor Laws and the Unemployed Workmen Act, in one direction or another. We do not regret this peremptory and insistent demand for reform. The present position is, in our opinion, as grave as that of 1834, though in its own way. We have, on the one hand, in England and Wales, Scotland and Ireland alike, the well-established Destitution Authorities, under ineffective central control, each pursuing its own policy in its own way; sometimes rigidly restricting its relief to persons actually destitute, and giving it in the most deterrent and humiliating forms; sometimes launching out into an indiscriminate and unconditional subsidising of mere poverty; sometimes developing costly and palatial institutions for the treatment, either gratuitously or for partial payment, of practically any applicant of the wage-earning or of the lower middle class. On the other hand, we see existing, equally ubiquitous with the

Destitution Authorities, the newer specialised organs of Local Government—the Local Education Authority, the Local Health Authority, the Local Lunacy Authority, the Local Unemployment Authority, the Local Pension Authority—all attempting to provide for the needs of the poor, *according to the cause or character of their distress*. Every Parliamentary session adds to the powers of these specialised Local Authorities. Every Royal Commission or Departmental Committee recommends some fresh development of their activities... Athwart the overlapping and rivalry of these half a dozen Local Authorities that may be all at work in a single district, we watch the growing stream of private charity and voluntary agencies—almshouses and pensions for the aged; hospitals and dispensaries, convalescent homes and "medical missions" for the sick; free dinners and free boots, country holidays and "happy evenings" for the children; free shelters and soup kitchens, "way tickets" and charitable jobs for the able-bodied, together with uncounted indiscriminate doles of every description—without systematic organisation and without any co-ordination with the multifarious forms of public activity. What the nation is confronted with to-day is, as it was in 1834, an ever-growing expenditure from public and private funds, which results, on the one hand, in a minimum of prevention and cure, and on the other in far-reaching demoralisation of character and the continuance of no small amount of unrelieved destitution.

Deferring our proposals with regard to the whole of the Able-bodied until Part II. of the present Report, we recommend:—

90. That, except the 43 Eliz., c. 2, the Poor Law Amendment Act of 1834 for England and Wales and the various Acts for the relief of the poor and the corresponding legislation for Scotland and Ireland, so far as they relate exclusively to Poor Relief, and including the Law of Settlement, should be repealed.

91. That the Boards of Guardians in England, Wales and Ireland, and (at any rate as far as Poor Law functions are

concerned) the Parish Councils in Scotland, together with all combinations of these bodies, should be abolished.

92. That the property and liabilities, powers and duties of these Destitution Authorities should be transferred (subject to the necessary adjustments) to the County and County Borough Councils, strengthened in numbers as may be deemed necessary for their enlarged duties; with suitable modifications to provide for the special circumstances of Scotland and Ireland, and for the cases of the Metropolitan Boroughs, the Non-County Boroughs over 10,000 in population, and the Urban Districts over 20,000 in population, on the plan that we have sketched out.

93. That the provision for the various classes of the non-able-bodied should be wholly separated from that to be made for the Able-bodied, whether these be Unemployed workmen, vagrants or able-bodied persons now in receipt of Poor Relief.

94. That the services at present administered by the Destitution Authorities (other than those connected with vagrants or the able-bodied)—that is to say, the provision for:—

(i.) Children of school age;

(ii.) The sick and the permanently incapacitated, the infants under school age, and the aged needing institutional care;

(iii.) The mentally defective of all grades and all ages; and

(iv.) The aged to whom pensions are awarded—should be assumed, under the directions of the County and County Borough Councils, by:—

(i.) The Education Committee;

(ii.) The Health Committee;

(iii.) The Asylums Committee; and

(iv.) The Pension Committee respectively.

95. That the several committees concerned should be authorised and required under the directions of their Councils, to provide, under suitable conditions and safeguards to be embodied in Statutes and regulative Orders, for the several classes of persons committed to their charge, whatever treatment they

may deem most appropriate to their condition; being either institutional treatment, in the various specialised schools, hospitals, asylums, etc., under their charge; or whenever judged preferable, domiciliary treatment, conjoined with the grant of Home Aliment where this is indispensably required.

96. That the law with regard to liability to pay for relief or treatment received, or to contribute towards the maintenance of dependents and other relations, should be embodied in a definite and consistent code, on the basis, in those services for which a charge should be made, of recovering the cost from all those who are really able to pay, and of exempting those who cannot properly do so.

97. That there should be established in each County and County Borough one or more officers, to be designated Registrars of Public Assistance, to be appointed by the County and County Borough Council, and to be charged with the threefold duty of:—

(i.) Keeping a Public Register of all cases in receipt of public assistance;

(ii.) Assessing and recovering, according to the law of the land and the evidence as to sufficiency of ability to pay, whatever charges Parliament may decide to make for particular kinds of relief or treatment; and

(iii.) Sanctioning the Grants of Home Aliment proposed by the Committees concerned with the treatment of the case.

98. That the Registrar of Public Assistance should have under his direction (and under the control of the General Purposes Committee of the County or County Borough Council) the necessary staff of Inquiry and Recovery Officers, and a local Receiving House, for the strictly temporary accommodation of non-able-bodied persons found in need, and not as yet dealt with by the Committees concerned.

PART II.—THE DESTITUTION OF THE ABLE-BODIED.

That the duty of so organising the National Labour Market as to prevent or to minimise Unemployment should be placed upon a Minister responsible to Parliament, who might be designated the Minister for Labour. Royal Commission on the Poor Laws and the Relief of Distress. *Minority Report* (Cd 4499), XXXVII, Chapter XII (1909), 999, 1031–2, 1215

82 National Committee for the Prevention of Destitution The Crusade

The Crusade, which was the official organ of the National Committee for the Prevention of Destitution, appeared monthly from February 1910 until February 1913. It contained articles on poor relief and other aspects of social reform, reports on the progress of the campaign and announcements of meetings of the various provincial branches of the NCPD. Its editor was the young Fabian Socialist, Clifford Sharp. On the demise of the *Crusade* in 1913, Sharp became the editor of a new weekly, *The Statesman*, which was intended to take over the work of *The Crusade*, though it covered far more than social policy.

It is now just a year since the two Reports of the Royal Commission on the Poor Laws were published, and it is scarcely too much to say that of the two only one remains. The Majority Report, with its proposals to thrust the Unemployed and the underfed school children back into the Poor Law, to give non-elected bodies uncontrolled power over public funds, and to reinstate the old Poor Law system under a new name, is to all intents and purposes dead. But for the activity of its critics and opponents, it would probably have failed to gain any attention, and would have survived only a few weeks. As it is, it has failed to gain any substantial support either from politicians or from the public, and it has survived only a few months.

The Minority Report, on the other hand, is undeniably alive. Handicapped at the start by the weight of influence against it, it has gained already such a volume of enthusiastic support as

will ensure its survival until its principles have been translated
into law. Had we no other evidence to justify this statement as
to the relative position of the two Reports, we might find ample
confirmation for it in the fact that the party which stands for the
status quo, and is bent on opposing changes of any sort in the
existing Poor Law, has recently given up the unnecessary task
of attacking the proposals of the Majority, and is now concen-
trating its hostile attentions on the Minority scheme. . . .

Of the ultimate success of the campaign there is now no
doubt. In the sphere of Poor Law reform the principles of the
Minority Report, as we have said, hold the field. The most
serious danger which we have to face is not the opposition of
rival schemes of reform, but the resistance of those who are
content with the present system. Our real opponents are the
party of the status quo, a party which, though as weak in controversy as we could wish, has behind it all the forces of
political inertia. It is always easier, in this country at all
events, to resist changes than to bring them about. We say this
not to discourage our friends, but to remind them that a great
deal of hard work has yet to be done if things are not to remain
as they are.

Given that hard work, however, there is every prospect of our
efforts being speedily crowned with success. It is a most striking
and hopeful fact that the question of Poor Law reform should
not have been swamped by all the great political issues which
have attracted so much attention during the past six months. It
would scarcely have been possible to select a more unfavourable
time for attempting to rouse public interest in a new scheme of
social reform. Yet, that public interest has been aroused to a
remarkable extent is proved not only by the rapid growth of our
membership, but perhaps even more by the attendance and the
enthusiasm shown at the meetings, numbering well over a
thousand, that have been held all over the country in support
of the Minority proposals. Everywhere that our lecturers, from
the Minority Commissioners themselves downwards, have gone,
they have received the welcome which comes to those who bear

long-awaited tidings. It is evident that when the Conservative
party, in 1895, put Poor Law reform on their programme they
rightly interpreted the wishes of the electors, and that the years
which have elapsed since then have served but to intensify the
demand for reconstruction. *The Crusade Against Destitution*, Vol 1,
No 1 (February 1910)

---

83 J. Austen Chamberlain   The Conservatives and the Minority Report

Joseph Austen Chamberlain (1863–1937) was the eldest son
of Joseph Chamberlain. He had served as Chancellor of the
Exchequer under Balfour from 1903 to 1905, and, after his
father's incapacitating illness in 1906, found himself charged
with the task of winning over the Conservative Opposition to
his father's policy of tariff reform. This task often brought him
into collision with the Conservative leader, Arthur James
Balfour (1848–1930), a nephew of Lord Salisbury and a
close friend of the Webbs, whose intellectual prowess he
admired.

Of the other personalities mentioned in this extract, George
Wyndham (1863–1913) was a chief secretary for Ireland from
1900 to 1905 and a Tory of the old landowning variety;
Walter Long (1854–1924), another landed gentleman, was
President of the Local Government Board from 1900 until
1905, and had steered the Unemployed Workmen Act
(77B) through Parliament; and Alfred Lyttleton (1857–
1913), a son of Baron Lyttleton, had been made Colonial
Secretary after Joseph Chamberlain's resignation in 1903 but
lost his seat at the 1906 General Election, was subsequently
re-elected and gave active support in Parliament to measures
of social reform such as the Trade Boards Bill.

A private member's bill, the Prevention of Destitution Bill,
which contained the main principles of the Minority Report
had been introduced in the House of Commons in February
1910 by Sir Robert Price. The Bill was finally talked out, but
only after a lengthy debate on the second reading which

included speeches both from the Prime Minister, Herbert Asquith, and the Unionist leader, A. J. Balfour.

After his speech and Wyndham's, A. J. B., Long, Lyttleton and myself retired to Balfour's room to consider our attitude to a private member's bill which embodies the policy of the Minority Report of the Poor Law Committee. Balfour, who had not read it or given much consideration to it but who had seen the Webbs, was the most favourably inclined to it. The rest of us, who had gone a little deeper into it, were agreed that it would not do, though I confessed to having been greatly attracted by it before I studied it. I think that our line will be that the first work for Parliament (and quite enough for one Parliament) is to carry out the recommendations on which both the majority and minority are agreed. These alone will work an enormous change and require all the care Parliament can give to them. The popular and *sound* objections to the minority scheme in its entirety are:

1. That it would cost about 50 millions!

2. That it establishes an intolerable bureaucratic tyranny. Five separate inspectors from the Local Authority might descend on any working man's home and carry off himself, his wife or any or all of his children to a municipal institution, feed, clothe or otherwise care for them, utterly ignoring both parental rights and parental responsibility, whilst it would rest with a sixth inspector not appointed by or under the control of the Local Authority to decide without appeal whether any and, if so, what part of the cost of this public assistance should be recovered from the family. And all the inspectors might act without any call for help from the individual, without there being any destitution and without there being anything in the nature of a criminal act or default on the part of the parents.

3. That the whole tendency of the Report is to make the position of the State-aided better than that of the ordinary decent working man taxed to support them.

"The Webbs," said Vivian to Lyttleton, "carry you on logically and imperceptibly from one point to another; but when you look at the whole, it's moonshine!"

Not a bad criticism. J. Austen Chamberlain. *Politics from the Inside 1906–14* (1936), 238–9

PART FIVE

The Break-up of the Poor Law 1914-30

The outbreak of the war with Germany in August 1914 brought with it fears that the pressures on the poor-law system which had been rapidly easing since 1908 might suddenly build up again. Concern was felt for the condition of families in which the breadwinner had volunteered for active service and for those thrown out of work by the war. There was a strong feeling that such unfortunates should not be subjected to the degradation of applying for poor relief (84). A special Government committee was established under the chairmanship of the President of the Local Government Board, Herbert Samuel, to discuss measures for the prevention and relief of distress caused by the war. This central committee urged local authorities to set up their own representative committees to decide on local projects to prevent distress; members of the local board of guardians were to sit on the committees, but this could not disguise the fact that once again the relief of hardship had been taken away from the poor law.

THE EFFECTS OF WORLD WAR I
In fact the early fears of increased destitution proved groundless. Total war soon showed itself to be an effective cure for pauperism. Unemployment fell rapidly as the armed forces called for more men, and war industries for both men and

women. Wives of fighting men received separation allowances from the Government, and both they and their elder children were often willing to boost the family earnings by taking over jobs vacated by men who had volunteered for, or, after 1916, been conscripted into, the army. Rising prices meant that this growth of earnings proved rather less in real than in monetary terms; but as the war went wearily on the Government, fearing that inflation might cause working-class unrest, introduced price controls, food subsidies, and finally, in 1918, rationing of certain essential foodstuffs.

This marked improvement in the economic condition of the working classes meant that the Poor Law was little called on (85). The numbers on relief fell, and able-bodied inmates left the workhouses, many of which were taken over by the military for use as hospitals or barracks. Casual wards closed down as tramps disappeared from the roads. No elections to boards of guardians were held during the war, and few inspections were carried out by the Local Government Board, whose annual reports as a result were much reduced in size and interest.

It seemed that the Poor Law would not survive the First World War. There was a growing determination during the war years that a better society must emerge with the coming of peace, a society in which the nineteenth-century poor-law system would have no place; and the Government established a Reconstruction Committee in 1916 to discuss plans for the new society. In the following year, a Ministry of Reconstruction was created, with a former professor of anatomy, Dr Christopher Addison, as its first head. Under the aegis of these bodies, a host of subcommittees were set up to examine social and economic problems. In July 1917, a subcommittee of fifteen members under the chairmanship of Sir Donald Maclean was given the task of enquiring into problems of local government, and in particular into the relationship of boards of guardians to town and county councils. It was hoped that some form of compromise could be arrived at between the ideas of the Majority and the Minority Reports of the Royal Commission of 1905–09, so the members of the committee included Lord George Hamilton and Sir Samuel Provis, signatories of the Majority Report, and Beatrice Webb, the chief protagonist of the Minority. It was hardly surprising, therefore, that the Maclean Committee should echo the Reports of 1909 in its suggestion that the boards of guardians be abolished and their functions transferred to borough and county councils (86).

84 Local Government Board   War Victims and the Poor Law

After the outbreak of war in August 1914, an appeal by the Prince of Wales for donations led to the establishment of a National Relief Fund to aid those suffering financial hardship as a result of the war. It was felt that the wives and children of men who had volunteered for the forces should not be subjected to the humiliation of poor relief. Even those who had already received relief were to have the sum repaid out of the National Relief Fund in order to remove the stigma of pauperism.

Local Government Board,
Whitehall, S.W.,
29th *August,* 1914.

Sir,

I AM directed by the Local Government Board to refer to their circular letter of the 21st instant with reference to the Poor Law relief granted since the outbreak of the war to dependants of soldiers and sailors (including territorials) who were not previously in receipt of such relief, and I am to inform you that it has been decided that the cost of such relief shall be repaid to the Guardians out of the National Relief Fund.

I am therefore to request that the Guardians will supplement the information sent in reply to the Board's circular letter of the 21st instant by a statement, which should be verified by yourself, after reference to the Army or Navy Paymasters or the Secretaries of the Territorial Associations, as the case may be, showing the total cost of all the relief afforded to the persons indicated in consequence of applications granted in your Union or Parish between the 2nd and 29th of this month.

I am further directed to state that, when the repayment of the relief granted has been made, this should be credited to the proper accounts, the names of the recipients and all entries identifying them in any way with the receipt of Poor Law relief should be erased from the records kept by the Guardians, and a statement in the Form below should be immediately forwarded to the recipients of such relief.

I am,

Sir,

Your obedient Servant,

H. C. MONRO,

The Clerk to the Guardians. *Secretary.*

THE Guardians of the Union direct me to inform you that the relief granted to you on the   has been repaid to the Guardians from the Prince of Wales's National Relief Fund. Such relief will therefore not be treated as Poor Law relief, and all entries showing that you have received Poor Law relief will be struck out of the records of the Guardians. You may regard yourself, therefore, as having received this assistance from the Prince of Wales's Fund and not from the Poor Law.

Clerk to the Guardians.

Dated this   day of   , 1914.
Parlt Papers (Cd 7603), Appendix 46 (1914)

---

85 Ministry of Health   The Reduction of Pauperism
As these Ministry of Health statistics, published in 1919, show the numbers on poor relief both in the country generally, and in London in particular, fell steadily during the war years. *Parlt Papers* (230), XLII (1919), 11

Items.	1915 (1 Jan., 1915).	1916 (1 Jan., 1916).	1917 (30 Dec., 1916).	1918 (29 Dec., 1917).	1919 (28 Dec., 1918).
ESTIMATED TOTAL POPULATION:					
ENGLAND AND WALES	36,960,000	37,270,000	37,540,000	37,580,000	37,510,000
London	4,520,000	4,540,000	4,610,000	4,490,000	4,430,000
ESTIMATED TOTAL *civilian* POPULATION:					
ENGLAND AND WALES	—	35,360,000	34,500,000	33,710,000	33,470,000
London	—	4,310,000	4,240,000	4,030,000	3,950,000
TOTAL NUMBER OF PERSONS IN RECEIPT OF POOR-LAW RELIEF on or about the 1st January, in:					
ENGLAND AND WALES:					
Number	762,000	685,000	637,000	587,000	555,000
Number per 1,000 of estimated total population ..	20·6	18·4	17·0	15·6	14·8
Number per 1,000 of estimated total *civilian* population	—	19·4	18·5	17·4	16·6
London:					
Number	125,000	108,000	100,000	91,000	83,000
Number per 1,000 of estimated total population ..	27·6	23·7	21·7	20·3	18·6
Number per 1,000 of estimated total *civilian* population	—	25·0	23·6	22·6	20·9
TOTAL NUMBER OF PERSONS (excluding casuals and insane) IN RECEIPT OF OUTDOOR RELIEF IN ENGLAND AND WALES:					
Number	389,000	*349,000	*316,000	*290,000	*281,000
Number per 1,000 of estimated total population ..	10·5	9·4	8·4	7·7	7·5
Number per 1,000 of estimated total *civilian* population	—	9·9	9·2	8·6	8·4

* Excluding an estimated number of insane in receipt of outdoor relief.
MINISTRY OF HEALTH,   15*th December*, 1919.

86 The Maclean Report

Containing as it did several members who had served on the Royal Commission of 1905–09, it is not surprising that the Maclean Committee should reiterate the demand that the boards of guardians be abolished and their functions transferred to borough and county councils. These would then make arrangements for the various types of pauper to be dealt with by their appropriate committees—children by the local education authority, the sick by the health committee and so on. A home assistance, or public assistance, committee would co-ordinate the work of relief by visiting those in need, supervising the administration of relief to them and keeping a register of those relieved. The unemployed would be dealt with by a separate distress committee. Shorn of its poor-law associations, it was argued, a comprehensive system of this sort would obviate the need to set up clumsy ad hoc committees such as had been established to administer the Health Insurance Act of 1911.

III.—*The Abolition of the Boards of Guardians.*

6. We have not attempted in this Report to deal with the whole problem of overlapping local authorities in respect of public assistance. We have limited ourselves to the largest and the most intractable case of overlapping, namely, that of the Boards of Guardians, on the one hand, and the County, Municipal and other Health and Education Authorities on the other. We are here faced by overlapping functions and areas, and by conflicting principles of administration. The resulting confusion has been aggravated by the growing popular prejudice against the Poor Law—a prejudice which does less than justice to the devoted work of the Guardians, and the continuous improvement in poor-law administration, especially in respect of the children and the sick. For the last decade Parliament has been unwilling to entrust the Boards of Guardians with new functions, and the provision for new services has had to be made by

other Local Authorities—in some cases new Local Authorities—
often to the increase of the confusion and overlapping. Further,
the classification by institutions and the specialised treatment of
recipients of assistance, almost necessarily involve an enlarge-
ment of existing areas of administration. The Royal Commission
on the Poor Laws and Relief of Distress, which sat for over three
years and took a very large amount of evidence, attached great
importance to these points; and both the Majority and Minority
Reports concurred in recommending the abolition of Boards of
Guardians and of the Poor Law Union.

We recommend the abolition of the Boards of Guardians and of the
Poor Law Union, and the merging of all the functions of the Poor Law
Authorities in those of the County Council and the County Borough
Council, subject to the necessary modifications set out in our Schemes
below for London and the other administrative counties.

27. The adoption of more suitable areas of administration is
no less important than the unification of services. The expenditure on Public Assistance has grown enormously in the last 25
years, and included in this expenditure is an increase of 6½
millions per annum on Poor Law Relief, which is due in the
main to the demand for a higher standard of administration,
and particularly to the recognition of the advantage of classification and the appropriate treatment of various classes of recipients of relief, to which both the Majority and Minority
Reports of the Royal Commission attributed so much importance. The expenditure on Public Assistance is partly central
and partly local, but, as the Committee on Retrenchment in the
Public Expenditure (Cd. 8200) observed, "if the national resources are to be conserved to the fullest possible extent, it is of
course necessary that every practicable economy should be
secured in local as well as in central administration." Such
economy cannot be secured unless the whole expenditure out of
public funds on Public Assistance is so accounted for that it can
be kept under continuous observation in total as well as in
detail. The unification of Public Assistance services which we

T

recommend would greatly facilitate such a system of accounting.

28. But whatever measures of economy may be necessary we cannot contemplate any withdrawal or reduction of services, advantageous to the community as a whole, which have been conferred by recent legislation. On the contrary, we are disposed to think that the effect of the war will be to stimulate the demand for the improvement of social conditions. If the fulfilment of that demand is to be reconciled with the duty of securing both economy and efficiency in public expenditure, it appears to us imperatively necessary that the reorganisation of public assistance, which we have recommended, should previously have been carried out, based, as we have shown, upon the unification of services, the reduction in the number of separate authorities and the choice of the most suitable area of administration. Report on the Transfer of Functions of Poor Law Authorities in England and Wales (Cd 8917), XVIII (1917–18), 4–5, 10–11

POST-WAR DEPRESSION AND POPLARISM

The prospects of some remodelling of the social services along the lines recommended by the Maclean Committee seemed fair immediately after the war. In 1919 the Local Government Board was disbanded and its place taken by a Ministry of Health under Christopher Addison. Although the new Ministry now became the central authority for poor-law purposes, it was hoped that this would be only a minor part of its work, and that, under a progressive minister like Addison, it would press forward with the integrated development of health and other social services. The need for the Poor Law, it seemed, was bound to lessen. The end of the war did not bring with it a rise in unemployment: demobilised servicemen were given gratuities and an out-of-work donation to tide them over while they were seeking employment; and the post-war economic boom meant that in most cases work was not too difficult to find, and for those who were unlucky, unemployment insurance had been extended so that most industrial workers were covered by 1920.

Hopes of rapid social improvement proved short lived, however. The boom of 1919 was a short-term highly artificial one. In the long term, Britain's industrial future looked bleak: world demand for the products of her old staple industries—coal, textiles, iron and steel—had fallen; new competitors such as Japan were making inroads on her overseas markets; and many of her new industries were undercapitalised. In these circumstances, unemployment increased rapidly in 1920, and until the outbreak of the Second World War, Britain was to be saddled with the burden of one million or more unemployed. Governments, whether Coalition, Conservative or Labour, believed in a policy of financial orthodoxy and thus failed to provide any national solution to the problem. The unemployment insurance scheme of 1911 had not been designed to cope with mass unemployment, nor with those who remained jobless for more than a few weeks; so the long-term unemployed soon exhausted their contributions, and had to be given 'uncovenanted' or 'transitional' benefits. Those who could claim no benefits, or who found them inadequate, were forced to turn to their local board of guardians for relief.

In this waste land of the early 1920s, the wartime plans for social rebuilding withered. The Coalition Government and its supporters among the business classes pressed for a return to 'normalcy', to the situation existing before 1914, and therefore demanded the removal of wartime controls. The decision to return to the gold standard at pre-war parity with the dollar involved the Government in a policy of deflation and retrenchment with disastrous results for education, health and other social services. The Ministry of Health failed to give the expected leadership, especially after 1921 when Addison was removed by Lloyd George under pressure from Conservative supporters of his Coalition Ministry. Given this lack of enthusiasm for change at the centre, there was little likelihood of powerful vested interests like the boards of guardians being disbanded.

By 1921 many of these boards of guardians, particularly those in urban industrial areas or on the coalfields, found themselves swamped with applications for relief from unemployed men and their families. The number of persons receiving poor relief in England and Wales had risen from 450,000 in November 1918 to 568,000 by December 1920, and to nearly 1,500,000 by July 1921. The boards of guardians were totally unprepared and unequipped to meet such a situation. The Ministry of Health could give no help beyond urging the guardians to exercise the strictest economy and reiterating the outworn 1834 formula of 'less eligibility' (87). Most boards found it impossible to observe both this principle and the regulation that outdoor relief must be adequate to the needs of the case. To enforce a workhouse test was impossible, and the alternative of a labour test proved to be of little more value. Throughout the nineteenth century there had been strong misgivings about forcing such tests on those willing but unable to find employment, and the war period with its generous aid for those in distress had reinforced this attitude. The Representation of the People Act of 1918 had abolished the regulation that those in receipt of poor relief should be disfranchised, and in many industrial towns the enlarged working-class element in the electorate had returned a majority, or a strong minority, of Labour members to the boards of guardians. Such members were pledged to deal generously with the unemployed and their families whatever the cost to the ratepayer. Many no doubt saw this as an opportunity to smash the hated poor-law system.

The most famous of these boards was the Poplar board of guardians, dominated by convinced socialists like George Lansbury, who from his first election as a guardian in 1892 had pledged himself to a policy of 'decent treatment and hang the rates'. This attitude had earned the Poplar Union the disfavour of the central authority, and had led to an official inquiry into its administration in 1906. In 1919 the Labour Party won massive majorities on both the Poplar borough council and the board of guardians. Rising unemployment in the borough in

1920 served to revive indignation at the situation, which had long rankled with Lansbury and his colleagues, whereby boroughs and unions in the East End of London had to support their many poor by rates raised from property of a low rateable value while the wealthy West End boroughs had few un-employed men or distressed families to maintain. In 1921 Poplar borough council protested against this by refusing to pay their share towards the revenue of the LCC and other metro-politan bodies; they defied a court order to pay and marched to prison behind the town band to the considerable embarrass-ment of the LCC, the Ministry of Health and the prison authorities.

A compromise was speedily arrived at. The imprisoned coun-cillors were released, and the Minister of Health, Sir Alfred Mond, agreed to introduce a Bill allowing for payments from the Metropolitan Common Poor Fund towards the cost of relief of all paupers and not just those on indoor relief as previously. In return Mond insisted that any out relief financed by the Common Fund should not exceed 25s od (125p) a week for a married couple plus 5s od (25p) for each child, or alternatively that any sum given should be at least 10s od (50p) less than the standard rate of wages in the area. The Poplar guardians, how-ever, regarded this 'Mond Scale' as a minimum rather than a maximum level, and continued their policy of generous relief. In March 1922, Sir Alfred Mond asked Mr H. I. Cooper, clerk to the Bolton Board of Guardians, to carry out another investi-gation into the administration of poor relief in Poplar. Mr Cooper's report alleged that the guardians were indulging in a policy of lavish relief without restrictions, that this was de-moralising the recipients and destroying all incentive to work, and that a more careful administration could save the rate-payers and the Common Poor Fund at least £100,000 a year. The Poplar guardians responded in a pamphlet in which they pleaded *Guilty and Proud of It* (89).

Although Mond seems to have been considering drastic action against the defiant guardians, the Government took no

very firm line. Nervous about the possibility of left-wing revolution and perhaps uneasy at its failure to create the promised
'land fit for heroes', the Government feared a further embar-
rassing demonstration of solidarity by George Lansbury and his
colleagues. In any case, this was a period of weak Governments.
The Coalition Ministry crumbled in 1923, to be followed by a
short-lived Conservative Government, and then by a minority
Labour administration. A rapid succession of Ministers of
Health meant that there was little possibility of any consistent
policy being followed.

The Press and a section of the public were indignant at the
phenomenon of 'Poplarism' or 'Protelarianism', as the Webbs
disapprovingly christened it (88). For some it was part of a
sinister Red plot to undermine the finances of London and the
nation, particularly when the Labour Minister of Health, John
Wheatley, repealed the Mond Scale in 1924. Yet the giving of
unconditional outdoor relief was far from being confined to
boards of guardians with a Labour majority: both the Manchester and West Derby (Liverpool) Unions gave outdoor relief
on a liberal scale, and the Sheffield board of guardians had to
submit to an official investigation into its affairs in 1923. No
boards of guardians—Ratepayer, Labour, Conservative or
Liberal—had any solution to mass unemployment; they were a
destitution authority, giving a dole but little else. In the prevailing conditions of mass unemployment, unconditional outdoor relief, relief scales, even relief in aid of wages began to
reappear. Those features which had so alarmed the reformers of
1834 were still active a century later.

87 Ministry of Health   Restrictions on Outdoor Re-lief

Article XII of the Relief Regulation Order of 1911 gave
guardians permission to give outdoor relief without a test to
any class of pauper, provided that they reported each departure from the regulations to the central authority. The

Ministry of Health's advice on out relief differed little from
that of its predecessors, the Poor Law Commission, the Poor
Law Board and the Local Government Board.

_____

POOR LAW RELIEF AND UNEMPLOYMENT.

SIR,—

In view of the distress arising from the continuance of exceptional unemployment and the large numbers who in various
parts of the country are dependent upon Poor Law relief at the
present time, the Minister of Health deems it desirable to draw
the attention of the Guardians to some of the more important
rules which should guide them in the administration of relief.
The Minister has had the advantage of consulting the Association of Poor Law Unions in England and Wales, and he is
assured that they are in entire agreement with him in attaching
importance to the observance of these rules.

It has long been recognised, both by the Central Department
and by Boards of Guardians generally, that relief given under
the Poor Law should be sufficient for the purpose of relieving
distress, but that the amount of the relief so given should of
necessity be calculated on a lower scale than the earnings of the
independent workman who is maintaining himself by his labour.
This is a fundamental principle any departure from which must
in the end prove disastrous to the recipient of relief as well as to
the community at large, and, although the Minister has no
desire unduly to fetter the discretion of the Guardians as to the
manner or method in which they afford relief, he will feel bound
to exercise the powers which he possesses and to disapprove a
departure from the Relief Regulation Order authorised by
Article XII thereof in any case in which the relief given is
contrary to this principle. The Minister thinks it necessary for
this purpose to require that, when reporting departures under
Article XII of the Relief Regulation Order, the Clerk to the
Guardians should give sufficient particulars as to the amount of
relief granted, either generally or in particular cases, to enable

the Minister to satisfy himself that the amount given is not in excess of what is necessary in accordance with the above-mentioned rule. Ministry of Health. Circular No 240 to Boards of Guardians on Poor Law Relief to Unemployed Persons (8 September 1921)

88 Pall Mall Gazette   Poplarism

The generosity of the Poplar board of guardians did not meet with the approval of the majority of newspapers, who saw it as either 'A Premium on Idleness' (*Daily Mail*), as 'Socialism Run Mad' (*Nottingham Guardian*) or even as a 'Policy of Sovietism' (*Evening Standard*). The *Pall Mall Gazette*, which in the late nineteenth century had been a crusader for social reform, proved to be no exception in this case. It attempted to give the public a foretaste of what to expect from the inquiry ordered by the Ministry of Health into the administration of poor relief in Poplar.

THE MISRULE OF POPLAR

REPORT ON SOCIALIST ABUSES THAT WILL AMAZE LONDONERS.

ONE IN FIVE IN RECEIPT OF RELIEF.

From a Poor Law Correspondent.

Mr. Cooper, the clerk to the Bolton Board of Guardians, has left London, having completed his inquiry into the affairs of Poplar.

It is believed that he has exposed some of the grossest abuses of the Socialist regime that has pauperised Poplar, and that his report will be studied with interest when it is published.

Naturally, Mr. Cooper is bound to secrecy as to the details of the report until it is actually published. But it is now in the hands of the printers, and should be available in a few days' time.

Inquiry at Poplar makes it clear that he has delved deep for his information, and that the report will reveal many amazing facts.

Proved Up to the Hilt.

Mr. Cooper conducted a searching investigation into the allegation that it is more lucrative for a working man to accept outdoor relief in Poplar than to carry on with his ordinary work. His report is likely to prove this charge up to the hilt.

Even the amateur investigator in Poplar can learn of cases where men have actually left their jobs in order to take advantage of Mr. Lansbury's generosity, given at the expense of the ratepayers.

The last report on Poplar was presented by Sir J. S. Davy to Parliament in 1906.

That proved conclusively that the local Guardians regarded themselves as the advocates of a policy first, and the representatives of the ratepayers afterwards.

As a result within ten years, while the rate of London pauperism only slightly increased, that of Poplar had nearly trebled. This led to the pauperisation of seven in every hundred of the population, to the growth of sweating, and to increased burdens on the local tradesmen.

Socialism led to sordid misdoings and gross injustices.

The Desire of "the Comrades."

This was sixteen years ago. To-day not one in fourteen, but one in five, of the population are in receipt of outdoor relief.

Mr. Cooper will tell a story of waste and extravagance that will amaze Londoners who have not taken the trouble to study the doings of this borough.

The motive behind continues to be political. Mr. Lansbury and his comrades make no secret of their desire that all the ratepayers of London should pay for their local extravagances. He declares that in a district like Poplar pauperism is bound to grow, and that the only permanent remedy is Socialism.

The forthcoming report will act as a douche of cold water upon such heated statements.

Facts will be given in plenty to illustrate that the average Labour man, elected to a position of power on his local council, is incapable of governing.

It will be a document of great value to the sociological student, and Mr. Cooper will have good reason to be proud of his work.

A Shrewd Observer.

He was not content to accept the information placed before him by interested parties, for he is known in Lancashire as one of the shrewdest of clerks, and one of the most dominating personalities ever in Bolton, the birthplace of Lord Leverhulme.

His independent spirit, together with his very lengthy and practical experience of poor-law administration, made him an ideal man to undertake this inquiry. He has not lost any time, and not left many stones unturned in Poplar in order to ascertain the truth.

The workhouse administration will be reviewed, including the cost of maintenance, as compared with other similar institutions, the efficiency of the management, and the spirit of the place.

Record Bamboozling.

The conditions of outdoor relief, which should be given after the circumstances of the applicant are taken into account, and the earnings of all the members of a household calculated, have been reviewed.

Poplar falls far short of other districts in the care with which the guardians investigate cases, and holds the record for the way they allow themselves to be bamboozled.

There is a branch workhouse at Laindon, in Essex, for the reception of male able-bodied paupers. There the men are supposed to improve their physical conditions, to learn habits of industry, and to become fitted to earn their own living.

School for Idleness.

The results to-day can hardly be said to be encouraging. Those who live in the district believe that it is a school for idleness, and a "cushy" home for ruining the morale of the inmates. Mr. Cooper will no doubt have something to say on this feature of Poplar's misrule.

But apart from the purely local issues involved, this report will have a far-reaching national effect. The Poor Law is at present bending under the strains of abnormal unemployment. A system, admittedly imperfect, but capable of reforms, will be broken unless those responsible perform their duties with a sense of responsibility.

Questions.

Democracy is indeed on its trial in the Poor Law world to-day. Shall Boards of Guardians be abolished? Will the existing system break under the present burdens? Are Mr. Lansbury and his colleagues, who profess idealist doctrines and declare that they hope for a happier and healthier world, really bringing their ideals nearer realisation? Is Sovietism a panacea for present ills?

Such questions are at present being debated by students of our present social system, and Mr. Cooper's report will help to provide a very definite answer, based on facts and figures, not on Bolshevist theories. *Pall Mall Gazette* (15 May 1922)

89 Poplar Board of Guardians   Poplar's Answer

In this twopenny pamphlet the Poplar guardians issued a challenging reply to the critics who accused them of extravagance. Taking the main criticisms of the Cooper Report, they attempted to answer each of them in turn.

POPLAR PLEADS GUILTY

Pure religion and undefiled before God and the Father is

this, to visit the fatherless and widows in their affliction.— JAMES i., 27.

INTRODUCTORY

THIRTY years ago five Labour men found themselves elected as Guardians of the Poor for parts of the parishes of Poplar and Bow and Bromley, which form the Poplar Union.

The advent of these men into public life caused a great commotion at the time, and their work in the intervening years has given rise to much discussion and criticism. Again and again the forces of reaction have attacked them. Public and private investigations into their administrative work have taken place. In spite of it all they have carried on their work, and have made such a mark on the public life of Poplar that Labour is now in complete control of all the local administrative bodies.

During these years, the poor and the needy, the sick and the infirm, the fatherless, the widows, and the orphans have been properly and decently treated. The spirit of Bumble has been driven out and supplanted by the spirit of humanity. This work has cost money, but the people of Poplar have steadily supported the view that the duty of members of the Board of Guardians is to be Guardians of the POOR and not Guardians of the interests of property. In Poplar there is no cringing or whining on the part of those who apply for public assistance. Those who need relief apply for it as readily as the unemployed workman applies for his unemployment pay. Relief is accepted without shame or regret—in fact, in exactly the same spirit as that in which ex-Cabinet Ministers, Royalties, and others accept their pensions and allowances from the Government.

In Poplar it is well understood that the poor are poor because they are robbed, and are robbed because they are poor. For thirty years, continuous propaganda has been carried on, but it must not be inferred from this that the movement has not been constructive. We have always demanded that Poplar should not be segregated from the rest of London, and compelled to face single-handed the problems of destitution and misery thrust upon it by the present industrial system. We have always maintained that the poor of Poplar were the nation's poor; but that while the nation refused to shoulder the burden, it was our duty to shoulder it ourselves and to try to get the richer Boroughs of London to take their share.

In pursuance of this policy, we compelled Mr. Balfour to pass the Unemployed Workmen's Act, 1905, and later on we forced Mr. Asquith to pay £200,000 a year out of national funds to put that Act into operation. It was mainly because of our work that the Royal Commission was appointed to inquire into the working of the Poor Law and relief measures for the unemployed. One of our members was given a seat on this Commission. Poplar's methods of administration have been copied throughout the land. There is not a Poor Law institution which has not been improved by Poplar's example and policy. Poplar's latest achievement was to compel Parliament to meet in Special Session last autumn, in order to pass two Bills, one for the purpose of continuing and increasing national grants to the unemployed, and the other to extend the operation of the Metropolitan Common Poor Fund, so that the cost of out-door relief, with certain limitations, should be spread over the whole of London. The second Act also provided for the equalisation of the cost of maintaining the poor in institutions to the extent of 1s. 3d. per head per day instead of 5d., as was previously the case. Before these measures were passed, thirty members of the Poplar Borough Council (many of them also Guardians) suffered imprisonment for six weeks. But this action saved the people of Poplar £300,000 on last year's rates, and will save them at least £250,000 every year. *The richer Boroughs have to pay these sums of money to Poplar and similar sums to other poor Boroughs.* This is the great crime. This is "Poplarism." This is what has caused the very name of Poplar to stir up hatred and malice in the hearts of those who stand for vested interests and the rights of property. This is what has caused the Ministry of Health to organise the gutter press in a campaign of slander and abuse against Poplar. Guilty? Of course we plead guilty!

Guilty, and proud of it. *Guilty and Proud of It. Poplar's Answer* (nd), 1-2

THE END OF THE BOARDS OF GUARDIANS

The General Strike of 1926, and the long drawn out coal strike which followed it, brought applications for relief up to a peak figure of 2,500,000. In some mining areas, 30-40 per cent of the population were on relief and guardians themselves were forced at times to solicit charity in order to avoid having to apply to their own board for relief. Poor relief to strikers was complicated by the Merthyr Tydfil judgement, a legal ruling made in the Court of Appeal in 1900 after some South Wales coalowners had sued the Merthyr Tydfil board of guardians for giving relief to striking miners. The Master of the Rolls, Lord Lindley, had ruled that a board of guardians could not give relief to men who were unemployed by their own choice, though the guardians were fully justified in giving aid to the wives and children of strikers. In a circular issued in May 1926, the Ministry of Health reminded boards of guardians of the limitations imposed on them by the Merthyr judgement, but these proved easy to evade. The guardians merely paid an increased grant to the striker's wife. Since women were not subject to the labour test, the Merthyr judgement made unconditional outdoor relief even easier.

Inevitably the Poor Law became involved in the bitter feuds waged on the coalfields of Britain in 1926. Where colliery owners or their representatives controlled the board of guardians, it was alleged that relief was deliberately reduced in order to force strikers back to work. Where the board was in the hands of miners and their union officials, there were complaints that the rates were being used to supplement strike funds and that miners who threatened to return to work had their relief stopped (90).

Whatever the truth of such claims and counter claims, the rapid increase in relief payments in 1926 proved a final blow to the already rickety finances of some unions. The economic de-

pression of the early 1920s had reduced the rate income of poor-
law unions at a time when demands on their funds were increasing. Guardians in depressed areas found their expenditure
far outrunning their income, and had to borrow from their
bankers. When this source failed, they were compelled to seek
aid from the Ministry of Health, and a committee was set up
under the chairmanship of Sir Henry Goschen to supervise the
grant of loans to insolvent unions. By 1926 these unions found
themselves bankrupt; they were forced to seek further Government aid while unable to redeem debts incurred up to five
years earlier (91).

The financial difficulties of the boards of guardians allowed
the Ministry of Health to demand that they economise or receive no further loans. The Minister of Health in the Conservative Government of 1925, Neville Chamberlain, was not, however, content to rely on such short-term expedients; he had
become convinced that the poor-law system needed reforming.
His first action was to arm himself with stronger powers than
had hitherto been available to deal with guardians who refused
to heed the instructions of the central authority. In the face of
bitter Labour opposition he pushed through a Boards of Guardians (Default) Bill giving the Minister power to dismiss an
elected board of guardians and replace it by his own nominees
(92 and 93). The first union to feel the weight of these new
powers was West Ham, where the guardians had run up a
massive debt during the General Strike and had defiantly maintained a 'Poplarist' policy in the face of warnings from the
Ministry. A month later, in August 1926, the Chester-le-Street
Union in County Durham was 'West Hammed', and the third
and last victim was the Bedwellty Union in South Wales (February 1927). Both these unions lay in mining areas and their
financial difficulties were aggravated, it was alleged, by gross
misuse of funds during the coal strike (94). Other unions were
subjected to detailed investigations by Ministry inspectors, and
ordered to enforce work tests on all able-bodied male applicants
for relief.

This disciplining of boards of guardians was only a preliminary to their complete abolition. In 1927 Chamberlain carried a Poor Law Act consolidating over one hundred poor-law statutes. Late in 1928 he introduced a Local Government Bill to abolish the guardians and transfer their powers to councils, as the Royal Commission of 1909 and the Maclean Report of 1918 had recommended. Subject to the approval of the Minister, councils were to decide on their own administration, the Bill merely requiring them to set up public assistance committees and urging them to give relief under other auspices than those of the Poor Law wherever possible (96). Not surprisingly the Bill attracted considerable criticism: those who believed in the principles of the Minority Report of 1909 argued that it did not go far enough, particularly in relief of the unemployed, and that it left too much power for good or ill in the hands of the local councils (95); on the other hand, leading members of boards of guardians attacked it as an unwarranted interference in their affairs. But despite their fiery speeches these guardians could raise no such support as the overseers and select vestries had raised in Lancashire and Yorkshire in the 1830s. In March 1929 the Local Government Act received the royal assent. On 1 April 1930, 643 boards of guardians in England and Wales were quietly dissolved with only a paragraph and perhaps a photograph in the local paper to mark their passing. The oldest boards were four years short of their centenary. The machinery of the nineteenth-century Poor Law, if not its spirit and substance, was no more.

90 Joseph Jackson　No Relief for Blacklegs

On anxious inquiry from the Ministry of Health, the Clerk to the Gateshead Union reported that this refusal of relief was due to a misunderstanding, though two similar complaints in the following month would seem to indicate that some guardians were using their position to attack those whom they felt were betraying their fellow workers.

Sir,

On applying as usual for my Guardian Relief I was refused owing to signing on for work at Rowlands Gill Colliery. At present there is no work for me and I have a wife and Two Children, what's to become of them in the meantime. Its the Policy of the members of the Board of Guardians to stop men's relief who have signed on as they say we are (Blacklegging) am I entitled to relief until Colliery starts?

Yours in anticipation,

Joseph Jackson.

PRO, MH68/67 (November 1926)

_____

91 Gateshead Union   The Guardians in the Red

The Coal Strike of 1926 brought financial disaster to the Gateshead Union as to most of its fellow Unions in mining areas. By the end of the year, the Gateshead guardians were £250,000 in debt. The ending of the strike brought with it no prospect of any alleviation of this position, since many miners could not find work but became eligible for poor relief since they were no longer on strike.

Given their chronic financial state, the guardians found it difficult to resist demands from the Ministry of Health that they should reduce their relief scales.

_____

POOR LAW UNION OFFICES,
GATESHEAD.

8th December, 1926.

Sir,

The letter of the 16th November, sent by direction of the Minister of Health, on the subject of the relief given to children who are dependent upon miners in the Union, was submitted to the Guardians of this Union at their meeting last night, when they resolved to increase the deduction from the scale of Outdoor relief in respect of meals supplied by Education Committees from 1/- to 2/- per week in cases where children are receiving two meals per day.

U

The Guardians also considered their present financial position, and unanimously resolved to ask the Minister to sanction a further overdraft for £70,000. A copy of a statement submitted to the Guardians as to their financial position is enclosed for the information of the Minister. It is not likely that any substantial amount due from the Overseers will be received during this year at any rate.

The Guardians have had requests for payment from tradesmen who have supplied goods in November and December to Outdoor recipients, and the Minister will observe that the Guardians have only £133 - 11 - 5 in the Bank.

It is not expected that there will be any substantial diminution of cost of Out Relief for the next two weeks at any rate. Since last night's meeting of the Guardians I have learned from one Relieving Officer that he anticipates his relief will probably increase owing to the large number (over 400) of applications from single men—miners—for relief who are not able to secure employment, and whose disability under the Merthyr Tydvil case to receive relief appears to have been removed by the termination of the trade dispute. Another Relieving Officer reports that he has 300 applications from such men this morning.

On Saturday in each week the available money is distributed to the different Relieving Officers pro rata to their requirements and the cash in hand. It would be convenient if the Minister could make a temporary grant, on account of the £70,000 applied for, by Saturday morning. He may take it that the Guardians' funds will not be materially different on Saturday.

> I am, Sir,
> Your obedient Servant,
> George Craighill
> Union Clerk.

Union Clerk, Gateshead, to Secretary, Ministry of Health (8 December 1926). PRO, MH68/67

---

92 John Wheatley Opposition to the Default Bill
John Wheatley (1869-1930), MP for the Shettleston Division

of Glasgow, had been an active Minister of Health in the short-lived Labour Government of 1923-4. One of his actions had been to release the Poplar board of guardians from the restrictions imposed on them by the Mond Scale. After the fall of the Government, he refused to sit on the Opposition front benches, but joined the militant group of ILP back-benchers.

———

Mr. WHEATLEY: May I say with regard to the Bill that it is more dangerously reactionary than the Eight Hours Bill[1] we discussed last week. No one will have difficulty in seeing that it came from the same stable and is of the same pedigree. The right hon. Gentleman has addressed the House for, I think, about 75 minutes, and I submit that in that time he has done more practical Communist propaganda than the Communist party working in poverty and isolation can do in 75 years. Indeed, he has given that party a much greater boost than even was done by his colleague when he sent its leaders to prison. Anyone familiar with Communist literature knows that thesis after thesis has been written to show that political democracy in capitalist countries is only a toy given to the workers to keep them quiet and obedient, but that as soon as they use that toy to the inconvenience of their masters it will be taken away. We have been told that they would have votes as long as they voted for their master's voice, that they would have local government while they carried out their master's policy, that they would have a Parliament as long as that Parliament did not seriously threaten their master's economic power. And the deduction which the reader was always expected by the author to draw was this—that while the working class of this country should try to capture political power in order to weaken the influence of their masters, they should not rely on it mainly as the means of their emancipation. We on this side have always questioned that reasoning. But what have we to say in future when they

[1] The Coal Mines Bill—a measure designed to increase the maximum underground working period for miners from seven to eight hours per day.

quote against us the action to-day of the right hon. Gentleman? Not only Socialists but Liberals have always in this country asked the Government and the people to put their faith in political action, and they have so successfully appealed to the people that there has grown up in this country a system of local government which, I think, in the main, as has been said, rests broadly on the will of the people.

To-day we are asked to pass a Measure which is a step towards the complete destruction of that system of government. I submit to the House that this is a very serious matter; that to attack the work of a century in political reform, is something that ought not to be done even by this Conservative House of Commons, without the deepest consideration of its probable consequences on the psychology of the country. The paltry excuse which the Minister submits as justification for his act, is not one which any independent House of Commons would accept. He has attempted to justify himself entirely on what has happened at West Ham. Local government in this country was not granted on condition that the locally elected representatives would satisfy a Tory Government. If that had been the basis of our system, it would have been the very negation of democracy. Socialists and Tories differ as to the rights of the poor. We have been appealed to, not merely by people on this side of the House, but by the party opposite, when impatient individuals created trouble for them, to reason with our fellows, to convert them to our point of view, to try to get a majority of our comrades where that majority at the time was against us, and to rely on that constitutional way and on that way only to establish in society the views for which we stood.

In the local authorities, in the boards of guardians which we are discussing here, and, indeed, in regard to every public authority in this country, that is exactly what has taken place. Labour and Socialist enthusiasts carried on their propaganda. In the course of time they got their majority, and replaced the Tory majority against which the propaganda had been conducted. Naturally, when the people secured a change in the character of the majority they expected a change in policy. If a Labour or Socialist majority were merely to carry out, in continuity, the policy of their Conservative predecessors, there would be no sense at all in making the change. Toryism is Toryism from whatever hand it comes, whether the hand be the hand of a Socialist, or the hand of a member of the Conservative party. I think it not unreasonable, when we allow for difference in views, to expect that the Socialist majority will give greater consideration and more generous treatment to the poor whose affairs they administer than the Conservative majority whom they have succeeded. When a Socialist majority proceed, quite naturally, to give effect to their views, they find themselves confronted by a Conservative Minister of Health. He says, in effect, when they come to him as they must come to him: "If your scale of relief or the manner of administering it"—it really amounts to the same thing—"if your assistance to the poor, under your Socialist administration, exceeds what is given under a Conservative administration, then I will take the earliest opportunity of smashing you when you are compelled to come my way." Hansard. *Parlt Debates*, 5th Series, Vol 197 (5 July 1926), Cols 1659–62

93 The Boards of Guardians (Default) Act

Under this Act the Minister of Health obtained powers which would have been regarded as intolerable in the nineteenth century (19).

An Act to provide in the case of default by a board of guardians for the reconstitution of the board; and for matters arising out of the default or consequential on the reconstitution.

[15th July 1926.]

1.—(1) Where it appears to the Minister of Health (in this Act referred to as "the Minister") that the board of guardians for any poor law union have ceased, or are acting in such a manner as will render them unable, to discharge all or any of the functions exerciseable by the board, the Minister may by order under this Act appoint such person or persons, as he may think fit (whether qualified or not to be guardians for the union), to constitute the board in substitution for the then existing members of the board (who shall on the making of the order vacate their office) for such period, not exceeding twelve months, as may be specified in the order, and the persons so appointed shall be deemed for all purposes to constitute the board.

Until the expiration of the term of office of the persons appointed by the order (in this Act referred to as "the appointed guardians"), no person shall become a member of the board otherwise than by the appointment of the Minister.

(2) The Minister may at any time, and from time to time, by order extend, for a period not exceeding six months, the term of office of the appointed guardians.

An order made under this subsection shall be laid before both Houses of Parliament as soon as may be after it is made, and if either House within twenty-one days after the order has been laid before it presents an address to His Majesty praying that the order may be annulled, His Majesty may by Order in Council annul the order and it shall thenceforth be void, but without prejudice to the validity of anything previously done thereunder, or the making of a fresh order.

(3) An order made under this Act may—

(a) contain such supplemental and consequential provisions as appear to the Minister to be necessary or expedient for the purpose of giving full effect to the order; and

(b) be amended, varied or revoked by a subsequent order made under this Act.

(4) There may, out of any moneys in the hands of the appointed guardians for the purpose of the exercise of the powers or the discharge of the duties of the board, be paid to the appointed guardians such remuneration, and to any persons appointed to advise the appointed guardians such reasonable

allowance on account of travelling expenses and by way of subsistence, as the Minister may approve.

(5) If before the date on which an order is made under this Act in respect of any board of guardians the clerk or any other officer of the board has, on the directions of the Minister, incurred any liabilities in connection with the relief of the poor in the poor law union, the appointed guardians may discharge those liabilities out of any moneys in their hands as aforesaid. *Law Reports. Statutes* (1926), 92–3

94 Chester-le-Street

The Chester-le-Street Union on the Durham coalfield was, like the neighbouring Gateshead Union, in serious financial difficulty by 1926. There were allegations that the board of guardians, two-thirds of whose members were miners, their wives or union officials, were supporting the strike with generous donations of outdoor relief. Late in August 1926 the Minister of Health, acting under the Default Act, dismissed the elected board. Three civil servants were appointed to administer the Union, and, in their first report to the Minister, they catalogued the misdemeanours of the previous board of guardians. The number of cases on outdoor relief were sharply reduced from 14,000 in July 1926 to only 3,000 by the end of the year.

GENERAL ADMINISTRATION OF OLD BOARD.

In order to make clear the general administration of the Union at the 30th August, it would be desirable to trace its history back to the industrial dispute of 1921, and consider the position arising out of the fact that, prior to the mining dispute which began on the 1st May, 1926, the mining industry in the Union area was very depressed and there was, as a consequence, a great deal of unemployment. In the limits of this report, however, it is impossible to do so, and the appointed Guardians propose to restrict their statement as far as possible to the period dating from the 1st May to the 30th August, 1926.

(1) NATIONAL STOPPAGE: EMERGENCY COMMITTEE.

At a meeting of the Guardians held on the 6th May, 1926, the following resolution was passed:—

"*National Stoppage:* The Chairman then drew the attention of the Board to the very serious position created by the National Stoppage, and proposed that an Emergency Committee be appointed, with power to act and to deal with the question of providing for the people in the present crisis on behalf of the Guardians. Five members were appointed to constitute the Committee with power to add to their numbers."

The Emergency Committee of five members held a meeting on the following day, the 7th May, 1926, and resolved:—

"That the remaining members of the Labour Party on the Board be added to the Committee."

The members of the Labour Party on the Board, including the 39 miners' representatives already referred to, numbered 47.

On the 12th May, 1926, 36 members of the Guardians attended a meeting of the Emergency Committee and thereafter in effect this Emergency Committee took over complete control of the Guardians affairs and continued to administer the affairs of the Union and grant relief.

Their minutes were subsequently confirmed by the full Board of Guardians as a matter of course.

The effect of this procedure was that the independent Guardians, numbering 12, practically ceased to attend the fortnightly Board Meetings, having been deprived of all reasonable opportunity of performing the duties for which they were elected.

(2) CO-OPERATIVE STORE PASS BOOKS.

At this meeting on the 12th May, 1926, the Relieving Officers were instructed not to require production of Co-operative Store Pass Books by Applicants for Relief. These Store Pass Books in a mining district are the best source of information from which

the Relieving Officers can ascertain the private means of applicants for relief. The Chairman of the Board was Chairman of
one of the largest Co-operative Societies in the district and the
Chairman of the Emergency Committee was Vice-Chairman of
the same Society.

It was not until the appointed Guardians took office that the
Relieving Officers were able to obtain the Store Pass Books. In
October, 1926, 24 persons were convicted on one day of obtaining relief to the total of £256 9s. 6d. by fraud. The Magistrates
only ordered repayment and inflicted fines, as they were of
opinion that the defendants had been misled by the old Board
of Guardians. The appointed Guardians shared the views of the
Bench of Magistrates. They came to the conclusion that the
administration of poor law in the Union since 1921 has had the
effect, so far as applicants for poor relief are concerned, of degrading and corrupting people who may otherwise be honest,
and gave instructions to the Relieving Officers to abstain from
prosecutions where persons who had obtained relief without
disclosing their means were willing to refund the amount paid.
Since these instructions were given 34 persons have agreed to
refund the relief granted to them and the sum of £324 1s. has
been recovered.

(3) ORDERS FOR CO-OPERATIVE SOCIETIES.

Efforts were made to secure the orders for all relief in kind for
Co-operative Societies, e.g., on the 13th May, 1926, the Birtley
Relief Committee passed the following resolution: "That all
relief vouchers given to recipients during this week be issued on
the various branches of the Co-operative Societies."

(4) COLLECTION FOR GUARDIANS.

At Birtley the relief was paid out every Friday at the local
Picture Hall, in the Co-operative Society's building. When the
recipients went out of the Hall they had to pass near the exit a
table at which sat, or stood, members of the local Unemployed
Organisation (four in particular, but occasionally others). Each

recipient passing was asked to remember the Local Guardians and a great majority contributed money to these men. None of the Guardians who lost their employment in the mining industry during the dispute has applied for relief. *Parlt Papers*, Cd 2818, XI (1927), 7–8

___

95 Sidney Webb   Speech on the Local Government Bill

Sidney Webb had been elected as MP for Seaham in 1922, and was President of the Board of Trade in the Labour Cabinet of 1924. Not unnaturally he was disappointed with Neville Chamberlain's scheme of poor-law reform, which ignored many of the proposals of the Minority Report of 1909, particularly with regard to the treatment of the unemployed. Neville Chamberlain, in his speech introducing the Bill, had paid tribute to his father as being one of the first to suggest that the powers of the boards of guardians should be handed over to the councils. Sidney Webb responded to this by his detailed reference to Joseph Chamberlain's attitude towards the treatment of the unemployed.

___

I must come now to what is after all my biggest interest and that is the Poor Law. The right hon. Gentleman's Bill with regard to the Poor Law is like the historic curate's egg. It is very good in that he should at last do what his father recommended 40 years ago and abolish the separate *ad hoc* destitution authority. Neither the right hon. Gentleman nor any of us would wish to cast any reflection on the public spirited men and women who serve as guardians but the evil of the system is, first that they are limited to the relief of destitution. They cannot step in before destitution has begun, in order to prevent it, and they cannot go on for a single minute after destitution has ceased, in order to prevent a relapse. They are limited to the moment of destitution. In the second place they are circumscribed in all sorts of ways in what they do, and the system is quite incongruous in relation to the treatment of the sick. The right hon.

Gentleman does not sweep the Poor Law away. He has abolished the boards of guardians but not the Poor Law. He has transferred the work of the boards of guardians with their powers and liabilities to the county councils and the county borough councils. That is a step and I thank the right hon. Gentleman for that step. It is said that the time-lag in England is 19 years, and the 19 years is up this year.

I have pointed out that the Poor Law is to be handed over intact, and that you will have a difference in right between one citizen in one county and another citizen in another county. Under the Poor Law, citizens all over England are supposed to have the same legal rights of relief. Now you are going to dodge about from county to county. County A will have taken over some of the Poor Law services, and County B will not have done so. The resident in County A will not be a pauper and the resident in County B will be a pauper. There is, however, a much more serious case, for Clause 4 enables the new authorities, if they like, to take over some part of the Poor Law service, some part only, and a small part, and it prevents them taking over all the rest of the Poor Law services. These are to continue to be Poor Law. I ask the right hon. Gentleman's particular attention to one Section of the Poor Law which is in as bad and chaotic a condition as it was in 1834. It is the relief of the able-bodied. There are as many able-bodied men being given outdoor relief from Poor Law authorities to-day as there were in 1834—not proportionate to the population, but literally as many. The right hon. Gentleman referred in a happy way to the suggestion of his illustrious father that the Poor Law ought to be handed over to the counties and county boroughs, but he might have reminded the House that his illustrious father, in making that suggestion, said emphatically that the unemployed workmen ought not to be degraded by the Poor Law at all. He said:

"The law exists for securing the assistance of the community at large in aid of their destitute members; and where the necessity has arisen from no fault of their own, the persons concerned, there ought to be no idea of degradation connected with such assistance. Those compelled to apply have probably paid rates and taxes in past time. The payment is, in fact, an insurance against misfortune."

The illustrious father of the Minister of Health was not able to get his own way then but he came into the Government, and he managed to do something. He sent out a circular, in which he said:

"It is not desirable that the working classes should be familiarised with Poor Law relief. The spirit of independence that leads so many of the working classes to make great personal sacrifices rather than incur the stigma of pauperism is one that deserves great sympathy and respect, and it is the duty and the interest of the community to maintain it by all means at its disposal."

If the author of these words could be here now, how surprised he would be to find that his equally illustrious son is proposing that the only class among those whom the guardians at present relieve which is not to be taken out of the Poor Law is the unemployed; that is the 100,000 men and their families whom the guardians are now relieving out of the Poor Rate, are to remain, because the Poor Law is to be handed over to the counties, and they are not to be taken out of it. They are to remain under the Poor Law, and the county or county borough council will have to go on doing what the guardians have been doing. That is not what Mr. Joseph Chamberlain suggested. His influence went further, and the Unemployed Workmen Act was passed in 1905 to enable the borough and city councils to make some other provision than out-door relief for the unemployed. This Bill proposes to repeal the Unemployed Workmen Act. These men are not only to be kept under the Poor Law but the door is locked, bolted, and barred against them by the repeal of this Act. The councils which are to take over the duties of the guardians are to be held within the limits of the powers that the guardians now have, and the powers which were given to them by the Unemployed Workmen Act are by this very Bill to be taken away from them.

This Bill fails to carry out the intentions of the right hon. Gentleman and the intentions of the Government, fails I am quite sure, to carry out the desires of the House in these matters; and I ask the right hon. Gentleman to see if there is not some substance in some of my points and to put in Amendments to carry out his own desires. But on the main point of whether able-bodied men are to remain under the Poor Law and without the aid of the Unemployed Workmen Act, whether the new authorities are to go to this new work crippled through having no more than the powers of the boards of guardians, it seems to me—we have had some Biblical quotations already—rather like the case of the potentate who hardened his heart and would not let the people go. It seems to me that the Poor Law authorities behind the right hon. Gentleman are not willing to let these able-bodied people go, and I ask him whether he had not better let them go like the sick, whom I am sure that he wishes to take completely out of the Poor Law, to be dealt with by the county and county borough councils in whatever way they find necessary, in preparation for the taking over by the Ministry of Labour of the whole of the able-bodied unemployed. Hansard. *Parlt Debates*, 5th Series, Vol 223 (28 November 1928), Cols 456–7, 463–5, 467

___

96 The Local Government Act (1929)

As its full title shows, the Act comprehensively covered several facets of local government. Part I alone dealt with poor-law matters, abolishing the boards of guardians and providing for the transfer of their functions to the town and county councils.

___

An Act to amend the law relating to the administration of poor relief, registration of births, deaths, and marriages, highways, town planning and local government; to extend the application of the Rating and Valuation (Apportionment) Act, 1928, to hereditaments in which no persons are employed; to grant complete or partial relief from rates in the case of the hereditaments to which that Act applies; to discontinue certain grants from the Exchequer and provide other grants in lieu thereof; and for purposes consequential on the matters aforesaid.

[27th March 1929.]

PART I.
POOR LAW.
Transfer and administration of Functions.

1. On the appointed day the functions of each poor law authority, shall, subject to the provisions of this Act and except as otherwise expressly provided by this Act, be transferred to the council of the county or county borough comprising the poor law area for which the poor law authority acts, or, if the poor law area is not wholly comprised within one county or county borough, the functions of the poor law authority so far as they relate to any county or county borough into which the area extends shall be transferred to the council thereof, and as from the appointed day all then existing poor law authorities shall cease to exist.

4. The council of every county and county borough shall prepare, and within six months after the commencement of this Act submit to the Minister, a scheme (hereinafter referred to as an administrative scheme) of the administrative arrangements proposed to be made for discharging the functions transferred to the council under this Part of this Act:

Provided that the Minister may on the application of a council extend the time within which a scheme is to be submitted if he is satisfied that there is reasonable cause for such extension.

5.—(1) A council in preparing an administrative scheme shall have regard to the desirability of securing that, as soon as

circumstances permit, all assistance which can lawfully be provided otherwise than by way of poor relief shall be so provided,
and accordingly any such scheme may declare that any assistance which could, after the appointed day, be provided
either by way of poor relief or by virtue of any of the following
Acts as amended by any subsequent enactment including this
Act (that is to say)—

(a) The Public Health Act, 1875:
(b) The Local Government Act, 1888:
(c) The Mental Deficiency Act, 1913:
(d) The Maternity and Child Welfare Act, 1918:
(e) The Blind Persons Act, 1920:
(f) The Public Health (Tuberculosis) Act, 1921:
(g) The Education Act, 1921:

shall be provided exclusively by virtue of the appropriate Act
and not by way of poor relief, but nothing in this subsection or
in any scheme shall diminish or otherwise affect the duty of a
council under section thirty-four of the Poor Law Act, 1927, to
provide relief for the poor.

For the purposes of this subsection, the expression "assistance" includes maintenance and treatment at hospitals and
other places, the education of children, and any other services
which could, after the appointed day, be provided either by way
of poor relief or by virtue of any of the above-mentioned Acts.

6.—(1) An administrative scheme shall provide for the constitution of a committee of the council (hereinafter referred to
as the public assistance committee), and may provide—

(a) that any other committee of the council shall act as the
    public assistance committee, or that the members for the
    time being of any other such committee, shall so act; and
(b) for the inclusion in the public assistance committee or
    among any members of another committee acting as
    such, of persons who are not members of the council,
    some of whom shall be women;

so, however, that of the whole number of members of the public assistance committee or committee or body acting as such, two-thirds at least shall be members of the council.

(2) Subject to the provisions of the last foregoing section, all matters relating to the exercise by the council of the functions (other than those specified in section two of this Act) transferred to them under this Part of this Act, except the power of raising a rate or borrowing money, shall stand referred to the public assistance committee, and the council before exercising any such functions shall, unless in their opinion the matter is urgent, receive and consider the report of the public assistance committee with respect to the matter in question.

(3) The scheme may provide for the delegation by the council to the public assistance committee, with or without any restrictions or conditions as they think fit, of any of the functions so transferred, except the power of raising a rate or borrowing money, and may provide for the discharge, on behalf of and subject to the general direction and control of the public assistance committee, of any of the functions of that committee by any of the other committees of the council. *Law Reports. Statutes* (1929), 49–54

Epilogue

I t was ironical that the boards of guardians should be destroyed by the very problem which they had been established after 1834 to deal with—the problem of how to relieve the able-bodied unemployed. Nor did their dissolution bring the problem any nearer to solution. The Act of 1929 proved a severe disappointment to those who hoped that a new deal for the poor might emerge from it. The economic depression of 1929–31 brought with it reductions in governmental and local authority expenditure, thwarting any ambitious ideas the more progressive councils might have entertained for tackling their newly acquired responsibilities. Relief under the public-assistance committee came to be little different from relief under the guardians; if the workhouse test and the labour test disappeared, they were replaced by the means test which became as emotive a symbol for the working man of the 1930s as the workhouse had been for his nineteenth-century ancestor. Public-assistance committees which attempted to adopt a 'Poplarist' policy and refuse to operate the means test were brought sharply to heel by the Ministry of Health. At Durham and Rotherham, the public-assistance committees were dismissed just as the West Ham, Bedwellty and Chester-le-Street boards of guardians had been. An inquiry into the state of Britain's social services in 1937 found over one million people being maintained by public assistance which 'remains one of the most important services in spite of the growth of other more specialised forms of social provision'.[1] George

[1] PEP. *Report on the British Social Services* (1937).

Orwell's *The Road to Wigan Pier* or Walter Greenwood's novel *Love on the Dole* presented a similar picture in more dramatic terms. The Act of 1929 had not destroyed the Poor Law.

It was the Second World War which forced the country to reappraise not only its administrative machinery for dealing with poverty but its attitudes towards the poor. The Luftwaffe did not distinguish between the deserving and the undeserving, and relief for those rendered homeless by bombing had to be given generously according to need. 'Less eligibility' and the means test had to be abandoned if civilian morale was to be maintained. The evacuation of schoolchildren from the big cities to the country brought many people face to face for the first time with the realities of urban poverty.

Experiences of this sort gave rise to a determination to provide a better society, without the Poor Law, after the war. Thus there was an enthusiastic reception in 1942 for Sir William Beveridge's *Report on Social Insurance and the Allied Services*. As Beveridge himself admitted, his plan for the future was a cautious one, 'a British revolution' based on the insurance principle of contribution in return for benefits, as pioneered by the Insurance Act of 1911. Beveridge saw the State as maintainer of full employment and provider of a free health service and family allowances. But the most attractive feature of the Beveridge plan was its universality: all citizens irrespective of income or class were to contribute and all were to be entitled to benefits. This notion was in sharp contrast to the Poor Law and most of the other pre-war social services, which had been seen as providing solely for the needs of the poor.

Despite the Government's cool reception of the Beveridge Report, the pressure of public opinion in its favour proved irresistible. Three White Papers of 1944 on *Social Insurance, Full Employment* and *A National Health Service* laid down the pattern of post-war welfare services, and the Labour victory at the General Election of 1945 ensured their adoption. The Family Allowances Act had already become law before the new Government took office, and there followed a stream of social legislation with the National Insurance and National Health Service Acts of 1946 and the National Assistance Act of 1948 prominent among them. On 5 July 1948 the new structure of social services was completed and the Poor Law was formally repealed.

Yet those who hoped that poverty would be banished from this 'Welfare State' were to be disappointed. Post-war inflation soon rendered the insurance benefits less than adequate for the subsistence of those dependent on them. Full-employment policies kept the bulk of the working population prosperous, but pensioners, and low-paid workers with large families, were still poor according to the standards of an increasingly affluent society. Far greater resort had to be made to National Assistance payments for supplementing insurance benefits than Beveridge had intended. Many refused to seek such aid because National Assistance still seemed to them to resemble public assistance and poor relief. In an era when private affluence was balanced by public squalor, the workhouse buildings of the nineteenth century often had to continue their life as hospitals, particularly for the mentally ill. Here was proof, if proof were needed, of the truth of the text, 'the poor ye have always with you'. Legislative provision, whether in 1834 or 1948, could not by itself solve the problem of poverty. Nor could slogans, whether they spoke of 'less eligibility' or the 'welfare state'. Patience, compassion and flexibility were required to meet the ever changing pattern of human need. This, if anything, was the lesson taught by the English poor-law system.

Suggestions
for Further Reading

There are two monumental histories of the English Poor Law which those with a serious interest in the subject must consult at some time despite their daunting bulk. The first is Sir George Nicholls. *History of the English Poor Law*, 3 Vols (Reissue 1904). This work was written by one of the members of the Poor Law Commission of 1834 and is partisan in its views. Nevertheless the first two volumes contain useful summaries of legislation and of key reports like that of the Royal Commission of 1832–4. The third volume, added to Nicholls's original two by Thomas Mackay, is interesting if only for its view of the nineteenth-century poor-law system through the eyes of a firm believer in the 'less eligibility' principles of 1834.

Nicholls's work was largely superseded in the 1920s by Sidney & Beatrice Webb. *English Local Government*, Vols VII–IX (1927–9, Reissued 1963). This detailed work of critical scholarship covers the whole field of English poor-law history from 1597 to 1929. It is complemented by the same authors' *English Poor Law Policy* (1909, Reissued 1963) which examines the policies of the Poor Law Commission, Poor Law Board and Local Government Board with regard to the various types of pauper. Although these volumes remain the classic work on the subject, their readers must bear in mind the close association of the Webbs with the campaign for poor-law reform, particularly from 1905 onwards.

On the last years of the Old Poor Law, the best short account is J. D. Marshall. *The Old Poor Law 1795–1834* (1968). E. M. Hampson. *The Treatment of Poverty in Cambridgeshire 1597–1834* (1934) is a detailed but by no means parochial study of the development of the poor-law system in a rural county. A more recent study of a different type of area is G. W. Oxley. *The Relief of the Permanent Poor in South West Lancashire under the Old Poor Law* in J. R. Harris (Ed) *Liverpool and Merseyside* (1969). D. Marshall. *The English Poor in the 18th Century* (1926) is a readable account of the life of the poor in eighteenth-century England. J. R. Poynter. *Society and Pauperism. English Ideas on Poor Relief 1795–1834* (1969) provides a thorough and much needed analysis of the multifarious schemes for poor-law reform advocated in this period. In the field of periodical literature, Mark Blaug's two articles, 'The Myth of the Old Poor Law and the Making of the New' and 'The Poor Law Report Re-examined', *Journal of Economic History*, XXIII (1963) and XXIV (1964), contain important and challenging reassessments of established views on the deficiencies of the Old Poor Law, particularly with regard to the allowance system.

J. D. Marshall. 'Nottinghamshire Reformers and the New Poor Law', *Economic History Review*, XIII (1961) discusses the importance of Nicholls, Becher and Lowe in the framing of the New Poor Law. A. W. Coats. 'Economic Thought and Poor Law Policy in the 18th Century', *Econ Hist Rev*, XIII (1960) examines changing opinions on poor-law reform in that century.

Biographies provide the best guide to the debate over the New Poor Law. S. E. Finer. *The Life and Times of Sir Edwin Chadwick* (1952) is the best modern biography of the most important figure in the poor-law history of this period. R. A. Lewis. *Edwin Chadwick and the Public Health Movement* (1952), though mainly concerned with Chadwick's career as a sanitary reformer contains a valuable discussion of his relationship with the Poor Law Commissioners. Nassau Senior's thinking on poor-law questions is covered by S. Leon Levy. *Nassau Senior* (1970) and also in an older work, M. Bowley. *Nassau Senior and Classical*

Economics (1937). J. T. Ward. *The Factory Movement 1830–1855* (1962) and M. Hovell. *The Chartist Movement*, 2nd Ed (1925) provide interesting accounts of the Anti Poor Law Movement and its relationship to the Ten Hours' Movement and to Chartism respectively. C. Driver. *Tory Radical. A Life of Richard Oastler* (1946) is a highly readable account of the life of a leading opponent of the New Poor Law. D. Roberts. *Victorian Origins of the British Welfare State* (1960) contains a useful, if at times erratic, analysis of the social background and careers of the leading members of the poor-law inspectorate. A. Redford. *Labour Migration in England 1800–1850*, 2nd Ed (1964) gives an account of the migration scheme and its difficulties. H. L. Beales. 'The New Poor Law', *History*, XV (1931) is an excellent and elegant brief discussion of the thinking behind the 1834 Act. R. Boyson. 'The Poor Law in North East Lancashire 1834–71', *Transactions of the Lancashire and Cheshire Antiquarian Society*, lxx (1960) and N. McCord. 'The 1834 Poor Law Amendment Act on Tyneside', *International Review of Social History*, XIV (1969) provide interestingly contrasted pictures of the working of the new system in these areas. R. A. Lewis. 'William Day and the Poor Law Commissioners', *University of Birmingham Historical Journal*, IX (1964) gives a full account of the career of the unfortunate Day as an assistant poor-law commissioner. M. E. Rose. 'The Anti Poor Law Movement in the North of England', *Northern History*, I (1966) discusses some aspects of the organised resistance to the new system in Lancashire and the West Riding, while D. Roberts. 'How Cruel was the Victorian Poor Law?', *Historical Journal*, VI (1963) examines in more general terms the allegations of inhumanity levelled at the New Poor Law by its opponents.

On the working of the Victorian poor law, M. Bruce. *The Coming of the Welfare State* (1961) contains the most recent general account. D. Owen. *English Philanthropy 1660–1960* (1965) analyses the many charities which supplemented poor relief in Victorian England. R. G. Hodgkinson. *The Origins of the National Health Service: The Medical Services of the New Poor*

Law 1834–1871 (1967) gives a detailed account of medical relief. M. B. Simey. *Charitable Effort in Liverpool in the 19th Century* (1951) is a valuable discussion of the development of philanthropic effort in face of the growing problem of urban poverty. E. Cannan. *History of Local Rates in England*, 2nd Ed (1912) is an invaluable brief guide to the complexities of the poor rate. W. O. Henderson. *The Lancashire Cotton Famine* (1934) provides the authoritative account of this important episode in the development of poor relief. Henry Mayhew's four massive volumes, *London Labour and the London Poor 1851–62*, have recently (1965) been reissued. A dip into them is a rewarding and exciting experience. There are two useful critical articles on Mayhew: J. R. T. Hughes. 'Henry Mayhew's London', *Journal of Economic History*, XXIX (1969) and E. P. Thompson. 'The Political Education of Henry Mayhew', *Victorian Studies*, XI (1967–8). B. Harrison. 'Philanthropy and the Victorians', *Victorian Studies*, IX (1965–6) gives a critique of the Victorian passion for good works. J. E. O'Neill. 'Finding a Policy for the Sick Poor', *Victorian Studies*, VII (1963–4) describes the campaign for the improvement of conditions in workhouse sick wards. E. P. Hennock. 'Finance and Politics in Urban Local Government 1835–1900', *Historical Journal*, VI (1963) discusses the financial difficulties of local authorities in this period.

The developments of the later nineteenth century are competently outlined in M. Bruce, op cit, and in K. de Schweinitz. *England's Road to Social Security* (1943). The full history of the influential Charity Organisation Society has yet to be written, but K. Woodroofe. *From Charity to Social Work* (1962), C. L. Mowat. *The Charity Organisation Society 1869–1913* (1961) and A. F. Young & E. T. Ashton. *British Social Work in the 19th Century* (1956) contain valuable insights into the work and ideas of the society and some of its leading members. By contrast with Mayhew, no publisher has as yet reissued the seventeen volumes of Charles Booth's *Life and Labour of the People in London* (1902). A. Fried & R. W. Elmer. *Charles Booth's London* (1969) provides selections from this work, while T. S. & M. B. Simey. *Charles*

Booth, Social Scientist (1960) is an indispensable critical account of the man and his work. Harold Pfautz. *Charles Booth on the City* (1969) should also be consulted. B. S. Rowntree. *Poverty. A Study of Town Life* (1901) is a more advanced and more manageable social survey than that of Booth. Asa Briggs. *Social Thought and Social Action. A Study of the Work of Seebohm Rowntree* (1961) gives a survey of the man and his achievements. Bentley B. Gilbert. *The Evolution of National Insurance in Great Britain: the Origins of the Welfare State* (1966) is the best modern account of the discussion and legislation on poverty and allied problems in late Victorian and Edwardian England, and ranges far more widely than its clumsy and uninspiring title implies. Beatrice Webb's two volumes of autobiography *My Apprenticeship* (1926) and *Our Partnership* (1948) contain lively accounts of her conversion to social investigation under the tutelage of Charles Booth and of her career as a member of the Royal Commission on the Poor Laws. U. Cormack. *The Royal Commission on the Poor Laws and the Welfare State*, reprinted in A. V. S. Lochhead. *A Reader in Social Administration* (1968) provides a useful corrective to the Webbian view of the Royal Commission and its findings. W. H. B. Court. *British Economic History 1870–1914. Documents* (1965) contains an excellent selection of source material on wages, living standards and poverty in this period.

The inter-war period has been very scantily covered as far as writing on the poor law, or even on the social services generally, are concerned. M. Bruce, op cit, and K. de Schweinitz, op cit, both give an outline of developments in social welfare between the wars. C. L. Mowat. *Great Britain Between the Wars* (Reissued 1966) contains the best short account of social and economic conditions in Britain in the 1920s and 1930s. K. Feiling. *Neville Chamberlain* (1946) gives a careful and sympathetic description of his subject's career at the Ministry of Health. PEP. *Report on the British Social Services* (1937) contains a detailed critique of the state of the social services in the 1930s. P. Abrams. 'The Failure of Social Reform 1918–20', *Past and Present*, XXIV (1963) is a stimulating essay on the failure of post-war reconstruction plans, though it concentrates on housing rather than on social security. B. Keith Lucas. 'Poplarism', *Public Law* (1962) is the best and clearest account of the tragi-comic Poplar episode and its consequences, details of which may also be found in R. Postgate. *Life of George Lansbury* (1951). As yet, however, the surface of the history of welfare problems in this vital period remains barely scratched.

Acknowledgements

I would like to thank the following for their kind permission to reproduce extracts from the works listed below:

The London School of Economics and Political Science (Beatrice Webb, *Our Partnership*); W. Heffer and Sons Ltd (G. Cuttle, *The Legacy of the Rural Guardians*); Messrs Cassell & Co Ltd (J. A. Chamberlain, *Politics from the Inside*); Messrs Constable & Co (George Lansbury, *My Life*). Transcripts of Crown-copyright records in the Public Record Office and extracts from Command Papers and Hansard appear by permission of the Controller of HM Stationery Office.

I am indebted for their assistance to the Keeper and staff of the Public Record Office, and to the Librarians and staff of Manchester University Library, the John Rylands Library, the Manchester, Leeds and Sheffield City Libraries, the Huddersfield and Tower Hamlets Borough Libraries, and to the Director and Goldsmith's Librarian, London University Library for permission to reproduce an extract from Nassau Senior's Diary.

I also owe debts of gratitude to my colleagues in the Department of History, University of Manchester, and particularly to Dr E. R. R. Green and Dr W. H. Chaloner for their unstinted help and advice, to Mrs M. Gissop, Mrs B. Bentham and Mrs J. Lockett who typed the manuscript so competently, to my wife for her help and sympathy and to Simon and Christopher who provided light relief. All errors and omissions are of course my own.

M.E.R.

Index

Acts of Parliament: 5 Eliz, c 4 (1563), 35, 36n; 43 Eliz, c 2 (1601), 11–12, 72, 85, 120, 150, 215, 275; 13 & 14 Ch II, c 12 (1662), 12, 28; 9 Geo I, c 7 (Knatchbull's Act 1722), 13, 18, 25n, 38; 22 Geo III, c 83 (Gilbert's Act 1782), 13, 18, 26–8, 71; 35 Geo III, c 101 (1795), 19, 28–30; 36 Geo III, c 23 (1796), 20, 38–9; 59 Geo III, c 12 (Sturges Bourne's Act 1819), 23, 67–9, 112; 4 & 5 Wm IV, c 76 (Poor Law Amendment Act 1834), 95–100 (framing of, 76, 87–90; opposition to, 103–5; praise of, 105–7); 7 & 8 Vic, c 101 (1844), 178; 9 & 10 Vic, c 66 (1846), 192, 199–201 (effects of, 201–3); 10 & 11 Vic, c 110 (Bodkin's Act 1847), 192–3; 26 & 27 Vic, c 70 (Public Works Act 1863), 138, 142–3, 158–60; 28 & 29 Vic, c 79 (Union Chargeability Act 1865), 193, 196, 206–7, 214; 30 & 31 Vic, c 6 (Metropolitan Poor Act), 162; 48 & 49 Vic, c 46 (Medical Relief Disqualification Removal Act 1885), 238; 56 & 57 Vic, c 73 (Local Government Act 1894), 238; 5 Ed VII, c 18 (Unemployed Workmen Act 1905), 157, 239, 260–2, 263, 274, 280, 301, 316–17; 16 & 17 Geo V, c 20 (Board of Guardians Default Act 1926), 303, 309–11 (attack on, 307–9); 19 &

20 Geo V, c 17 (Local Government Act 1929), 13–14, 135, 304, 317–20, 321–2

Addison, C., 284, 290, 291

Aged Poor, 139, 141–2, 146, 149, 161, 168, 237, 238, 241, 249, 252–4, 254–6, 276

Agricultural Labourer, condition of, 19, 30–2, 62–4

Agriculture, poor rate burden on, 198–9, 214–15

Allowance System, 19, 22–3, 37; continuance after 1834, 141–2, 148–50, 154–5, 222, 226–8, 294; 1834 Act and, 99–100; Hindon (Wilts) scale, 60–1; in Coventry, 54–6; Ld Althorp on, 91; Select Committee (1824) on, 52–4; Speenhamland (Berks) scale, 33–5

Althorp, Lord, 76, 87–8; speech on PL Amdt Bill, 90–2

Andover Union, enquiry (1846), 122, 127

Anti-Pauper System, The, 24, 72–4

Anti-Poor Law Movement, 109–11, 118–20

Apprentices, 54–5, 178

Arnold, R. A., 138; on board of guardians, 138–40

Aschrott, P. F., 231–2; on Charity Organisation Society, 232–4

Assistant Commissioner, to Poor Law Commission, 101, 103–4, 109, 121–2, 123–6; to Royal Commission (1832–4), 75, 77–9

Baines, E., 90, 92–3
Balfour, A., 263, 267, 280–1, 301
Barnett, Canon S., 235, 237, 248; criticisms of poor law, 248–50
Becher, Rev J. T., 24, 71–2; on poor law reform, 72–4
Bentham, J., 46, 76, 118
Bitter Cry of Outcast London, The, 235, 236
Blatchford, R., 236, 239–40; criticism of poor law, 240–1
Bodkin, W. H., 192–3
Booth, C., 242, 263, 264, 268, 271; survey, 236
Booth, W., 235, 236
Buller, C., 194, 207–8; on vagrancy, 208–9

Chadwick, E., 76, 101, 122, 123; criticism of Poor Law Commission, 127, 130–1; report of 1834 and, 84–7
Chalmers, Rev T., 21, 224
Chamberlain, Joseph, 258–9, 314, 316; Circular, 157, 239, 259–60
Chamberlain, J. Austen, 280–1; on Minority Report, 281–2
Chamberlain, Neville, 303, 314
Charity, criticism of, 223–4, 226; Royal Commission (1905–9) on, 272–3
Charity Organisation Society, 142, 231–2, 248; formation, 224–5; influence on Royal Commission (1905–9), 263–4, 265, 272; organisation, 232–4
Children: boarding out, 179, 188–91, 256; cottage homes, 257; district schools, 178–9, 183–5; in workhouse, 256–7; industrial schools, 178–9, 185–8, 222, 231, 256; Minority Report (1909) on, 276; Poor Law Commission on, 180–1; scattered homes, 238–9, 256, 257–8; treatment and education of, 178–191ff
Close Parishes, 195–8, 214

Cobbett, W., 76, 90; speech on New Poor Law, 93–4
Colquhoun, P., 21, 46–7; on poverty, 47–9
Coode, G., 193, 203; on settlement laws, 203–5
Cotton Famine, Lancashire, 142–3, 156–60, 214, 222, 239
Crusade, The, 266, 278

Davies, Rev D., 30; on agricultural labourer, 30–3
Davy, J. S., 263, 264, 271, 297
Day, W., 123–6; on poor law finance, 217–19
Dickens, C., 171, 185; on Manchester pauper school, 185–8

Eden, Sir F. M., 21, 39, 42; on poor laws, 42–3
Ellison, J., on 1834 Act, 112–13; on settlement, 205–6

First World War, effect on poor law, 283–90ff

General Strike (1926), 302, 304–6, 311–12
Gilbert, T., 26
Goschen, G. J., 142, 222, 225; Minute (1869), 223–4, 226–8
Grey, Sir G., 122, 132; speech on Poor Law Commission, 132–4
Guardians, Board of, 135–40ff; abolition, 285, 288–9, 304, 318; attitude to poor, 138–40, 240–1; composition, 136, 220, 238, 252; corruption, 137–8, 252; duties, 136, 138–40; established, 101; financial difficulties, 215–19, 302–3, 305–6; opposition to New Poor Law, 118–20, 125; relations with central authority, 136–7, 141, 148–50; Royal Commission (1905–9) on, 264–5, 274–5, 275–6; under Gilbert's Act, 26–8; voting for, 135, 238, 292

Guardians, Boards of: Bedford, 179–81; Blackburn, 148–50; Bradford, 194–5; Chester-le-Street, 303, 311–14; Gateshead, 304–6; Huddersfield, 118–20; Manchester, 138–40, 230–1; Poplar, 238, 250–2, 292–4, 296–302; Sheffield, 238, 294; South Wales, 124–6, 215–19
Guilty and Proud of It, 293, 299–302

Health, Ministry of, 290, 291; on outdoor relief (1921), 294–6, 302
Hill, Octavia, 232, 234, 263

Irish Poor, 23, 192–3, 202, 204, 205–6

Kay, J. P., 181–2; on pauper education, 182–5

Labour Rate, 22, 57–8
Labour Test, 22, 58–60, 71, 150, 151–2, 249, 259–60, 303; Order (1842), 140
Lancet, The, 161–2, 172–3, 222; on workhouse infirmaries, 173–5
Lansbury, G., 238, 250, 264, 271, 292–3, 294, 297, 299
Leeds, effect of 1846 Removal Act in, 201–3
Less Eligibility, 73–4, 85, 179–81, 224, 249, 292, 295
Lewis, G. C., 122, 127, 130
Lewis, T. F., 101, 122, 127; on Chadwick, 130–1
Liverpool, poor rates in, 220–1; relief administration in, 69–71, 294; vagrant ward, 210–11
Local Government Board, 222; abolition, 290; influence on Royal Commission (1905–9), 263–4; on aged poor, 252–4; on outdoor relief, 223, 228–30
Long, W., 260, 280

Maclean Committee (1918), 284–5, 304; report, 288–90

Magistrates, 26, 28, 33, 101, 313; powers of relief, 38–9
Malthus, Rev T. R., 21, 43–4; on poor law, 44–6
Manchester, education of pauper children, 178–9, 185–8; relief administration in, 23, 64–7, 223, 230–1, 294; workhouse in, 169–71
Marcus, 111, 116–18
Marshall, A., 237, 247; on poor law, 247–8
Merthyr Tydfil Judgement, 302, 306
Metropolitan Common Poor Fund, 162, 293, 301
Migration Scheme (1835), 102, 107–9
Minimum Wage, 35–6
Mond, A., 203; Scale, 293, 294, 307

National Committee for the Prevention of Destitution, 266–7, 278–80
National Relief Fund (1914), 285–6
Nicholls, G., 24, 72, 101, 123, 124

Oastler, R., 110, 113, 119–20; on New Poor Law, 113–14
Outdoor Relief, 140–6off; amount (Poplar), 152, (Stepney), 153, (Skipton), 154–5; criticism of, 142, 153, 226–8; Local Govt Bd Circular (1871), 228–30; Min of Health Circular (1921), 294–6; Prohibitory Order (1844), 140, 143–5; Regulation Order (1852), 141, 146–8, 149, (1911), 294–5; Regulations (1835), 102–3; Regulations of Manchester Guardians (1875), 230–1
Overseer, assistant, 23, 67, 68–9; collection of poor rate, 219; criticism of, 61–2; in Manchester, 64–7

Pall Mall Gazette, 296; on Poplar, 296–9

Pitt, W., 20, 35; poor law reform plan, 36–7

Poor Law Board, 122, 133–4; abolition, 222; regulations on relief, 146–8

Poor Law Commission: abolition, 122–3, 132–4; established, 101; powers under 1834 Act, 76–7, 87–90, 95–100; procedure, 127, 130; regulations on relief, 102–3, 120–1, 143–6; weaknesses, 121–2

Poor Law Union: Birmingham, 223; Camberwell, 257–8; Clerk, refusal to elect, 118–20; Docking, 196; formation of, 101; in Essex, 255–6; Greenwich, 257; Poplar, 150–2, 223, 292–4, 296–302; Sheffield, 223; Skipton, 154–5; Uckfield (Sussex), 105–7

Poor Relief, costs, 40–1, 128–9, 105, 263, 268–70; numbers on relief, 263, 268–70, 284, 286–7, 292, 302

Poverty, 47; causes, 236–7, 243–4; cycle, 242, 243–5; line, 242; primary and secondary, 242, 245–6

Public Assistance: committee, 265, 288, 319–20, 321; registrar, 265, 277, 281

Rates, after 1834, 213–14; difficulty of collection, 215–19, 302–3, 306; in agricultural areas, 198–9, 214–15; inequalities of, 214–15, 215–17, 220–1, 292–3

Rathbone, W., 219, 224; on poor rates, 220–1

Rawlinson, R., 158–9; on Public Works Act (1863), 159–60

Reconstruction, Ministry of, 284

Rogers, J., 137; on boards of guardians, 137–8

Roundsmen, 22, 56–7

Rowntree, B. S., 236, 241–2; survey of York, 242–7

Royal Commissions: on Aged Poor (1895), 237, 238, 252–3; on Poor Laws (1832–4), 75–6, 79–84, 84–7, 266–7; on Poor Law (1905–9), 248, 261, 262–82ff, 284–5, 288, 304 (Majority Report, 271–4; Minority Report, 274–8)

Select Committees: on Aged Deserving Poor (1899), 238, 253; on Labourer's Wages (1824), 52–4; on Poor Laws (1817), 21, 49–51; on Poor Relief (1861–4), 223

Select Vestry, 23, 67–9, 73, 112–13

Senior, N., 76, 77, 84, 87, 95; on drafting of New Poor Law, 88–90

Senior, Mrs N., 188; on boarding out, 188–91

Settlement and Removal, 23, 28–30, 191–207ff; after 1834, 191–2; changes in legislation, 192–3; illegal removal, 194–5; opinions on reform, 203–6

Shaw-Lefevre, J., 101, 130

Sick Poor: improvement of conditions, 162, 175–8; infirmaries, 175–8; in workhouse, 161–2, 171–2, 248–9

Smith, Dr E., 162, 172; on workhouse diets, 164–9

Stephens, Rev J. R., 110, 116

Sturges Bourne W., 49, 67, 87, 88

Taine, H., 169; on Manchester workhouse, 169–71

Times, The, 76, 121; on New Poor Law, 94–5

Torrens, W. M., 156–7; on relief to unemployed, 157–8

Unemployed: alternatives to poor relief for, 239, 259–60, 316–17; numbers of, 283–4, 291, 292; Royal Commission (1905–9) on, 265–6, 276, 277–8

Vagrants, 193–4, 206; Poor Law Board on relief of, 208–9; vagrant ward, regulations, 210–11; writings of, 211–13

Webb, B., 268, 285; campaign to break up poor law, 266–7; on Royal Commission (1905–9), 263–4, 271

Webb, S., 266, 268, 274, 314; on Local Government Bill (1929), 314–16

Wheatley, J., 294, 306–7; on Boards of Guardians (Default) Act (1926), 307–9

Whitbread, S., 20, 35; minimum wage proposal, 35–6

Widows, relief of, 142–3, 146, 179, 199–200, 227, 230–1, 249

Workhouse, 160–78ff; alleged cruelties in, 133–5; critics of, 25, 161; diets, 162–9, 170, 249–50; expenditure on, 88–90, 97–8; in Huddersfield, 171–2; in Liverpool, 69–70; in Manchester, 169–71; opposition to, 110–11; Royal Commission (1832–4) on, 85–6; under New Poor Law, 160–1

Young, Sir W., 25; on workhouses, 25–6